LESSONS ON
THE ANALYTIC
OF THE SUBLIME

M E R I D I A N

Crossing Aesthetics

Werner Hamacher

& David E. Wellbery

Editors

Translated by
Elizabeth Rottenberg

Stanford
University
Press

Stanford
California
1994

LESSONS ON THE ANALYTIC OF THE SUBLIME

(Kant's 'Critique of Judgment,'
§§23–29)

Jean-François Lyotard

'Lessons on the Analytic of the Sublime'
was originally published in French
in 1991 under the title
'Leçons sur l'analytique du sublime,'
© 1991, Editions Galilée

Assistance for this translation
was provided by the French
Ministry of Culture.

Stanford University Press
Stanford, California

© 1994 by the Board of Trustees of the
Leland Stanford Junior University

Printed in the United States of America

CIP data appear at the end of the book

Stanford University Press publications
are distributed exclusively by
Stanford University Press
within the United States,
Canada, and Mexico; they are
distributed exclusively by
Cambridge University Press
throughout the rest of the world.

Contents

Preface

This is not a book but a collection of lessons. Or rather a file of notes in preparation for the oral explication of the Analytic of the Sublime (Kant's *Critique of Judgment,* §§23–29). This book does not exempt one from reading Kant's text; on the contrary, it requires one to read it.

These notes have not received their final "polish," and in a sense the professor will never be finished with his class. From this two-fold negligence there comes a twofold fault: the writing retains the heaviness and the repetition of the oral explication, which follows Kant's text step by step; but at the same time, the whole is far from "covering" the text—I am not speaking of the "content," which is inexhaustible; it cannot even "cover" the text according to the "letter" of the text.

These lessons have only a modest scope. They used to be called *explication de texte*, in which one of the rules was to find the explication of the text in the text, with no outside resource. This is what I have done, although I have extended the references to all three *Critique*s, as the Analytic of the Sublime forces one to do.

Why publish these notes in this state? The question always exceeds what the "author" can advance by way of reasons or excuses. Here are a few. He imagines that these notes will be helpful in avoiding certain errors in the reading of Kant's text, that they will be helpful in discussions, begun and to come, with his colleagues who are philosophers. He is also convinced that this book, once it has been published, will lighten the load of the one that is in progress. He would also like for the visible marks of oral presentation, which remain, to turn this file into something of an awkward homage, and a farewell, to this strange "profession": one "teaches philosophy" only by learning how to philosophize. Just as it is, I dedicate this collection to the students who for years have endured its working and reworking.

If one had to summarize in a few words what is here said, one could say that these lessons try to isolate the analysis of a differend of feeling in Kant's text, which is also the analysis of a feeling of differend, and to connect this feeling with the transport that leads all thought (critical thought included) to its limits.

Earlier versions of Chapters 1 and 7 have appeared in the *Revue Internationale de philosophie* 4, no. 1975 (1990), and in the collection *Du sublime* (Paris and Berlin, 1988), respectively. I wish to thank the editors of these publications.

Abbreviations

ANTH   *Anthropology from a Pragmatic Point of View.* Ed. and trans.
Mary J. Gregor. The Hague: Martinus Nijhoff, 1974.

KPV   *Critique of Practical Reason.* Trans. Lewis White Beck. New
York: Macmillan, 1956. *Kritik der praktischen Vernunft.*
Hamburg: Meiner, 1974.

KRV A, B   *Critique of Pure Reason* (A: 1781; B: 1787). Trans. N. Kemp
Smith. New York: St. Martin's Press, 1929. *Kritik der reinen
Vernunft.* Hamburg: Meiner, 1956.

KU   *Kant's Critique of Judgement* (1790). Trans. J. C. Meredith.
Oxford: Clarendon Press, 1952. *Kritik der Urteilskraft.* Hamburg: Meiner, 1974.

ORIENT   "What is Orientation in Thinking" (1786). In *Kant's Political
Writings,* ed. Hans Reiss, trans. H. B. Nisbet. Cambridge,
Eng.: Cambridge University Press, 1970, pp. 237–49.

FI   "First Introduction to the *Critique of Judgment*" (1789). In
Critique of Judgment, trans. Werner S. Pluhar. Indianapolis:
Hackett, 1987, pp. 383–441.

N.B.: For the three *Critiques*, reference is made first to the English
translation and then to the German edition (in italics). All references that
are not preceded by an abbreviation refer to the *Critique of Judgment.* The
abbreviation "t.m." following a reference to the English translation indicates that the French translation has been modified in Lyotard's text. All
English spelling including quotations conforms to the standard adopted
by *Webster's Ninth New Collegiate Dictionary.* Unless otherwise noted, the
use of italics for emphasis reproduces such uses in the French version.

LESSONS ON
THE ANALYTIC
OF THE SUBLIME

§1 Aesthetic Reflection

System and Feeling

The task assigned to the *Critique of Judgment*, as its Introduction makes explicit, is to restore unity to philosophy in the wake of the severe "division" inflicted upon it by the first two *Critiques*. One reading, correct but overly confident in the letter, sees this task accomplished in the regulative Idea of a finality of nature that is introduced in the second part of the third *Critique*. This Idea, in effect, serves as the sought-after "bridge" between the theoretical and the practical, spanning the gulf previously created between the knowledge of objects according to the conditions of possible experience and the realization of freedom under the unconditional of moral law. In the opening of this passage, the critique of aesthetic judgment fulfills, according to the aforesaid reading, an essentially preliminary function: taste at least, if not the feeling of the sublime, offers the paradox of a judgment that appears, problematically, to be doomed to particularity and contingency. However, the analytic of taste restores to judgment a universality, a finality, and a necessity—all of which are, indeed, subjective—merely by evincing its status as reflective judgment. This status is then applied to teleological judgment in order, precisely, to legitimate its use. In this way, the validation of subjective pleasure serves to introduce a validation of natural teleology.

This reading would seem fully justified by the way reflection is presented in the Introduction to the third *Critique*. The faculty of judging is said to be "simply *reflective*" when "only the particular is given and the universal has to be found" (18; *15*). This is what the *Anthropology* (§44) calls *Witz, ingenium,* or "discovering the universal for the particular," finding an identity in a multiplicity of dissimilar things. If reflection is, therefore, assigned the task of reunification, it is because of its heuristic function: although the faculty of pure judgment may not have "a special authority to prescribe laws," it may well have "a principle peculiar to itself upon which laws are sought" (15; *12*). In the terminology of judicial spheres of influence employed in paragraph II of this Introduction (11–12; *9–10*), although the faculty of judging will have "no field of objects appropriate to it as its realm" in which it legislates in an autonomous fashion, its peculiar principle does apply to "some territory." Precisely because it does not legislate, this principle can supplement the determinant legislations of understanding in its theoretical realm and of reason in its practical realm, and consequently reconcile the two. The "weakness" of reflection thus also constitutes its "strength."

The weakness of the principle peculiar to reflection is manifest in that it is a principle that is "merely subjective *a priori*" (15; *12*). This principle does not concern itself with the determination of objects, such as the world for understanding, or freedom for reason. Still, it must be remembered that the objects thus determined were not determined by the two preceding *Critiques* except as being possible *a priori*. Reflective judgment concerns itself with these objects in their particularity, as they are given. It judges them as if the rules that determined their possibility *a priori* were not sufficient to account for their particularity. It endeavors to "discover" a generality or a universality in them which is not that of their possibility but of their existence. The critical question is thus to determine the principle by which reflection is guided on the path to this discovery.

A problem is posed by this question, for the principle of judgment can be found neither in the realm of theoretical understanding nor in the realm of practical reason. It cannot be borrowed from any other authority save the faculty of judging itself. It "can only give as a law from and to itself" a "transcendental principle" (19; *16*). Such is the "subjectivity" of the principle: the faculty that exercises it is the same faculty that invents it. This principle, the result of art rather than reason, which can only be applied with art, cannot have the same objective validity as the categories for understanding or the law for practical reason, which are deduced by argumentation. The principle of judgment is, as we know, the principle of a teleology of nature for freedom. In judging according to this principle, knowledge permits itself to think the "particular natural laws" as forming a "system of experience" such that our faculty of cognition in general (that is, knowledge itself) might have determined "for [its] benefit" (*zum Behuf unserer Erkenntnisvermögen*: 19; *16*). An Idea that is merely regulative, and not legislative, thus unites the separate realms of nature and freedom, without losing any of their heterogeneity.

There can be no question, therefore, of reflection being summoned at the opening of the third *Critique* merely in its heuristic capacity: it invents its own principle, finality, and lets itself be guided by this principle in deciphering the empirical laws of nature. For the project of unifying philosophical knowledge with itself, this is sufficient, as the finality of nature can only be known analogically, *nach der Analogie* (15; *12–13*), with the finality of reason in its practical usage, where finality is causality by way of the Idea. It is proper, therefore, to introduce the faculty of reflection between understanding and reason in order to provide the indispensable supplement for this project.

However, the text of the Introduction does not stop here. It invokes "a further ground" for linking the theoretical and the practical. And the connection that one may expect on this ground "appears to be of even greater importance" than the one previously mentioned. The latter is "logical" (15; *12*) in the transcendental sense of determining realms of jurisdiction and territories of legislation. The former, judged "of even greater importance," is concerned with "the faculties of the soul" (ibid.). One might say that it belonged to transcendental psychology were it not that this expression closely resembles that of "rational psychology," and the paralogisms of the first *Critique* clearly show that rational psychology "owes its origin simply to misunderstanding" (KRV B, 377; *415*). This is not the place to debate the distinction, enigmatic as it is, between the (logical) faculties of knowledge and the "faculties of the soul generally"; the famous table (39; *36*) at the end of the Introduction sets these faculties in a parallelism that can only be "uneven." The distinction, and the parallelism it implies in turn, are, however, so important that they contain perhaps the whole secret of the problem of reflection. For "logically" reflection is called judgment, but "psychologically," if we may be permitted the improper use of this term for a moment, it is nothing but the feeling of pleasure and displeasure. As a faculty of knowledge, it is devoted to the *heuristic*, and in procuring "sensations," the meaning of which will become clear, it fully discloses its *tautegorical* character, a term by which I designate the remarkable fact that pleasure and displeasure are at once both a "state" of the soul and the "information" collected by the soul relative to its state. This it does in such a way that one cannot easily distinguish, at first, the role that the aesthetic will play—that the analysis of the *a priori* conditions of these "subjective" sensations will play—in the grand strategy of supplementation.

Paragraph VII of the Introduction does, indeed, set out to justify the aesthetic. However, it is no coincidence that the force of the argument consists in referring the pleasure of taste as faculty of the *soul* back to the agreement (to "the harmony" [*die Angemessenheit*]: 32; *27*), most certainly subjective, of the two faculties *of knowledge* that are always brought into play in any relation to an object: the faculty of presentation and the faculty of concepts, imagination, and understanding. The grounds for pleasure, the "psychological" state par excellence, are converted into a very logical harmony. There is thus a finality to be found even for pleasure, in the relation of objects—according only to their forms (for pleasure never becomes an element of cognition)—to the faculties of knowledge. The relation of the faculties of knowledge to each other gives taste the authority to lay claim to universality (see Chapter 8). A very subjective claim indeed, yet one that is nevertheless universal, for the interaction of understanding and imagination regarding the form of an object suffices, "without any reference to a concept" (*ohne Rücksicht auf einen Begriff*: 30, t.m.; *28*), to arouse in thought the pleasure that the affinity of these two faculties of knowledge gives it in general (31; *28–29*).

The subjective finality found in aesthetic pleasure seems of little importance to the general project as stated in the Introduction to the third *Critique*, where aesthetic reflection is declared to be simply "a special faculty" that judges things "according to a rule, but not according to concepts" (36; *32*). The teleological faculty, on the other hand, "is not a special faculty, but only general reflective judgment" (ibid.). And the reason, surprising at first, for this eminence is that the teleological faculty proceeds, "as it always does in theoretical cognition," "according to concepts" (*nach Begriffen*: ibid.). This can only be the concept of finality or, in other words, a causality of the end. The teleological faculty merely uses this concept of finality as it proceeds, "with respect to certain objects of nature, following special principles" (36; *32*). These principles are themselves "of a judgment that is merely reflective" (ibid.). This faculty prescribes that finality be employed, in effect, as a regulative and not as a legislative Idea. The fact remains that as Idea, finality is a concept. And this is enough to place teleological reflection on the side of knowledge—"it belongs to the theoretical part of philosophy"—whereas aesthetic reflection, which "contributes nothing [*nichts beträgt*] to the cognition of its object . . . must *only* be allocated [*gezählt*] to the critique of the judging subject" (ibid., t.m.). The argument concerning the aesthetic thus ends with the following statement: "A critique [of the judging subject] . . . is the propaedeutic of all philosophy" (ibid.).

A classical reading of the third *Critique* that puts the accent on teleology is, as we see, firmly rooted in the letter of the Introduction. Even when the Introduction sees in aesthetic pleasure something of great "importance," it does so only in order to show how aesthetic pleasure relates to the faculties of knowledge, that is, to a subjective finality. Moreover, the subjective quality of this finality allows the "importance" of the aesthetic to be immediately limited to that of the propaedeutic. Conversely, the conceptual, therefore *expoundable* (211–12; *201–2*) use of teleology and its application to objects of nature (even when teleology finds itself attached to "as if" clauses or to the "regulative" employment that is reflection's "peculiar principle") earn teleology the place of honor in the strategy of unification. The strength of reflective weakness can be explained by the heuristic function of reflection; the tautegorical aesthetic shares in the weakness of this strength.

I would argue that an importance of an entirely different order may be accorded the "Analytic of Aesthetic Judgment," that of being a propaedeutic to philosophy, a propaedeutic that is itself, perhaps, all of philosophy (for "we can at most only learn how to philosophize [*höchstens nur philosophieren lernen*]," but we cannot learn philosophy: KRV, 657, t.m.; *752*). One must be able to see beyond the strictly thematic reading that I have evoked and that Kant's text strongly encourages. The thematic reading remains faithful to the concern for a system that haunts the Introduction to the third *Critique*. However, aesthetic judgment conceals, I would suggest, a secret more important than that of doctrine, the secret of the "manner" (rather than the method) in which critical thought proceeds in general. The manner (*modus aestheticus*) "possesses no standard other than the *feeling* of unity in the presentation," the method (*modus logicus*) "follows definite *principles*" (182; *174*). "Fine art . . . has only . . . a *manner* (*modus*)" (226; *215*) and not a method. The mode of critical thought should by definition be purely reflective (it does not *already* have the concepts it seeks to use); moreover, aesthetic judgment reveals reflection in its most "autonomous" state, *naked*, so to speak. In aesthetic judgment, reflection is, as we have seen in the text of the Introduction, stripped of its objective, teleological function, even, one could say, of its heuristic function in general, because aesthetic judgment, considered from the point of view of the "soul," has no claim to knowledge and because, as pure pleasure, it has nothing other than itself to pursue. It perpetuates itself: "The contemplation of the beautiful . . . strengthens and reproduces itself. The case is analogous (but analogous only) to the way we linger [*Verweilung*]" on an attractive object, on an object that renders the mind "passive" (64; *61*).

Before an inquiry into the *a priori* conditions of judgments can be made, critical thought must be in a reflective state of this sort, if it does not want—and it must not want—these *a priori* conditions to be in any way prejudged in its investigation. Otherwise the latter will be nothing but delusion, and its discoveries mere semblances. Thought must "linger," must suspend its adherence to what it thinks it knows. It must remain open to what will orientate its critical examination: a feeling. The critique must inquire into the "dwelling place" of a judgment's legitimation. This dwelling place is constituted by the set of *a priori* conditions of possibility for the judgment. Yet how does it know that there is a dwelling place, and how does it know where to find it, if it has not *already* been informed of its address? Even informed of the address, thought would still need to orientate itself in order to find that dwelling place. Yet orientation, for thought as for the body, requires "a feeling." To orientate myself in unfamiliar places, even if I know the astronomical points of reference (the points of the compass), I must, in concrete terms, "necessarily be able to feel a difference within my own *subject*, namely, that between my right and my left hands" (ORIENT, 238). Otherwise, how would I know, for example, that when I face south the Orient is to the left? Kant draws attention to this point: "I call this a *feeling* because these two sides [right and left] display no perceptible difference as far as external intuition is concerned" (ibid.). Consequently, "I orientate myself *geographically* purely by means of a subjective distinction" (ibid., 239). (Can a feeling, which guides a manner, be called a *principle*, which commands a method? But it is subjective.)

Transposed into the realm of thought, the question is thus one of a "subjective distinction" that allows "reason" to determine its *Fürwahrhalten*, namely, how it is that reason can regard as true an object of thought in the absence of "objective criteria of knowledge" (ibid., 240). The problematic of the empirical use of concepts that are "already" determined (here, the points of the compass) is indeed the problematic of a pure reflection. Kant will respond to this problematic, in the article that I quote, by appealing to the "feeling of a *need* that is inherent in reason" (ibid.). However, his response is itself orientated by the stakes of the discussion to which the article is devoted, the "controversy" over pantheism between Jacobi and Mendelssohn. As regards aesthetic reflection, the "subjective distinction" should only be the feeling of pleasure and displeasure. It alone can give or refuse to give the *satisfecit* to reflection, depending on the orientation reflection chooses to take, and this it does immediately, "subjectively," in the absence of any objective criterion. Even so, this pleasure and its opposite must be "pure," for otherwise they proceed necessarily from the satisfaction of another faculty, theoretical or practical, rather than from pleasure or displeasure, or from a simple, empirical enjoyment. Thus they lose all value of discernment for reflection, and, above all, they attest that the legislations, yet to be discovered, already exercise their criteria of satisfaction on the knowledge that seeks to house them. Thought would not have truly lingered.

We will see that Kantian thought cannot escape this final predicament (of the type you would not look for me if you had not already found me), nor can the predicament be avoided. However, not being able to escape it is one thing, and knowing what to escape is another. This ideal "knowledge" is given to reflection in aesthetic judgment because reflection finds in aesthetic judgment the most autonomous model for its "manner." The reading that I advocate—without at all contesting the legitimacy of the other reading—consequently admits that if the third *Critique* fulfills its mission of unifying the field of philosophy, it does so, not primarily by introducing the theme of the regulative Idea of an objective finality of nature, but by making manifest, in the name of the aesthetic, the reflexive manner of thinking that is at work in the critical text as a whole.

Sensation as Tautegory

Let us turn now to the distinction between the two kinds of operations that are delegated to reflection and not easily articulated with one another: guidance operations that I have called heuristic for the transcendental activity of thought, and "sensations" that inform thought of its "state." The difficulty here resides in the combination of the two dispositions. The following two-part question, admittedly a bit summary, would be right on the mark: How can feelings orientate a critique? Why should the latter have any need for them?

We must first examine feeling itself. In the third *Critique*, as we know, the term "aesthetic" is subject to an important semantic displacement in relation to its usage in the first *Critique*. I must pass over these indeed primordial questions that are associated with this small revolution. The revolution does, in any case, prohibit one from freely transposing questions raised by the pure *a priori* forms of sensibility to the analysis of judgments on the beautiful and the sublime.

Initially, as regards the question of the conditions of knowledge in general, "aesthetic" means to grasp the givens of sensible intuition in the *a priori* forms of space and time. In the third *Critique*, the term designates reflective judgment, only insofar as it excites the interest of the "faculty of the soul" that is the feeling of pleasure and of displeasure. Kant insists that the term "sensation" that is "a determination of the feeling of pleasure or displeasure . . . is given quite a different meaning [*etwas ganz anderes*]" from the sensation that is "the representation of a thing" (45, t.m.; *42*). Sensation is an indispensable block in the "building" of the conditions of possibility for objective knowledge in general, the essential articulation of which consists in the subsumption of an intuitive given, already synthesized by a schema, under the synthesis of a judgment by concepts for which understanding is responsible. In the analytic of taste, sensation no longer has any cognitive finality; it no longer gives any information about an object but only about the "subject" itself.

According to this second meaning, sensation informs "the mind" of its "state." Let us say that the "state of mind," the *Gemütszustand*, is a nuance. This nuance affects thought as it thinks something. The affection occupies a position in a range that extends from extreme pleasure to extreme displeasure; affections occupy a position similar to that of the right and the left in pure reflective thought. Sensation, the *aisthēsis*, signals where the "mind" is on the scale of affective tints. It could be said that sensation is already an immediate judgment of thought upon itself. Thought judges it to be "good" or "bad" given the activity in which it is engaged. This judgment thus synthesizes the act of thinking that is taking place before an object, with the affection that this act procures for it. The affection is like the inner repercussion of the act, its "reflection."

From this brief localization of sensation there follow two remarkable characteristics, both of which relate to the aesthetic subject and to aesthetic time. The first is that sensation is always there. I would not say that it is permanent, knowing the problem that the idea of permanence raises for critical thought especially when applied to a "subject." I will come back to this. By "always there" I mean only that it is there "every time" there is an act of thought, what Kant calls "knowledge" or "representation." The term "act of thinking" presents its own difficulties. We can hope to lessen these difficulties by limiting its scope to the notion of actual thought as opposed to active thought, or occurring rather than performing: "for, *in so far as it is contained in a single moment* [in einem Augenblick enthalten] no representation can ever be anything [*niemals etwas anderes*] but absolute unity [*als absolute Einheit*]" (KRV A, 131, t.m.; *143*; emphasis in the text).

The occurrence of sensation accompanies all modes of thought, whatever the nature of thought may be. To use the terms that Kant himself employs to place them in the "serial arrangement" of representations (KRV, 314; *354*), whether one "intuits" or "conceives," whether one forms a "notion" or an "idea," there is always sensation. The dichotomy with which this classification begins concerns our question directly. It distinguishes perceptions that are representations "with consciousness," knowledge *Erkenntnis* (*cognitio*), objective perceptions, from sensations *Empfindung* (*sensatio*) or perceptions "which relate . . . solely to the subject as the modification of its state" (ibid.). Intuition, like sensation, is an *immediate* representation, but of the object rather than the "subject." Thus it is a "knowledge." Despite the immediate presence of the state of thought it signals or perhaps because of it, sensation is not the knowledge of a subject. In the passage quoted above, it is not said that sensation is present every time there is "representation," that is, conscious representation. But we will see in the "deduction" of "common sense" in paragraph 21 of the third *Critique* (see Chapter 8, pp. 198–202) that such must be the case if aesthetic judgment is not to be reduced to a particular opinion tied to a simple empirical agreeableness (48–50; *46–48*). We encountered the same argument in the Introduction (32; *28*), where the argument rested on the universality of the *a priori* conditions of knowledge in general (of thought) and was used to legitimate taste's claim to universality.

Any act of thinking is thus accompanied by a feeling that signals to thought its "state." But this state is nothing other than the feeling that signals it. For thought, to be informed of its state is to feel this state—to be affected. The sensation (or the feeling) is both the state of thought and a warning to thought of its state by this state. Such is the first characteristic of reflection: a dazzling immediacy and a perfect coincidence of what feels and what is felt. This is true to such a degree that even the distinction between the active and the passive nature of this "feeling" is improper to feeling, for it would introduce the beginnings of an objectivity and with it a knowledge. I call this a matter of reflection because sensation refers solely to the criterion of differentiation between pleasure and displeasure (and not at all to the distinction between true and false or just and unjust). The faculty *of the soul* that is responsible for this difference is the feeling of pleasure and displeasure, to which the simple "faculty of judgment" corresponds on the side of the said *cognitive* faculties (39; *36*). Yet in its purest mode, the latter is reflective. Pure reflection is first and foremost the ability of thought to be immediately informed of its state by this state and without other means of measure than feeling itself.

In paragraph 9 of the third *Critique*, Kant introduces sensation. The question is to know how in a judgment of taste we become

conscious of the agreement of the faculties (of knowledge) that
are in free play, whether it is by sensation or "intellectually." The
answer to the question is argued in the following way:

> If the given representation occasioning the judgment of taste were a
> concept that united understanding and imagination in the estimate
> [*Beurteilung*] of the object so as to give a cognition of the object, the
> consciousness of this relation would be intellectual (as in the objective
> schematism of judgment dealt with in the critique). But then, in that
> case, the judgment would not be laid down with respect to pleasure
> and displeasure, and so would not be a judgment of taste. But now,
> the judgment of taste determines the object, independently of con-
> cepts, as regards delight and the predicate of beauty. There is, there-
> fore, no other way for the subjective unity of the relation in question
> to make itself known [*kenntlich machen*] than by sensation. (59–60;
> *57*)

Further (§36), when he proceeds to the "deduction" of judgments
of taste by answering the question How are judgments of taste
possible?, Kant distinguishes this question from the question about
the possibility of judgments of knowledge in the following terms:
in judgments of taste in contrast to judgments of knowledge, the
faculty of judging "has not merely to subsume [the givens] under
objective concepts of understanding . . . and does not come under
a law, but rather . . . it is itself, subjectively, object as well as law
[*Gegenstand sowohl als Gesetz ist*]" (145, t.m.; *138*).

In this last passage in particular one begins to detect the other
characteristic of reflection, namely, a capacity that I will call a
domiciling capacity. Thinking can defer to the power of understanding for a knowledge of the object. For the taste it has for an
object, however, it relies on its own competence, its "law," the
"subjective principle" we have already encountered. Thought only
judges according to its state, judging what it finds pleasurable.
Thus this state, which is the "object" of its judgment, is the very
same pleasure that is the "law" of this judgment. These two aspects of judgment, referentiality and legitimacy, are but one in the
aesthetic. By moving the term "aesthetic" away from Schelling's
particular use of it (although the problem is a similar one), I mean

to draw attention to the remarkable disposition of reflection that I call *tautegorical.* The term designates the identity of form and content, of "law" and "object," in pure reflective judgment as it is given to us in the aesthetic.

The effect of sensation's recurrence with every occurrence of (conscious) thought is that thinking "knows" the state (without cognizing it, but sensation is a representation with consciousness, a perception) in which it finds itself *in this occurrence.* Sensation is thus able to pass through the different spheres of thought that the critique distinguishes. Sensation is there on the occasion of any object that thought can think, wherever it may be in the "field" of possible knowledge. For sensation never takes place except on the occasion of a thought. The differences that have allowed a hierarchy to exist between the simple "dwelling place" of an object of thought in relation to a "territory" in which its knowledge is possible, and a "realm" in which thought legislates *a priori* (12–13; *9–10*), do not prevent thought from being able to *feel itself* on every occasion. Thought must still be able to feel itself as it relates to objects in the "unbounded . . . field" (13; *11*) of the supersensible, even if one only finds in it Ideas of reason about whose objects one can have no theoretical cognition (ibid.).

One might contend that this transitiveness is assured from the moment that one has presupposed *one* mind, *one* thought, *one* subject, and that, therefore, reflection is nothing more in the end than the predicate of one of these entities. So that the recurrence of sensation would only translate, in succession, the permanence of a substrate. This objection raises nothing less than the question of the subject in Kantian thought. We will come back to this. But as to the presupposition of a substrate "bearer" of sensation, the refutation of such a hypothesis is simple. If there is a substrate in Kantian thought, it exists as the regulative Idea, for the substrate is the supersensible about which we have no knowledge (213–15; *203–5*). The idea that we have of it cannot even be unique, for it must be suited to each of the antinomies proper to the three highest faculties that are the object of the critique. To represent this substrate one needs not one but three Ideas: that of the "supersensible of nature in general," that of a "subjective finality of nature for our cognitive faculties," and that of a finality of freedom in accord with the finality in the moral sphere (215; *205*; see Chapter 8, pp. 215–18).

It is striking that little mention is made of a subject in the great majority of Kant's texts that touch on reflection. In general the exceptions are to be found in the Introduction. Whatever the case may be, the notion of a "subject" in its substantive form does not seem necessary to the understanding of what reflection is. The notion of actual thought (in the sense evoked above) is sufficient. On the contrary, the adjectival or adverbial forms, "subjective," "subjectively," abound in these texts. They do not designate an instance, subjectivity, to which sensation refers. They allow one to distinguish the information that sensation provides thought from the information that a knowledge of the object brings thought. We have read (59; *57*) that Kant places sensation in a kind of symmetry with the schema. The parallel is quickly abandoned, for the schema makes knowledge possible, whereas sensation provides no knowledge at all. However, something of the symmetry may be preserved: just as the schema unites the two faculties, imagination and understanding, in order to make knowledge of an object possible—on the side of the object, so to speak—so sensation is the sign of their union (pleasure) or of their disunion (displeasure), *on the occasion* of an object and on the side of thought. In both cases, it is indeed a relation between the same faculties. It is nevertheless a fact that the schema is determinant of the object of knowledge, and the sensation is a simple sign for thought of the state of thinking this object. The sign provides an indication of this state every time that thought thinks. One could say that thought is reflected there, on the condition that one accept a reflection without representation in the modern sense of the word (Freud, for example, conceives of affect as a "representative" without representation).

In order to account for this disposition, Kant introduces the notion of a supplementary faculty—rather neglected until now, especially in its "tautegorical" aspect—the simple capacity to feel pleasure or displeasure. It has no more need than do the other faculties of referring back to a substantial "subject." In critical thought, these other faculties are, after all, or should simply be sets of conditions that make synthetic judgments possible *a priori*. As to its logical implication, a faculty can be reduced to a group of "primary" propositions that are *a priori* conditions: the definition of thinkable objects, the axioms of the syntheses that can be performed on them. What Kant calls the "territory" or the "realm" of the faculty corresponds to what the logician calls the domain of application of a set of axioms (*mutatis mutandis...*).

"Subjective" always determines a state of thought (of "mind," one could say, although the *Gemüt* of *Gemütszustand* is more of a sentimental mode than it is a *Geist*). The term "subjective" forces the critique to question what thinking feels when it thinks and what it cannot fail to feel in every case or, as Kant writes, on all occasions. If one can speak of the occurrence of sensation in all of the uses of thinking, let there be no mistake: this occurrence is but the insistence of a shadow thrown by a certain actual thought on itself, and not the persistence of a substantial predicate attached to "thinking." In sensation, the faculty of judging judges subjectively, that is, it reflects the state of pleasure or displeasure in which actual thought feels itself to be. This almost elementary characteristic on which the deduction of the subjective universality of taste will lean comes to light in aesthetic judgment. This is because, in the case of aesthetic judgment, judgment has no objective validity, and the faculty of judging has, in effect, only to judge a state of pleasure or of displeasure, which is by this time already the judgment.

The "Subjective"

The second observation relates to what the first implied as to the nature of an aesthetic temporality. I can only begin to outline it here, for the latter certainly merits a study of its own. An indispensable element of this study lies in the analysis of the pleasure experienced in taste from the perspective of the faculties of knowledge in general. There is a certain minimalism to the *a priori* condition of pleasure provided by the beautiful: "Now the concepts in a judgment constitute its content (what belongs to the cognition of the object). But the judgment of taste is not determinable by means of concepts. Hence it can only have its ground in the subjective formal condition of a judgment in general. The subjective condition of all judgments is the judging faculty itself, or judgment" (143; *136–37*). Here we see why the "deduction" of the judgment of taste is "so easy": "It is spared the necessity of having to justify the objective reality of a concept" (147; *141*). This minimalism on the side of the faculties of knowledge prevents pleasure from being attributed to a subject. On the contrary it leads to an analysis of the part played by the two other faculties, imagination and understanding, in the "state" of thought that is pleasure. The nuance *of* this state or that in which this state consists is to be found in the relation of these faculties to one another outside of any cognitive aim.

The analytic of the judgment of taste makes this clear under the double heading of quantity and modality. We will come back to the use of categories in this analysis (see pp. 43–49 and Chapter 2). If taste is not to lapse into the particularity and contingency of a determined empirical agreeableness, one should be able to discover in it a universality and a necessity, despite its wholly "subjective" nature. We know the solution given to this problem by the analytic: a judgment of the beautiful is not immediately universal, but it immediately "imputes" (*sinnt . . . an*), "waits for" (*erwartet*), "promises itself" (*sich verspricht*) (56–57 t.m.; *54*) a subjective universality in the name of a *Gemeingültigkeit*, of a universal validity (54; *52*). This for its quantity. For its modality, the judgment of taste unites, in a necessary way, the "favor" (*Gunst*: 49; *47*) that distinguishes it from other delights with the form judged beautiful: this form cannot fail to please. But this necessity cannot be demonstrated, nor can it be anticipated by a reasoning. It is said to be "exemplary" (*exemplarisch*: 81; *78*) because judgment, in the singularity of its occurrence on the contingent occasion of an object's form, only gives the "example of a universal rule that one cannot formulate [*die man nicht angeben kann*]" (ibid., t.m.). This form *cannot* fail to please.

The quantity and the modality thus defined depart notably from what they would have to be if they were categories of understanding. They admit restrictive clauses that turn them into something like logical monsters. But one must see precisely in these distortions the sign that we are dealing with "places" of the reflective topic that are subjective modes of synthesis, provisional or preparatory to the categories as they are described in the Appendix to the analytic of the first *Critique* entitled "Amphiboly of Concepts of Reflection" (KRV, 276; *309*). (I return to this below. To facilitate matters I will refer to this text simply as the Appendix.) In place of what will be the quantity of a determinant judgment, reflection can already compare givens under the "heading" (*Titel*) of their identity or their difference, and in place of what will be the modality of a determinant judgment, it can compare givens under the "heading" of their determinability or determination (KRV, 277, 281–82; *310, 315–16*). The distortion or the monstrosity that affects the categories by means of which the analysis of taste proceeds, results from the fact that here the movement of reflective anamnesis works from the objective to the subjective. If the categories were applicable to taste just as they were, taste would be a determinant judgment. (However, it is true, and we will try to understand why it is, that this judgment that is not determinant must be analyzed by means of the categories in order to appear paradoxically as such.)

This judgment is reflective, and thus it is singular or particular, but it nonetheless involves a double claim to the universal and the necessary. Is this claim legitimate? It is, given the condition of a principle authorizing it. This principle is obviously a "subjective" one. It "determines . . . by means of feeling only and not through concepts" (*welches nur durch Gefühl und nicht durch Begriffe . . . bestimme*: 82; *79*). It can be formulated: there must be a *Gemeinsinn*, a "common sense." This sense is not at all an "external sense" (an allusion, perhaps, to the computing of a sixth aesthetic sense by Dubos and by Hutcheson), but "the effect arising from the free play of our powers of cognition" (83; *80*). This is the same principle that was presupposed in paragraph 8 under the name "universal voice" (*die allgemeine Stimme*: 56; *54*). The term *Stimme* appears very rarely and perhaps just once in the text of the third *Critique*. *Stimme* is quite different from the French *voix*; it evokes the accord of voices, and the mood of a soul (*Stimmung*), and the beginnings of its determination as destination (*Bestimmung*). The term leads one directly to the analysis of *Gemeinsinn*. What is in accord in the latter are the voices of understanding and imagination, the faculties of knowledge taken only in their respective dispositions, the one to conceive and the other to present, taken thus precisely "before" they operate in a determining way.

The interpretation to be given to this common sense has provoked much debate. I will attempt to show how its *ratio essendi* consists not in the assent that empirical individuals give one another in regard to the beauty of an object but—insofar as it makes the *a priori* feeling of aesthetic pleasure possible—in the unison in which the two "voices" of the faculties are to be found: the "proportionate accord" (*proportionnierte Stimmung*: 60; *58*), "accord" (*Stimmung*), "proportion" (*Proportion*) in which their "ratio" (*Verhältnis*) is "best adapted" (*zuträglichste*: 83; *80*). This argument will be elaborated further (see Chapter 8). For the moment I will simply support it with the following passage from paragraph 31: "Now if this universality [of taste] is not to be based on a collection of votes [*Stimmensammlung*], a recollection of voices and interrogation of others as to what sort of sensations they experience, but is to rest, as it were, upon an autonomy of the subject passing judgment on the feeling of pleasure (in the given representation), i.e., upon his own taste, and yet is also not to be derived from concepts" (135–36, t.m.; *130*). This text in particular, in which the problem of the universality of taste is posed, should be enough to discourage all sociologizing and anthropologizing readings of aesthetic common sense, although other passages of the third *Critique* seem to lend themselves to it (150–52; *144–45*). I am thinking in particular of Hannah Arendt's reading, but she is not the only one. The "autonomy of the subject" here invoked by Kant can be nothing other than what I call the reflective tautegory. It leads us back to our question about aesthetic time.

The pleasure of the beautiful promises, demands, gives the example of a communicated happiness. There will never be proof that this happiness is communicated, even when individuals or cultures empirically agree to recognize forms given by nature or art as beautiful. There can never be proof of this because a judgment of taste is not determinant and the predicate of beauty is not objective (41–42, 50–51; *39–40, 48–49*). However, if taste involves this demand it is because taste is the feeling of a possible harmony of the faculties of knowledge outside of knowledge. And as these faculties are universally and necessarily required in any thinking that judges in general, so must their greatest affinity be in any thinking that judges itself, that is, that feels itself. Such is, in summary, the "deduction" of the principle of common sense, the argument of which paragraph 21 (83–84; *80–81*) gives an outline (addressed in §9; 57–58; *55–56*). The deduction rests on the "fact," provided by the pleasure of taste, that there is a degree of optimal agreement between the two faculties. This degree of optimal agreement exists even when the faculties are released from the constraints of knowledge and morality, and have no way of grasping what it is that provides this pleasure, i.e. the form of the object: "free play" (*freie Spiel*: 58; *55*), "quickening" (*Belebung*: 64, *143*; 61, *137*), "stirs" (*erweckt*), "puts" (incites; *versetzt*: 154; *147*; see Chapter 2, pp. 60–67).

Thus this unison only takes "place" whenever the pleasure of taste is experienced. It is only the "sensation" of this unison here and now. It releases a horizon of unison in general but is itself singular, tied to the unpredictable occurrence of a form. The union of faculties is felt on the occasion of a certain sunset, on the occasion of this particular Schubert allegro. Universality and necessity are promised but are promised singularly every time, and are only just promised. There could be no greater misunderstanding of judgments of taste than to declare them simply universal and necessary.

Aesthetic Temporality

I consider this unison to be singular and recurrent and always as if it were occurring anew, as if it were something that appeared every time for the first time, like the outlines of a "subject." Each time a form provides the pure pleasure that is the feeling of the beautiful, it is as if the dissonances that divide thought, those of the imagination and the concept, were on the wane and left the way open, if not to a perfect agreement, then to a peaceful conjugality or at least to a benevolent and gentle emulation resembling the one uniting fiancés (see Chapter 7). The subject would be the perfect unity of the faculties. But taste does not *result* from this unity. In this sense it cannot be felt by a subject. It results from the "engagement" of the two faculties and thus announces the hoped-for birth of a united couple. There is not one subjectivity (the couple) that experiences pure feelings; rather, it is the pure feeling that promises a subject. In the aesthetic of the beautiful the subject is in a state of infancy.

It finds itself in this state each time pleasure arises from the beautiful. It does not *remain* in infancy. For it to remain so, the synthesis with its "promises of unity" would have to be possible in a unity that persisted identical to itself over time. For the condition of persistence is one that must be found in the concept of a subject. We see, however, that the condition is contradictory: if a unity of promises were possible, promises of unity would be impossible or fallacious. The aesthetic would be merely a muddled logic.

Yet even logically, the condition for the unification of the diversity of representations in a subject encounters great difficulty. This synthesis is attempted in the second edition of the first *Critique* under the heading "Transcendental Deduction of the Pure Concepts of Understanding." Whether or not this deduction (in the critical sense: KRV A, 120; *126*) misses its object or not will not be discussed here. I will only remind the reader that "the principle of the synthetic unity of apperception," also called the *Ich denke* or the "self as identical" (KRV B, 153, 155; *140*, *145*), which the deduction establishes or claims to establish whatever its intrinsic ground, refers only to a thinking that knows objects objectively. In arguing to legitimate this principle (KRV B, §19), Kant insists on this to such an extent that he makes it the force of the said deduction: for want of being bound to the *a priori* principle of this *Selbst*, judgments about objects merely have a "subjective validity" (ibid., 159; *154*), are "only subjective" (ibid., 159; *154–55*) as in the case of "perception" and "association" (ibid.).

Without going into the intrinsic difficulties of this deduction, it would be wrong to look for the aesthetic "subject" in a synthesis similar to that of the *Ich denke*, the sole purpose of which is to guarantee the objectivity of judgments. I would venture further. A reading, even one like Heidegger's, endeavoring, not without reason, to demonstrate that in the end the authentic principle of the synthesis is not the "I think" but time—such a reading is valid (if it is valid) only for knowledge and can only refer to determinant theoretical judgments. It is clear that morality (for example), if only because of the supposition of an unconditioned causality that escapes by hypothesis the serial time of the conditions of determination—a supposition that must be made in order to deduce morality—requires a notion of time or of temporality more heterogeneous than that required by knowledge (see Chapter 5, pp. 131–37). This is all the more true for aesthetic time. Judgments of taste determine nothing of their object. To be synthesized with each other in succession and eventually in a subject, they themselves must nevertheless be taken as objects for this synthesis. This is always possible. But by its very nature this synthesis is the one that unites the diversity of judgments of taste under the concept of their determination and under the schema of their succession. It is thus theoretical and objective, like the *a priori* unity of apperception, and not aesthetic and subjective.

One needs to venture further still. The first edition of the first *Critique*, in its Preliminary Remark or more precisely the *vorläufige Erinnerung* that constitutes the body of the second section of the deduction (KRV A, 131–33; *141–47*), focuses on the three elementary syntheses of apprehension, reproduction, and recognition (ibid., 132–33; *140–41*) that apply to the givens upon which understanding makes its judgments of knowledge. These syntheses, Kant writes, "point to three subjective sources of knowledge that make possible understanding itself—and consequently all experience as its empirical product" (KRV A, 131; *141*). A few lines earlier Kant already notes that these sources are "subjective," when he indicates that they "form the *a priori* foundation of the possibility of experience" that comes to fill in the categories of understanding. The "objective reality" of the categories of understanding finds sufficient authorization in the proof that one cannot think without them. But "more than" (*mehr als*) the unique power of thinking as understanding is at stake here. What is at stake is understanding insofar as it knows objects. The "subjective sources" (the syntheses) establish the transcendental possibility of the knowledge of objects.

These syntheses are of crucial importance to aesthetic judgments in their relation to time. In the third *Critique* it is no accident that from a "mathematical" point of view, the "Analytic of the Sublime," under the category of quantity, or under the "heading" of its *subjective* analogue, focuses almost entirely on the "apprehension" (*Auffassung*) and the "comprehension" (*Zusammenfassung*), also called the *comprehensio aesthetica* (99, 102, 107; *95, 98, 104*), of the elements of a given form (see Chapter 4, pp. 102–9). The analysis is conducted from the perspective of space, but it is easy and interesting to carry it over to the form of time. The painful character proper to the sublime feeling proceeds notably from the aporia of the judgment it involves from a quantitative point of view (see Chapter 4). Transposed into time, this aporia signifies an inability to synthesize the givens by containing them within "*a single moment*" (in einem Augenblick: KRV A, 131; *143*). If in apprehension, consequently, the intuition, limited here to its *subjective* status because it is not a question of knowing the object, is thwarted if not impossible (see Chapter 5, pp. 141–46), one must ask oneself how the synthesis of "reproduction in imagination" that is "inseparably bound" to it (KRV A, 133; *148*) can take place at all. Not to speak of the third synthesis, the "recognition in a concept." Moreover, one does not see how in the absence of the elementary syntheses, "subjective sources" that "make possible understanding," the unity of a subject (here, the subject of the sublime feeling) could be deduced.

I have chosen the example of the sublime judgment because it responds clearly, that is, negatively, to the question of the possibility of a subject and an aesthetic temporality (both sublime) constituted according to the model of the *Ich denke* and the temporality required for theoretical thinking. There seems to be no question that the most elementary conditions (the syntheses of time) for the synthesis of a *Selbst* are lacking here.

Yet this failing does not in the least prevent the feeling of the sublime from being a feeling, that is, a "sensation" by which a thought, reflective in this case, is made aware of its state. This state is certainly complex, ambivalent as to the quality of the judgment that is made about the object, for thinking says both "yes" and "no" to the latter, according and refusing the object its "favor": thinking is both "attracted" (*angezogen*) and "repelled" (*abgestoßen*: 91; *88*). It remains that "the judgment itself [that is, the sublime feeling] all the while steadfastly preserves its aesthetic character, because it represents, without being grounded on any definite concept of the object, merely the subjective play of the mental powers" (107; *103*). I conclude that the properties that prevent the deduction of a sublime subject are the same ones that allow the sublime to be maintained in the order of the "subjective."

The "subjective" can and must persist as the sensation of itself that accompanies any act of thinking the instant it occurs. This it must do even when the most elementary synthesis required by knowledge, that of a minimal apprehension of the givens in a single instantaneous grasp, is no longer assured by the imagination, the faculty whose responsibility it is to ensure this apprehension. In such a case where this synthesis is wanting in the order of determination, the *lack* of synthesis is felt just as strongly in the order of reflection. This is the case because the only synthesis relevant for reflection is the synthesis that puts the faculties at work in thinking in contact with each other. If imagination succumbs in its duel with reason, it is signaled in and as a "state" of thought; it is felt. It is a displeasure.

When it is a matter of taste, the relation between partners is good, well proportioned, and "free" because it is not subject to the legality of understanding that constrains the imagination by schematism and principles to prepare the givens for their sub-sumption under concepts. This freedom is manifest in the gentle, reciprocal emulation between the faculty of concepts and the fac-ulty of presentation, without the former taking over with its "sur-feited" excess (89; *85*) of order (of geometry, for example), or the latter with a fantasy so uncontrolled it would escape all subjective finality (85–88; *82–84*). This euphonic disposition (to return to the motif of *Stimme*) is examined in the analysis of taste from the per-spective of the relation, which, here, is finality (61–81; *58–77*). This finality is subjective in that it puts the components of the thinking of the beautiful, that is, of imagination and understanding, to-gether in such a way as to suggest their accord. Thus it is, I repeat, that *one* "subject," a subject, that is, *one* is promised.

To say on the contrary that the relation of the faculties in ques-tion in the sublime feeling—imagination and reason—is cacopho-nous does not change the general disposition that places any aes-thetic on the side of the "subjective" or reflective judgment. It seems the feeling must be the opposite of what it is in taste, for what is felt in the sublime is not the proper proportion in the free play of the two faculties that are being exercised, but their dispro-portion and even their incommensurability: an "abyss" (*Abgrund*) separates them. An abyss that repels and attracts an imagination (107; *103*) is enjoined to present the absolute. The paradox of Kant's analysis (which here, no matter what he says, closely fol-lows Burke's analysis of *delight*) is that it discerns in this cacopho-ny a secret euphony of superior rank (see Chapter 5).

However, the partners have also changed; reason has been re-placed by understanding in the challenge to imagination, and *be-cause of this* another finality is revealed in the ruins of the agree-ment of the faculties that made the beautiful pleasurable. Due to the change of imagination's partner, a conflict, which at first ap-pears to be merely "mathematical" in the antithetical sense of the first *Critique*, turns into a "dynamical" conflict. From a conflict in which reflection dismisses both parties with its double "no": nei-ther of you, neither one nor the other, has any legitimacy to claim what you claim—we move to a conflict in which it credits both of them with a double "yes": imagination is justified in trying to present the unpresentable and in not being able to succeed; reason is right to demand that it make this vain effort, because reason here is practical and the Idea to be presented is unconditioned causality, freedom, which constitutively requires its present realization but also constitutes the supreme "destination" of the mind (see Chapter 7, pp. 171–73).

Thus the question of whether the subject of the sublime is the same as the subject of the beautiful makes no sense. There cannot be a subject as synthesis, as container, or as agent of sublime feeling any more than there can be a subject of taste. To say that the sublime feeling is subjective means that it is a reflective judgment and as such has no claim to the objectivity of a determinant judgment. It is subjective in that it judges the state of feeling, and judges according to the state of feeling, in a tautegorical fashion. As with taste, the filtering of the analysis of this aesthetic judgment through the categories allows one to determine a concept of this "state." The procedure reveals the degree to which the unity of the faculties is precarious, lost almost—this is the component of anguish in this feeling. The "aptitude" for Ideas of reason must be developed in order for the perspective of a unity to reemerge from the disaster and, to say it simply, for a sublime feeling to be possible. This is its component of elevation that makes it similar to moral respect. Taste promises everyone the happiness of an accomplished subjective unity; the sublime speaks to a few of another unity, much less complete, ruined in a sense, and more "noble" (*edel*: 125; *120*). By recalling these various predicates, one is painting shades, the nuances of feeling; one is not constructing a subject. In the singularity of its occurrence, aesthetic feeling is pure subjective thinking or reflective judgment itself.

For Kant, what one calls the subject is either the subjective aspect of thinking, and as such consists entirely in the tautegory that makes feeling the sign, for thought, of its state, thus the sign of feeling itself because the "state" of thinking is feeling; or else the subject is only a ground zero where the synthesis of concepts is suspended (in the first *Critique*) or is the ever receding horizon of the faculties' synthesis (in the third *Critique*). In both cases it is an Idea the paralogisms of which the first *Critique* enumerates and that reflexively attach themselves to a transcendental appearance if one is not careful (KRV, 328–83; *370–436*). It is precisely through reflection, using the subjective state as a guide for thinking, using the feeling that accompanies it in all its acts, that one can locate this appearance and restore all proper domiciliations. And when the act of thinking is directed at the subject, it is with reflection again that one can critique the notion of subject.

The Heuristic

We will now examine the consequences for critical thinking and for the critical text of the other trait that characterizes reflection, the one I have called heuristic. It does not amount to very much to say that reflection, as sensation, accompanies all acts of thinking: it guides them. Nor to say that it passes through the topic of the faculties' spheres of influence: it elaborates the topic. Nor does it amount to very much to say that reflection is itself elaborated in a transparent manner in the aesthetic insofar as the latter is subjective: reflection is the (subjective) laboratory of all objectivities. In its heuristic aspect, reflection thus seems to be the nerve of critical thought as such.

Kant introduces reflection in its heuristic aspect starting with the first *Critique*, in the Appendix to the analytic of principles (KRV, 276–94; *309–31*). He calls reflection, *Überlegung*, "that state of mind in which we first set ourselves to discover [*ausfindig zu machen*] the subjective conditions under which we are able to arrive at concepts" (ibid., 276; *309*). To a great extent the text is devoted to the critique of intellectualist philosophy, to the philosophy of Leibniz in particular. Faithful to the inspiration that rules the transcendental aesthetic, Kant reminds us here that phenomena are not objects in themselves and that a certain use of "concepts" that Leibniz mistakenly attributes to understanding alone must be repatriated to the territory that belongs to sensibility.

The question concerns the domiciliation of the syntheses. Not every synthesis is the doing of understanding. But how do we know it? One would need to have at one's disposal a "topic" that could distinguish in advance not only the "places" (ibid., 281; *315*) in which the syntheses could precisely take "place" but also the conditions in which the application of these syntheses was legitimate and those in which it was not. The "logical topic" (ibid., 281; *316*), which has its source in Aristotle, distinguishes the different "headings" (ibid., 281–82; *315–16*) under which a plurality of given "representations" can be assembled. But this determination reveals a "doctrine" (*eine Lehre*: ibid., 281; *315*) that already confuses these "headings" with logical categories as if any synthesis were legitimate from the moment that it obeyed a rule of understanding, a mistake perpetuated by intellectualism.

The preliminary question to a logical topic is thus the following: How is the use of these "headings" determined? How are they different from categories? This is the question of the "transcendental topic." It does not prejudge the "headings" it distinguishes as being applicable to things themselves. What is presented in the "headings" is only "the comparison of the representations that is prior to the concept of things" (ibid., 281; *316*). These "headings" regroup the spontaneous ways of synthesizing givens. One might say that they all respond to the question, What does this (this given) remind us of? They are always comparisons. But one may compare according to various "headings." Kant thus enumerates four ways of comparing, four "headings" that he discusses in the first part of the Appendix: identity/difference (*Verschiedenheit*), agreement/opposition (*Widerstreit*), inner/outer, determinable (or matter)/determination (or form).

How are they different from schemas when they seem to occupy a similar intermediary place? The function of the schematism is, let me repeat, to make possible the modes of synthesis already defined and attributed, respectively, to the unifying power given in the forms of sensibility and to the unifying power proper to the categories of understanding. The schemas are in "third" rank, so to speak, as intermediary operators in the transcendental elaboration of the conditions of possibility for knowledge in the strict sense. However, the various reflexive "headings" that put representations in relation to each other are "places" "in a state of mind" (ibid.,

278; *310*). The relations they enable look for their "right determining" (ibid.) of their assignment to a faculty, either understanding or sensibility. Once domiciled, the syntheses that these relations indicate only "*subjectively*" (ibid.) are legitimized in their objective, cognitive usage. The "headings" are thus not even "concepts of comparison" (ibid.), as one might be tempted to call them, but only places of provisional and preparatory localization. They can be compared to the *topoi* that for Aristotle and the rhetoricians (ibid., 281–82; *315–16*) support an argumentation of opinion, with the difference that the critique will retain "no more than the above-mentioned four" already cited (ibid., 281; *316*) and that it will not grant them any cognitive validity. These places are immediate. It is up to the reflection that detects them to turn them into authentic conditions for the possibility of syntheses, into transcendental locations, into forms or categories. This expected transformation is what allows them to be called "concepts of reflection" (ibid., 288; *324*).

It is subjectively through reflection that they first become present to thought as possible syntheses *felt* by thought "before" thinking turns them toward the knowledge of objects. It is again reflection, reflection alone that will assure their "right determining" by domiciling their use with one of the two faculties. For reflection is, writes Kant, "the consciousness of the relation of given representations to our different sources of knowledge" (ibid., 276; *309*). In Kant's text the term "consciousness" generally includes reflection: thinking is conscious insofar as it is aware of its state, that is, insofar as it feels itself. Reflection thus does not only feel thinking spontaneously synthesizing in such or such a manner—four all together—it also subjectively feels that a certain manner or a certain "heading" of synthesis belongs to sensibility, another to understanding. Thus it is that "we first set ourselves to discover the subjective conditions under which we are able to arrive at concepts" (ibid.), as we have read. This is how the "transcendental topic" operates, entrusting to reflection the determination of faculties in which every synthesis whatever its "heading" finds its legitimate dwelling place: "We must first resort to transcendental reflection in order to determine for which cognitive faculty they [the objects of these "headings"] are to be objects, whether for pure understanding or for sensibility" (ibid., 282; *316*).

An example: under the "heading" identity/difference, two objects whose predicates are all identical are logically indiscernible, according to Leibniz. However, if they are intuited in different regions according to the forms of space and/or of time, though it be at the same exact instant, it is necessary to think them as two distinct objects. "Certainly, if I know a drop of water in all its internal determinations as a thing-in-itself, and if the whole concept of any one drop is identical with that of every other, I cannot allow that any drop is different from any other. But if the drop is an appearance in space, it has its location not only in understanding (under concepts) but in sensible outer intuition (in space)" (ibid., 283; *318*). Leibniz's principle of indiscernibles is thus no more than "an analytic rule for the comparison of things through mere concepts" (ibid., 284; *318*).

It is not only the critique of intellectualism that is operative in the text of the Appendix. The Appendix is already the detection of the "transcendental appearance" (expounded a few pages later) that makes one believe that only the purely conceptual determination of a relation between phenomena (their identity) is valid; yet phenomena are given in a spatiotemporal intuition (that precisely makes them phenomena) and admit of other relations that may be in contradiction to the first. Although logically indiscernible, two objects can be aesthetically discernible (in the sense of the first *Critique*).

In the Appendix to the analytic of principles this confusion is still but a "transcendental amphiboly" (ibid., 282; *316*), that is, a confusion of address: the drops of water are identical if they are domiciled in understanding, different if they are addressed to sensibility. This is because thinking has a sensible intuition of the drops of water. Thus it is not a matter here as in the transcendental "appearance" (KRV, 297–307; *334–47*) of a finitude of the faculty of presentation forgetting itself in the use of concepts, but of negligence in the topical reflection on the conditions of knowledge of objects that are effectively knowable.

In face of the "illusion" that pushes thought to grant the same cognitive value to concepts of reason (without the corresponding intuition) as it does to those of understanding, which are legitimately associated with sensible intuitions, reflection is up against much more than the ignorance of the amphiboly mentioned in the Appendix. For this "logical precept [that pushes us] . . . to advance towards completeness by an ascent to ever higher conditions" (ibid., 307; *346*) reflects "a natural and unavoidable dialectic of pure reason" (ibid., 300; *337*). The appearance of logic that gives rise to the amphiboly can be dispelled, and the intellectualism that is its victim and representative refuted. But one cannot avoid the transcendental appearance (ibid., 298–300; *335–37*). The transcendental dialectic can only prevent the "natural dialectic" of reason from abusing us without, however, being able to do away with it. It is in fact the "actual principles [*wirkliche Grundsätze*] that incite us to tear down all those boundary fences" (ibid., 299; *336*) that "the critique" opposes to the use of concepts outside of experience.

However, the question raised in these conditions by appearance and illusion for the transcendental dialectic cannot be elaborated, let alone resolved, except by reflective work. Meditating on the notion of appearance and taking sensory appearance for his model, Kant assimilates the erroneous judgment it contains to a "diagonal," "the diagonal between two forces . . . that determine the judgment in different directions that enclose, as it were, an angle" (ibid., 298; *335*). This complex effect must be decomposed into the effects proper, respectively, of the two forces in question, sensibility and understanding, for the illusion to be dispelled—this is what must be done "by transcendental reflection" "in the case of pure *a priori* judgments" (and no longer in perceptive empirical judgments: ibid.). Its function we are reminded ("as we have already shown": ibid., that is, in the Appendix) is to assign "every representation . . . its place in the corresponding faculty of knowledge" (ibid.). Thus the heavy task, the infinite task of distinguishing speculative syntheses from cognitive syntheses, which is one of the most important tasks of the dialectic of the first *Critique*, also belongs to reflection.

We must conclude the following: it is based on the feeling thinking experiences while it proceeds to the elementary syntheses

called "headings" or "concepts of reflection" that thinking "first"
(*zuerst*: ibid., 276; *309*) guides itself in determining the dwelling
place or places of the faculties that authorize each of the syntheses.
Only in a certain realm can a particular synthesis legitimately take
"place" because it will have been localized and circumscribed by
the conditions of possibility of its tutelary faculty. But this domiciling requires that thinking have the faculty of being able to orientate itself. The relative uncertainty, the amphiboly of the reflective "headings" leaves room for hesitation as to the proper address,
whereas the determination of syntheses under the categories of understanding presupposes on the contrary a legitimate dwelling
place already known and occupied.

This conclusion must be corroborated with other remarkable
moments of the critique, the moments when the critique circum-
scribes the "territories" and the "realms" of validity of judgments.
In particular for ethical judgment, and of course for aesthetic judgments. We will only be able to present some of the testimonies.
However, judging by the Appendix to the analytic and the Introduction to the dialectic, two related texts that constitute the turning point of the first *Critique*, we can already diagnose the following: with reflection, thinking seems to have at its disposal the critical weapon itself. For in critical philosophy the very possibility of
philosophy bears the name of reflection. The heuristic power to
undertake a critique, *Urteilskraft*, is the power to elaborate the
proper *a priori* conditions of possibility, that is, the legitimacy of
an *a priori* synthetic judgment. But this elaboration (analysis and
"deduction") itself requires synthetic judgments of discrimination.
Thus the power to critique must have the enigmatic capacity to
judge the proper conditions of judgment "before" being able to
make use of, before having the right to make use of these conditions in judging whether they are the proper ones. Yet reflection is,
as we have said, tautegorical in that it is nothing but the feeling,
pleasant and/or unpleasant, that thinking has about itself while it
thinks, that is, judges or synthesizes. The operators of the syntheses that it produces are "first" reflected or reflexive, under the
"headings" or "concepts of reflection," as spontaneous assemblages
of "representations," as blurred "comparisons" that have not yet

been domiciled, that are pre-conceptual, felt. And it is precisely because these "headings" are felt and not yet determined in their objective use (having only "subjective" value) that reflection can legitimate or delegitimate their use according to the faculty that takes hold of them.

The reader of Kant cannot fail to wonder how the critical thinker could ever *establish* conditions of thought that are *a priori*. With what instruments can he formulate the conditions of legitimacy of judgments when he is not yet supposed to have any at his disposal? How, in short, can he judge properly "before" knowing what judging properly is, and in order to know what it might be? The answer is that critical thinking has at its disposal in its reflection, in the state in which a certain synthesis not yet assigned places it, a kind of transcendental pre-logic. The latter is in reality an aesthetic, for it is only the sensation that affects all actual thought insofar as it is merely thought, thought feeling itself *thinking* and feeling itself *thought*. And because thinking is judging, feeling itself judging and judged at the same time. In this subjective presence of thought to itself there is the domiciling gesture that sends the spontaneous syntheses (under their "headings") to their tutelary faculties thus limiting their use and establishing their legitimacy.

Such is the aspect of reflection that I have called heuristic. Together with the tautegorical aspect, it transforms the apparent aporia of thinking, of a critical thinking that can anticipate its *a priori*'s, into a legitimate paradox. Critical thought thus seems able to escape many of the objections made to it, in particular from the perspective of speculative thought. But I will not get into this.

Anamnesis

I will insist instead upon two observations. The first is that the reflexive "moment" should not be understood as if it had its place in a genealogy. The *a priori* conditions, the categories of understanding, for example, or the forms of intuition are strictly *a priori*; they did not wait for reflective thought to produce them on the basis of subjective comparisons in order to "exist." Besides the fact that, strictly speaking, they have never existed and will never exist, they are "always already" what must be called upon to legitimate a judgment's claim that it knows its object. In the Appendix the question is to know how their *legitimate* use can be discovered and not how they are produced. This is why reflection, in assuming this task, fulfills a function that is not constitutive but, instead, "heuristic." Much more than a genealogy, one should see in the reflexive moment a kind of *anamnesis* of critical thought questioning itself about its capacity to discover the proper use of the transcendental locations determined in the "Transcendental Doctrine of Elements" formed by the Aesthetic and the Logic. One is thus led to calculate that the further critical thought moves from the safe places of synthesis that are the forms of intuition and the categories of understanding (with schemas), that is, the further it moves from the examination of *a priori* conditions of knowledge, the more manifest the tautegorical aspect of reflection becomes. There are signs of it in the more frequent occurrence of operators such as regulation (in the "regulative Idea" or the "regulative principle"), guidance (in the guiding thread), and analogy (in the "as if"), which are not categories but can be identified as heuristic tautegories. Because of these curious "subjective operators," critical thought gives itself or discovers processes of synthesis that have not received the imprimatur of knowledge. Knowledge can only draw on them reflexively, inventing them as it does according to its feeling, though it may have to legitimate their objective validity afterward. If this assessment is correct, one could say that following the theory of the elements of the first *Critique*, the anamnesic tone of the Kantian text is better heard the closer critical thought comes to objects as little knowable (*stricto sensu*) as the Ideas of theoretical reason, moral law, taste and the sublime feeling, and last the historical, political judgment. For the latter objects of critical thought, the act of dispelling an amphiboly occasioned by a failing in the domiciling faculty is not enough to discover the proper use of their *a priori* conditions of possibility.

From this first observation the second naturally follows: with the aesthetic (I set politics aside, it having not been the object of a *Critique*) one must be very far advanced in the anamnesis of critical thought. The "object" of the critique of the aesthetic faculty of judging is in fact nothing other than reflective judgment itself, in its purest state. Yet what does "pure" here mean? That it is the "sensation" that refers thinking to itself and in so doing informs it of the "sentimental" state, the pleasure or displeasure in which it finds itself, because this "sensation" is this state. It follows that the movement of critical thought must reverse itself here if we compare it to what it was in the first *Critique*.

In the latter, as we saw when we examined it in the Appendix to the principles, the interest of reflection consisted mainly in its heuristic function. It was a matter of showing how critical thought could distinguish among the spontaneous comparisons to which thinking proceeds when it redistributes them to the competent faculties for the faculties to legitimate. I have not yet studied the role that the categories play in this redistribution. I will do so, but it cannot escape the reader of the Appendix that everything happens as if the four important, pure concepts of understanding— quality, quantity, relation, and modality—exerted their control from high and from afar, but did this through the anamnesis in which reflection discovers in itself the four "headings" under which thinking subjectively feels the comparisons to be possible. This teleguidance of reflection by the categories of understanding can perhaps be explained here by the fact that reflection, in its heuristic aspect, has only to discover the proper use of the categories of understanding for knowledge *stricto sensu*.

As for aesthetic judgments, which are only sensations considered to be judgments and which must be analyzed as such, the tautegorical function of reflection must on the contrary win out over its heuristic function, for in this case sensation does not and should not lead to anything but itself. Furthermore, sensation does not "prepare" thinking for any possible knowledge. The locations of legitimacy that sensation discovers must remain *its* locations, nothing more than the "headings" under which thinking feels the comparability of the givens to be. And if it is true that these "headings," as they are enumerated and examined in the Appendix to the first *Critique*, are still overly affiliated with or connected to the categories of understanding, then the critique must find a way to break this subjection and leave the proper domiciling of the "headings" (the "headings" of reflective thinking reduced to itself, that is, to sensation) to the purely tautegorical reflection that aesthetic judgment alone engages. Sensation is in itself the whole of taste and of the sublime feeling from the perspective of the faculties of the soul.

Yet critical thought does not take this path. The "Analytic of the Beautiful" and the "Analytic of the Sublime" are indeed involved in correctly domiciling these two aesthetic judgments and circumscribing their exact legitimacy—tautegorical reflection. But they cannot accomplish this without the help of the categories of understanding. One might say that the analysis of purely tautegorical, "reflective" judgments (for taste, at least) cannot take "place" without recourse to the principles of legitimation discovered for determinant judgments in the first *Critique*. An abrupt end is thus put to reflective anamnesis at the precise moment where, with taste, it seemed that anamnesis would be forced to reflexively reveal the depths of reflection. It seems that we are never to know more about the "headings" and the "places" of pure reflective synthesis than what we can know by means of the pure concepts of understanding. Did the Introduction not say the following about taste: "Here, now, is a pleasure that—as is the case with all pleasure or displeasure that is not brought about through the agency of the concept of freedom . . . no concepts could ever enable us to regard as necessarily connected with the representation of an object. . . . It must always be only through reflective perception that it is cognized as conjoined with this representation" (31, t.m.; *28*). Can the critique, then, not speak the language of this "reflective perception" upon which, according to all indications, it ceaselessly orientates itself? Or perhaps this "reflective perception" has no language at all, not even the voice of silence? What is at stake here is the relation of the tautegory to the category, of the reflective to the determinant.

Reflection and Category in the Theoretical and Practical Realms

Let us return for a moment to what the Appendix of the first *Critique* has to say about this relation. The "headings" under which the purely subjective syntheses are regrouped, the "comparisons" made by simple reflection, are four in number, as we have seen: identity/difference, agreement/opposition, inner/outer, determinable/determination (KRV, 277–96; *310–33*). These "headings" may seem somewhat enigmatic. But Kant explains them, leaving no doubt as to their function. Thus the comparison of a set of representations under the "heading" of identity is the subjective movement of thought that will lead it to a universal judgment; if the comparison is made under the "heading" of difference, then it will not be possible to regroup all the representations under the same concept and the judgment that can be made will be a particular one. It is clear that the reflexive "heading" identity/difference is the subjective "threshold" through which a comparison passes when it goes to place itself under the category of quantity. Similarly for quality, agreement and opposition subjectively indicate affirmative and negative judgments. The "heading" of inner prepares for the category of inherence (or subsistence), that of outer for the category of causality (or dependence), both being categories of relation. Finally the determinable (or matter) gives rise to problematic judgments, the determination (or form) to apodictic judgments. A translation of a merely determinable subject into the terminology of modalities is as follows: I do not judge it impossible to attribute this predicate to this subject; and of a subject of that is fully determined: I judge it impossible not to attribute this predicate to this subject.

From this exposition, which is bolstered by the many critiques that Kant directs against Leibniz's intellectualism and which may seem to make it somewhat obscure, we see that the reflexive "headings" are almost reduced to being merely the subjective reflections of the categories of understanding. A little as if the cognitive *a pri-*

ori still to be found already controlled the search by subordinating to itself what should have been a reflective *a priori*.

Invoking the fact that thinking's knowledge of itself is subjected to the same *a priori* conditions as any other knowledge and that consequently one should find in it the same formal conditions as in the knowledge of objects does nothing to justify this inversion. This argument carries no weight because reflection *is not* a form of knowledge. "I do not know myself through being conscious of myself as thinking," we are reminded in the paralogism of the first *Critique* (KRV B, 368; *377–78*). It is true that the consciousness in question in this passage is more logical (the "I" is a concept) than it is reflective. But the conclusion is all the more true *a fortiori* for reflective consciousness, which is immediate and without concept, without even the concept of an "I think": it is a sensation or "a perception that relates solely to the subject as modification of its state" (KRV, 314; *354*).

To justify reflective anamnesis being predetermined by the conditions of objective knowledge, we could invoke what we have already said: that reflection does not produce understanding. It discovers in itself modes of synthesis that are similar to those of understanding. The latter are always already there to make knowledge possible. As for the reflexive "headings" that do not entitle reflection to a consciousness of itself, one might say that they were reflexive "manners" of comparing givens, although in thought these manners would only be the subjective echo of the use of categories.

If we confine ourselves to this answer, we give up the heuristic function of reflection. The search seems even to work in the opposite direction: because of the categories, reflection is able to reveal spontaneous modes of comparison about itself, which are only approximate figurations of pure concepts. Yet there had to have been a reflective heuristic act because the critique was able to write itself; the transcendental can be constituted on the basis of the empirical. It would be more correct to say that the reflexive "headings" operate as principles of subjective distinctions similar in their role to the role ascribed to the difference between right and left in

"What is Orientation in Thinking" (ORIENT, 239). It is not enough
to have the four points of the compass to orientate oneself in
space; one also needs the subjective non-congruence of the right
and the left (first elaborated in "Concerning the Ultimate Foundation of the Differentiations of Regions in Space"). The category
is not enough to orientate oneself in thinking. Thinking also needs
a principle of differentiation that has only subjective value but
with which the use of the category is made possible and legitimate. What I have called domiciling consists precisely in this. The
reflexive "headings" guide domiciliation toward suitable dwelling
places.

   Therefore in the text of the Appendix the critique of Leibniz's
thought is attached to the exposition of the "concepts of reflection." What the critique of intellectualism—which slips into the
explanation of the "headings" of reflection—in fact shows is that
by itself the category is blind. The category applies its mode of
synthesis and thus authorizes the judgment that results from it on
all the givens with which it is presented without distinction. The
judgment that attributes a predicate to the totality of a subject,
which is universal, has for its only condition the complete enu-
meration of the logical properties that define the subject. Thus
two drops of water will be identical for understanding because
they are logically identical. But guided by its identity/difference
"heading," which is not the category of quantity, reflection remarks, however, that they are not absolutely identical, for they are
localized differently in space. Consequently these "same" objects of
thought require different syntheses, depending on whether they
are thought logically or aesthetically (in the sense of the first *Critique*): identifying synthesis in the former, disjunctive synthesis in
the latter. The heuristic function of reflection is so important that
it discovers a "resistance" of the forms of intuition to their unwar-
ranted assimilation into the categories of understanding. This discovery dispels the confusion proper to intellectualism and legitimates the modes of synthesis according to the dwelling place of
their faculties. Reflection is certainly discriminating, or critical, for
it is opposed to the ill-considered extension of the concept outside

its realm. It domiciles the syntheses with the faculties or, in what amounts to the same, determines the transcendentals that the faculties are by comparing the syntheses each can effect on objects that appear to be the same: the two drops of water are and are not identical.

As we have said, the same separating power of the reflective heuristic act enables one to locate the transcendental appearance and denounce the illusion resulting from it. I will cite the particularly distinguished case of the antithetic of the first *Critique* here because it has a decisive impact on the reading of the "Analytic of the Sublime." I will call it the act (in the sense of enacting and not acting) of the procedure (KRV, 461–64; *519–22*). We know that with the first two conflicts reason has with itself in regard to the cosmological Ideas of the beginning and the simple element, reflection dismisses both parties merely by showing how these concepts have no corresponding intuition in experience and that the differend is undecidable in the realm of knowledge's competence through understanding. The conflicts are about the quality and quantity of phenomena that belong to the world. The syntheses of givens effected in the name of these categories—their being placed in regressive series toward the simple and toward totality, respectively (ibid., 387–88; *441–43*)—are said to be "mathematical" (ibid., 462; *520*) because they combine "homogeneous" elements (ibid., 463; *521*). The condition of a phenomenon must be a phenomenon that is itself conditioned; a part of a composite must in turn be composite. With these terms we see the inability on the part of understanding to rule on questions (if there is something called the simple, if there is a beginning in the world) that imply the Idea of an absolute (undecomposable, the unconditional), which belongs to speculative reason.

But we know the opposite is also true, that when a thesis and antithesis present themselves on the subject of causality, i.e., a category of relation (either there is or there is not a free causality in play in the phenomena of the world), reflection recognizes that both positions are acceptable on condition that they are domiciled in different faculties: the first in speculative reason, which admits of the Idea of unconditioned causality; the second in knowledge through understanding where every cause is itself an effect. The elements synthesized here in the name of the causal relation are heterogeneous (the conditional and the unconditional) and their synthesis is said to be "dynamical" (ibid., 462–63; *520–21*). "The suit may [thus] be settled [*verglichen werden kann*] to the satisfaction of both parties [with] a procedure" (ibid., 462; *521*). Understanding is justified in accepting only the conditional in the explication, and reason only the unconditional, which under the title of freedom is an *a priori* condition of morality. Yet this solution is presented as a jurisprudential supplement: "the judge [supplementing] . . . what is lacking in the pleas" (*der Richter den Mangel des Rechtgründe . . . ergänzt*: ibid.). If reflection can thus supplement the category, it must have at its disposal a principle of subjective discrimination that belongs to no faculty, but that enables it to restore the legitimate limits of the faculties by exploring the confines they dispute. The act of procedure is thus an example of the reflective heuristic act in its domiciling function. We see here that the relation of the reflective act to the category does not involve a subjection of the former to the latter, but rather the opposite.

It would not be difficult to show that the same is true in the *Critique of Practical Reason*. In the search for the "concept of an object of practical reason" (KPV, 59–74; *68–84*), the critique can only refute the doctrines of the good by determining the limit that reflection imposes on the use of the category of causality in the realm of morality. In judgment, this category is indeed necessary in making possible the synthesis of an act with the moral cause (the Idea of the good) of which it is the effect. But reflection dissociates this causality from a causality applicable to the knowledge of objects of nature, to which actions regarded empirically also belong. The cause must remain without content if the act is to be something other than the effect of a natural determination (interested). Thus reflection retains only the notion of an empty legality of the theoretical use of pure concepts (as "type": ibid., 70–74; *79–84*) by prohibiting the content of what reflection brings together from being determined. The use of the category (of relation), i.e., causality, is thus subject to far more than a limitation. It undergoes a reorientation of such great importance that what results from it, the Idea of the unconditioned cause, ceases to be assigned to the realm of understanding in order to pass into that of reason.

We can be sure that reflection is what accomplishes the work of discrimination if we look at the chapter entitled "Incentives of Pure Practical Reason" (ibid., 74–93; *84–104*). The concept of incentive "presupposes the sensuousness [feeling] and hence the finitude of... beings" (ibid., 79; *89*). It requires that thinking, in morality, be immediately informed of its state by way of the sensation that it has of this state, and which is this state itself, i.e., feeling. Thus reflection in its tautegorical aspect shows that respect is the only moral feeling. Respect alone is the "heading" of a subjective synthesis that corresponds to the "logical" demand for a causality or for an empty or merely formal legality. For respect is not "the incentive to morality" but is "morality itself, regarded subjectively as an incentive" (ibid., 78; *89*). When morality is thought of as pure obligation, *Achtung* is the feeling. Here the pure tautegory of feeling confers upon the feeling its heuristic value. Reflection isolates respect *unto itself* by comparing it to other possible incentives as the only subjective "state" suitable to pure law.

The text fully acknowledges that this discovery takes place through reflection, as a "manner" rather than as a "method," which allows one to remark that the inversion of the relation between content (the good) and form (the law as duty) is indeed a proper "method" (ibid., 65, 66; *74, 75*), but that this method is not without "paradox" (ibid., 65; *74*). Yet what is a paradoxical method if not a manner? And how could it be otherwise, especially given the chapter on incentives where, as we have seen, morality's "aesthetic" is examined from the angle of feeling? As in the instance of the drops of water, one must depart from a logical application of the categories to morality—the "method" proper (see the table of categories of freedom: ibid., 68–69; *78*)—and this departure, through the paradoxes it discovers and that it uses, suffices to ensure that the heuristic proceeds, rather, as a "manner" (*modus aestheticus*).

This manner allows one to explain "the enigma" (*das Rätsel*) of the critique (ibid., 5; *5*) that "renounce[s] the objective reality of the supersensible use of the categories" while it grants objective reality to them when it is a question of the "objects of pure practical reason" (ibid.). The inconsistency is only apparent. Knowledge concerns itself with phenomena to which the categories must be applied for them to be determined. But morality rests on a "fact" (*ein Faktum*: ibid., 5; *6*), the fact of a supersensible causality, or freedom, which can only be "thought of" (*bloß gedacht*: ibid.) without being determined, the way causality must be in its cognitive usage. The use of the categories is "different" (*einen anderen Gebrauch*) in the theoretical and in the practical. Yet what is the power that estimates their proper use, that orientates them, if not reflection? Reflection is "consistent" thinking.

With this same paradoxical manner of proceeding, so removed from a "systematic construction" proper to the constitution of a science (ibid., 7; *6*), one should associate the term used for it in the preface to the second *Critique* to legitimate the accumulation of paradoxes or of "inversions" that surprise the reader of the critique. This term is *konsequente Denkungsart*, a consistent manner of thinking, a consistent manner in thought.

This term reappears in the third *Critique* in the episode devoted to the "maxims of common sense" (153; *146*). It designates the third of these maxims, "always to think consistently" (*mit sich selbst einstimmig denken*: 152; *145*), as "the hardest of attainment" (153; *146*) because it requires that the two preceding maxims also be observed, "to think for oneself" and "to think from the standpoint of everyone else" (152; *145*), and because to be "attainable" it requires a "repeated observance" (*nach einer öfteren Befolgung*: 153, t.m.; *146*). The spirit of a systematic topic pushes Kant to attribute—but only in a problematic manner ("we may say": ibid.)— the first maxim to understanding thus charged with emancipation in relation to prejudices, the second maxim to the faculty of judging, which thus finds itself entrusted with the supervision of a universality not yet guaranteed by a concept, and the third maxim to reason. It seems to me more faithful to the thinking of the transcendental topic to ascribe all three maxims to reflection, and in particular the last one. For in the first place a manner that cannot be acquired, but whose "attainment" is acquired through "repeated observance," which cannot be learned ("since learning is nothing but imitation": 169; *161*), resembles a "judgment" (*having* judgment) far more than it does reason. It could even characterize the genius in art (§§46–49). If this manner is nonetheless attributed to reason we must be reminded once again that "philosophy" itself, while it is a "rational science," can "never" be "learned": "as regards what concerns reason [and not its history], we can at most learn to *philosophize*" (KRV, 657; *752*). The third "maxim of common sense" calls on this reason, which counts only on itself, a reflective heuristic reason. This reason makes the "rationalism" of the *Critique*s a critical rationalism. But, above all, what could it mean "always to think consistently" if not to listen to a free reflective capacity in order to guide thinking and the syntheses it ventures according to the feeling that thinking has of itself in the very act of thinking?

Reflection and Category in the Territory of the Aesthetic

In light of what precedes, we will perhaps be able to see more clearly the reason for the categorical "paradoxes," which are just as plentiful in the third *Critique* as they were in the second. The distortion undergone by the concepts of understanding seems so violent that one might justifiably ask oneself what the filtering of the aesthetic analytics through the categories can bring to our understanding of aesthetic judgments. After all, as I have shown with the aesthetic—the examination of pure sensation—reflection seems to be in sensation as it is nowhere else. In its innermost aspect as tautegory it is exempted from every task, even a heuristic one. It does not even have to search for its own condition of possibility. The latter, as has been previously noted, is only "the subjective formal condition of a judgment in general . . . the judging faculty itself, or judgment" (143; *137*). With the aesthetic, reflection seems only to need the capacity to reflect in order to judge reflexively. Its

a priori condition is logically reduced to something called a "faculty," being here the faculty to feel, that is, to judge im-mediately. We
find a simplicity, a meagerness in the *a priori* condition of aesthetic judgment, and perhaps even a lack. This minimalism should
make a "method" of analysis useless and even harmful when it is
governed by the categories of understanding.

Is evidence of a "forcing" through the categories in the analytic
of taste not provided by the proliferation of negative or privative
clauses that follow one another and neutralize the determination of
the judgment of taste under the heading of each of the four categories? It is qualitatively affirmative (it says "yes" to pleasure—it is
a delight), but with no motive. For quantity, it is singular but
claims to be universal. As for relation, it is final but of a perceived
and not conceived "finality" (80; *77*). Finally *modality* is apodictic,
but its necessity is not demonstrable; it is "exemplary" (81; *78*).
The blurring is constant, and obvious. There is no reason to be
surprised, it seems, for it stems from the application of the determinant to the reflective. What is surprising on the other hand is
that the determinant must be applied to a manner of judging from
which it is excluded.

There is a polemical purpose to this paradox. The Appendix to
the first *Critique* affirmed that a reflective topic was necessary to
avoid the mistake of intellectualism. Symmetrically, the use, diverted in the extreme, of the categories of understanding to analyze
the aesthetic feeling would aim to make manifest the uselessness of
their direct application. We recall that in a note to the first *Critique*, Baumgarten's "attempt" "to bring the critical treatment of
the beautiful under rational principles" was declared "fruitless"
(KRV, 66–67; *64–65*). The paradoxical inversion that the reflective
critique introduces is thus announced: these principles or rules,
which are in fact empirical, "can never serve as determinant *a priori* laws by which our judgment of taste must be directed. On the
contrary, our judgment is the proper test of the correctness of the
rules" (ibid., 66; *65*). The categorical filtering (or "forcing") would
only suggest in the end *a contrario* the necessity of introducing a

principle of "subjective distinction" allowing for the proper use of the categories.

Moreover, it is difficult to see which principle of subjective discrimination the aesthetic feeling might need in order to domicile itself, because it *is*, as we have already seen, this principle: aesthetic feeling discriminates between the beautiful and the ugly through the "favor" or "disfavor" it bestows on the form, without mediation. It is no accident that quality takes the place of quantity at the head of the categorical analysis of taste: the "yes" and the "no" of feeling are not a simple logical property of judgment contained by the feeling; they determine whether or not *there is* beauty. They belong to a kind of "existential" determination, similar to the distinction between right and left in the sphere of perception.

Perhaps, though, because it is a matter of pure reflective judgment, understanding simply has no competence in the judgment whatsoever? Would the "proper test" not lie solely in aesthetic feeling, after all? And should one not conclude that reflection, when left to itself, can only say, "I feel, I feel" and "I feel that I feel" tautegorically? Just as genius in art "cannot indicate scientifically how it brings about its product" because it "gives the rule as *nature*" (168; *161*)? Must one consent in the end (or at the beginning) that the "consciousness" that pure reflection is, i.e., sensation, is unconscious like "nature"?

I think the trial is far enough along for the moment to have come to judge. Pure aesthetic feeling does not have the means of constructing the *a priori* conditions of its possibility, by definition, because it is immediate, that is, without a middle term. It cannot even search for itself, as we said, and, moreover, it is missing even the "places" of comparison that reflection can put under its "headings" or provisional "concepts" when thinking undertakes to *know*. Even the pure feeling of respect, which is tautegorical, is only pure insofar as it "says" at once a state of thought and the *other* of thought, the transcendence of freedom with its "complete incomprehensibility" (KPV, 7; *8*). The pure feeling is the ethical "manner" in which transcendence can be "present" in immanence (ibid., 49;

57). But with taste (in this regard the sublime feeling must be set apart) the reflexive immediacy does not refer to any objectivity, either world to know or a law to realize.

The roles here must thus be reversed. Thinking undertakes the heuristic act of reflection by means of the categories. The categories openly serve (I would say bluntly) as "principles of discrimination" to orientate thought in the muteness of pure feeling. This means is not fruitless, and the filtering of feeling through the quadrangle of understanding is not a forcing of feeling by understanding. Rather, we see an opposite effect: the pure concepts only apply to feeling on the condition, a reflective condition, as it were, that they bend to feeling's resistance and that they distort the straight syntheses authorized in their realm in order to remain faithful to feeling. Thus it will be shown four times that taste only lets itself be understood by the category on the condition that it escape the category's logic. The judgment it contains has a "distorted" quantity, quality, relation, and modality, and these it has merely by analogy. What are thus discovered are the reflexive "headings," the pre-categories of thought. But this time thinking no longer thinks objects, as in the Appendix to the first *Critique*, nor does it think acts, as in the second, but thinks only states of itself. The paradoxical anamnesis of reflection, conducted by means of logic, discovers the analogic in a recurrent way.

Thus the pure concept of understanding fulfills the function of a principle of discrimination in discovering the "subjective." Such is the reversal of roles that where one expected "manner" itself as a heuristic procedure, one instead finds "method." The inattentive reader therefore suspects some forcing. But in truth, if indeed the categories can and must be thus employed to domicile the *a priori* conditions of taste, the dwelling place sought after is not understanding, for none of these conditions perfectly satisfies its conditions. Nor is it reason, even in the sublime (see Chapter 7). If there is a dwelling place, it would have to be called, as we know, the reflective faculty of judging. But one may doubt whether this does indeed constitute a dwelling place, for it is the very heading, in critical thought, of thought in general and of critical thought in particular: domiciling.

Finally and above all, we must ask ourselves how the reversal that we point to is possible, after having attempted to understand its necessity. Who or what proceeds to the paradoxical anamnesis by which logic discovers analogy? It can only be reflection. In the "Analytic of the Beautiful," thinking persists obstinately in *reflecting* through what in general it *determines*. Although it employs concepts under which the givens must be subsumed in order to arrive at knowledge, thinking maintains that these concepts are not suitable, as they stand, in determining what it seeks to determine with them, i.e., taste. Reflection is thus revealed as an excess of determination, in the presumption of this impropriety.

There is much evidence of this to be found in the text. Let us examine, for example, the antinomy of taste in the "Dialectic of Aesthetic Judgment" (§§56–57). The antinomy only admits of pure feeling, leaving no room for any *disputatio* (thesis: 206; *197*), because it is immediate, yet it would require an *expositio* (antithesis: 206, 209–11; *197, 200–202*) devoted to establishing its universality and necessity objectively, that is, by means of arguments and by concepts. The first trait reflects the sentimental tautegory. The second presupposes a heuristic (taste looks to be communicable). We have shown how the heuristic aspect of reflection is absent in pure aesthetic feeling, which seeks nothing. The "promises," the "expectations," the "exigencies" of universality and necessity that the analysis reveals in aesthetic feeling should be thought of as immediate, purely "subjective." At most they indicate the "headings" of possible comparisons from the point of view of reflection. If one were to go by the verdict reached by understanding on the judgment of taste by means of its categories, the judgment is determined in all *logic* as particular (or singular) and merely assertoric. An exposition and discussion conducted by concepts will not fail to show this. They will always conclude by saying: to each his own taste.

However, this same use of categories of quantity (particular) and

modality (assertoric) reveals and awakens at the heart of the immediacy of feeling the "headings" of comparison or the "reflective
concepts" under which feeling lays claim, no less immediately, to
opposing properties. Let us recall that in the Appendix to the first
Critique, the "heading" identity/difference is the reflective analogue of quantity and that the "heading" determinable/determi-
nation that of modality. When taste "demands" or "promises" that
the beauty it attributes to the present form be attributed to itself
absolutely, that is, quantitatively, in totality, it prevents other aesthetic judgments made on this form from being justified in refusing it beauty under any other aspect. The reflective judgment of
taste would remain particular if it included a restriction implying
that, in another aspect, the form judged beautiful does not induce
the immediate feeling of a subjective harmony. But the "state" of
thought that corresponds to taste remains, on the contrary, *identical* to itself. It persists; it does not allow for *difference* in judgment
upon the beautiful. Logically evaluated, this quantitative property
could be called universality. But the logical quality of a judgment
remains particular (or singular). Thus it is only by subjective comparison under the "heading" of identity that a universality emerges,
a universality consequently that we will call "subjective."

    The same is true for modality. For understanding, the judgment
of taste is, at best, assertoric: a form is beautiful because it provides a pleasure connected to beauty; this is a fact. But here again,
the reflective demand, at work even in the use of categories, revives, in the immediacy of the sentimental assertion, an opposite
"heading," the one that *prevents* the form from *not being* felt, that
is, judged beautiful. This demand for the absolute necessity of
judgment, present in subjective feeling, calls for the communication of the subjective feeling by everyone. And here again this
claim thwarts the validity of simple assertion that logic must attribute to it (because this judgment does not have the means to
demonstrate its own necessity). Thus the analytic does not acknowledge the judgment of taste as having an apodictic necessity
in its immediacy. Instead one finds a pre-modal "heading" under
which reflection can group its comparisons, and which is called

determination ("form," in fact) in the Appendix to the first *Critique.*

These procedures are paradoxical only from the point of view of understanding for an intellectualist philosophy. They are legitimate when one sees that the categories are maneuvered by reflection in a heuristic function that exceeds the determinant function of the categories, nonetheless indispensable to the analysis. The reflective heuristic is at work in the text of the analytic of taste, and it discovers a latent heuristic (the claims of taste) in a feeling that seems devoid of any taste. But the mediation of the categories is necessary for the discovery to be possible. The result is a twisting of the effects of determination that were expected from the application of the categories. This twisting that the reflective act exercises upon what is determinant produces or invents the logical monsters that we know: a delight without incentive or motive, a subjective universality, a perceived finality, an exemplary necessity. Designations borrowed from the logic of understanding but diverted by unexpected epithets as works of art, these names are, in proper method or rather in proper manner, those of the "places" that the reflective heuristic discovers, even in tautegory, by means of the category.

We will tackle the reading of the "Analytic of the Sublime," keeping in mind the principle of this reversal that is demanded of reflection by the aesthetic. These reflective places reveal themselves in sublime feeling, again by means of the categories. But we will see that this occurs only with a further twisting of the categories, i.e., a distortion. The price is the one that pure reflection forces determinant judgment to pay in Kant's text in order that determinant judgment determine the reflective more effectively than the reflective would be able to if left to itself.

§2 Comparison of the Sublime and Taste

Why an Analytic of the Sublime?

The textual organization of the "Analytic of the Sublime," of what Kant calls its _Enteilung,_ its subdivision, deserves close attention (93; *90*). This partition is of great significance to the "content" of the analytic, and at times even exceeds it.

The analysis begins with a transition, an *Übergang* (§23), leading the reader from the capacity of estimating (*Beurteilung*) the beautiful to that of estimating the sublime. There are not two faculties of judging but two powers that the faculty of judging has of estimating aesthetically, and that proceed in different ways. Both feelings, that of the beautiful and that of the sublime, belong to the same family—that of aesthetic reflection—but not to the same branch of the family.

Why the transition to the examination of the sublime? Kant does not explain it. Is he concerned with saturating the analysis of aesthetic feeling? Is it to make a place for himself in the dispute that had raged throughout Europe for a century over the sublime? Does it have an intratextual motive, a contextual motive? The impact of the latter was evident in his *Observations on the Feeling of the Beautiful and the Sublime*, published in 1764. Kant had read Baumgarten's *Aesthetica* (1750), which he rejected, as we have seen, in a note to the first *Critique* as an "abortive effort . . . to bring the critical treatment of the beautiful under rational principles" (KRV,

66; *65*). He will only read the *Enquiry into the Origin of Our Ideas of the Sublime and the Beautiful* (1757) in Garve's German translation (1773). In the third *Critique* he places "the enquiry" under the rubric of "psychology" or "empirical physiology" (130–31; *125*). It describes correctly and even cleverly the kinds of delight that the *ego*, body and soul, experiences when it judges an object beautiful or sublime. But such an exposition is incapable of accounting for the demand to be communicable that the aesthetic feeling immediately entails. The empirical description has no access to this demand, or else it attributes it to a desire for "sociability," thus losing all specificity of aesthetic feeling. The empirical description does not have, by hypothesis, the means of elaborating an *a priori* principle to justify the fact that the ego, in experiencing the beautiful (and perhaps the sublime; see Chapter 9), requires that the *alter* experience it too (130–32; *125–27*). It does not have the means, in short, of elaborating a transcendental critique of the community called for by the aesthetic.

This, briefly, is the immediate context and place of the Analytic of the Sublime in the text. As for the textual completeness that the analysis of the sublime would enable, the feeling of the naive reader is, rather, the opposite: the Analytic of the Sublime creates a breach, not to say a break, in the examination of the aesthetic faculty of judging.

In truth the question—Why an analytic of the sublime?—is itself naive. What does "why" mean? The analytic is certainly not "introduced," if we are to go by the "surface" of the text. Its necessity is not "deduced" in the critical sense. The same can be said for the beautiful, the analytic of which also begins *ex abrupto*. However, the critical, philosophical function assigned to taste, as aesthetic reflective judgment in view of the unification of the theoretical and the practical, has been well argued in the Introduction (beginning with §III). Its function was legitimated at that time: the pleasure provided by the beautiful, in natural forms or quasi-natural (artistic) forms, presupposes, as Idea, an affinity of nature with reflective thinking that Kant calls a "subjective finality of nature for our cognitive faculties" (215; *205*). This affinity will be extended to the Idea of an objective finality of nature for freedom, an

Idea that is the object of the second part of the third *Critique*. Thus, critically speaking, the compatibility (no more) is made possible between the Idea of nature as mechanism, subject to the legislation of understanding that constitutes experience (first *Critique*), and the Idea of nature as art that authorizes and even calls for, as its end, as its horizon, the supernatural works of freedom ([Part II] 97; *302*). This compatibility is announced subjectively, minimally, so to speak, in the simple pleasure of the beautiful.

We will see that the same cannot be said for the sublime feeling. The relation of thinking to the object presented breaks down. In sublime feeling, nature no longer "speaks" to thought through the "coded writing" of its forms (160, t.m.; *153*). Above and beyond the formal qualities that induced the quality of taste, thinking grasped by the sublime feeling is faced, "in" nature, with quantities capable only of suggesting a magnitude or a force that exceeds its power of presentation. This powerlessness makes thinking deaf or blind to natural beauty. Divorced, thinking enters a period of celibacy. It can still employ nature, but to its own ends. It becomes the user of nature. This "employment" is an abuse, a violence. It might be said that in the sublime feeling thinking becomes impatient, despairing, disinterested in attaining the ends of freedom by means of nature.

Following this, it is hard to see how the analysis of sublime feeling could contribute to the project of philosophical unification that inscribes the whole of the critique and in particular the section on the aesthetic. The Introduction, devoted to expounding the project, makes no mention of the sublime, save in a short passage at the end of paragraph VII (33; *29*). There it is said that if aesthetic pleasure is possible it is not only because the object can offer a finality to reflective thinking (as in the beautiful, which is nature "in" thought) but also because, conversely, thinking can feel its own finality on the occasion of a form, "or even formlessness" (ibid.): this is the case in the sublime, which is "the subject" without nature. There is not another word in the Introduction about this reversal of finalities, however remarkable it is. One might say that Kant almost forgot to mention the Analytic of the Sublime in the exposition of the project of unification. Or that he wants it to be forgotten in recalling it so summarily. The First Introduction was more explicit on the subject of the sublime (FI, 437–41).

Moreover, and to return to our "transition" from the beautiful to the sublime, Kant makes no mystery of the incongruity of this analytic when he concludes the aforementioned transition with the aporetic form of the following assessment: "Hence we see that the concept of the sublime in nature is far less important and rich in consequences than that of its beauty. It gives on the whole no indication of anything final in nature itself, but only in the possible *employment* [Gebrauch] of our intuitions of it in inducing a feeling [*fühlbar*] in our own selves of a finality quite independent of nature. . . . This is a very needful preliminary remark. It entirely separates [*ganz abtrennt*] the ideas of the sublime from that of a finality of *nature*" (92–93; *90*). This is why, he adds, "the aesthetic estimate of the finality of nature," the "theory" of the sublime, is "a mere appendage" (*einen bloßen Anhang*: ibid.).

What is added to nature finalized aesthetically is, in short, the loss of its finality. Under the name of the Analytic of the Sublime, a denatured aesthetic, or, better, an aesthetic of denaturing, breaks the proper order of the natural aesthetic and suspends the function it assumes in the project of unification. What awakens the "intellectual feeling" (*Geistesgefühl*: 33; *29*), the sublime, is not nature, which is an artist in forms and the work of forms, but rather magnitude, force, quantity in its purest state, a "presence" that exceeds what imaginative thought can grasp at once in a form—what it can *form*.

The "mere appendage" to the critical elaboration of the aesthetic by natural finality thus takes a menacing turn. It indicates that another aesthetic can be not only expounded but "deduced" according to the rules of the critique. This other aesthetic appears to be "contra-final" (*zweckwidrig*: 92; *88*). The feeling that is analyzed is indeed aesthetic, for it immediately informs thinking of its "subjective" state. But the quality of the "state" of thought is provided by pure quantities that defy the imagination.

A negative aesthetic, one might say. But the word is vague. Taste is also negative; it denies understanding the capacity to resolve in concepts the feeling of the beautiful and the judgments that constitute it. The Analytic of the Beautiful proceeds *according* to the categories but can never get to the bottom of taste by categories *alone*; it must partially deny their power (see Chapter 1, pp. 43–49). The sublime denies the imagination the power of forms, and denies nature the power to immediately affect thinking with forms.

The Analytic of the Sublime is negative because it introduces an aesthetic without nature. We can call it modern in the way that Rabelais or Hamlet is modern. I would even venture to say that, in view of this analytic and everything in Western thought that had been building toward it—the Christianity insistent in Longinus's treatise—the aesthetic in general, which is the modern thought of art (which takes the place of a poetics of the natural order that had become impossible), contains from the moment of its appearance the promise of its disappearance. Despite the efforts of speculative thought and Romanticism, at the end of the nineteenth century, confidence in natural forms was shaken, and beyond forms or in their very depth, thought was made liable, *empfänglich*, for something that did not speak to it in good and due form.

Thus historically speaking, the Analytic of the Sublime is not incongruous: it comes from afar and it goes far. Critically speaking, it is an enigma. "Fallen in an obscure disaster," if one were to speak with pathos. What we are looking at today is how the critical procedure enables one to determine the place of this aesthetic feeling of the an-aesthetic in the play of faculties, in their "economy" and their dynamic. The result of the critical elaboration of the sublime is not insignificant for us today. This effort does not contribute to the general project of reconciling nature and freedom, that is, of unifying philosophy. In the second part of the third *Critique*, teleology also will not make use, at least explicitly, of the results of the analysis of sublime feeling. It is not hard to understand why this is. Sublime violence is like lightning. It short-circuits thinking with itself. Nature, or what is left of it, quantity, serves only to provide the bad contact that creates the spark. The teleological machine explodes. The "leading" that nature with its vital lead was supposed to provide for thinking in a movement toward its final illumination cannot take place. The beautiful contributed to the Enlightenment, which was a departure from childhood, as Kant says. But the sublime is a sudden blazing, and without future. Thus it is that it acquired a future and addresses us still, we who hardly hope in the Kantian sense. But this is still only history.

Seen in critical terms, the Analytic of the Sublime finds its "legitimacy" in a principle that is expounded by critical thought and that motivates it: a principle of thinking's getting carried away. As it is expounded and deduced in its thematic, sublime feeling is analyzed as a double defiance. Imagination at the limits of *what* it can present does violence to itself in order to present *that* it can no longer present. Reason, for its part, seeks, unreasonably, to violate the interdict it imposes on itself and which is strictly critical, the interdict that prohibits it from finding objects corresponding to its concepts in sensible intuition. In these two aspects, thinking defies its own finitude, as if fascinated by its own excessiveness. It is this desire for limitlessness that it feels in the sublime "state": happiness and unhappiness.

It is all too obvious that this desire for limitlessness is useless, that it should be relegated to inevitable illusion, that the critique must finally place the sublime close to insanity, showing it to have no moral value, that in the end the analysis of this feeling must be given over to the aesthetic with the simple title of appendage, without significance. However, this stage comes "second" and is, if I may say so, reactive. What is "first," active, and what motivates these protective measures is the outburst of imaginative and rational thought. If the critique multiplies the reminders of what is "permitted" or "legitimate," it is because thinking is irresistibly tempted to overstep them.

In this regard the sublime feeling is only the irruption in and of thought of this deaf desire for limitlessness. Thinking takes "action," it "acts" the impossible, it subjectively "realizes" its omnipotence. It experiences pleasure in the Real. I ask the reader to forgive me for using terms of the idiom of Freud and Lacan to situate this

violence. I am not the first to do it. But I do not intend to pursue
it in this way. There is plenty to designate this state in the critical
language itself. What critical thought does, in short, is to look for
the *a priori* conditions of the possibility of judging the true, the
just, or the beautiful in the realms of knowledge, of morality, and
in the territory of the aesthetic. The project seems modest and reasonable. However, it is motivated by the same principle of fury
that the critique restrains. *A priori* conditions of possibility must,
by hypothesis, be unconditioned, or else they would not be *a priori*. Yet if the critical examination can establish them as such, it
must be able to see the nothingness of the condition that is "behind" them. In other words, reflection pushes the analysis of its
own conditions as far as it can, in accordance with the demand of
the critique itself. Reflection thus touches on the absolute of its
conditions, which is none other than the impossibility for it to
pursue them "further": the absolute of presentation, the absolute of
speculation, the absolute of morality. All thought is a being put
into relation—a "synthesis," in the language of Kant. Thus when
thinking reaches the absolute, the relation reaches the without-
relation, for the absolute is without relation. How can the without-
relation be "present" to relation? It can only be "present" as dis-
avowed (as metaphysical entity), forbidden (as illusion). This dis-
avowal, which is constitutive of critical thinking, is the avowal of
its own fury. It forbids itself the absolute, much as it still wants it.
The consequence for thought is a kind of spasm. And the Analytic of the Sublime is a hint of this spasm. The significance of this
"appendage" thus significantly exceeds the exploration of an aesthetic feeling. It exposes the "state" of critical thought when it
reaches its extreme limit—a spasmodic state.

The Beautiful and the Sublime Compared in the Quality and Quantity of Judgment

Let us return now to the "transition" that leads from the beautiful to the sublime. Kant's manner here is almost Scholastic. The
beautiful and the sublime "agree" (*das Schöne kommt . . . mit dem*

Erhabene überein: 90; *87*) on certain points, but also present "important and striking differences" (*namhafte Unterschiede*: ibid.). Both the former and the latter are distributed according to the categorical quadrangle.

On the side of agreement, there is quality: the beautiful and the sublime please "on their own account" (*für sich selbst*: ibid.). The delight they provide, or, rather, that they are, is independent of all interest, whether empirical or rational, inclination or concept. We will see that things are not so simple for the sublime (see Chapter 7). As with taste, the sublime pleasure is provided by presentation. The faculty of presentation, the *Darstellungsvermögen*, which clearly designates the imagination here, is in *Einstimmung*, in harmony, with the faculty of concepts in general, whether understanding or reason, "in a given intuition" (*bei einer gegebene Anschauung*: 90; *87*). But it is specified further: imagination is in harmony with the faculty of concepts, understanding or reason " *als Beförderung der letzteren*" (ibid.). Philonenko translates this last expression as "to the benefit of the latter," i.e., reason. However, because it is also a question of the beautiful, I would read it as follows: "as assistance to these," the concepts, both of understanding in the case of the beautiful, and of reason in the case of the sublime. We will see how the beautiful also involves an excitation of understanding through imaginative presentation (see pp. 60–67).

On the side of agreement there is also quantity. Both feelings are singular judgments, but both profess to be universally valid. This universality is not objective; it does not attribute a predicate to the concept of the given object of pleasure. It is only concerned with the "attribution" of a state, delight, to thinking when the latter relates to the beautiful or sublime object. It is subjective.

Following these concessions to the agreement of the two aesthetic feelings—most of which will be invalidated by the subsequent analysis—the differences are not long in coming. They are many. After all, if such were not the case, there would be no need for a "transition."

These differences are "striking" (90; *87*). The first appears to involve a simple difference in accent. Kant returns to the quality and quantity of both judgments. Taste, which is a judgment of the beautiful, is induced by the form of the object. The sublime feeling "can also refer to an object even devoid of form" [*an einem formlosen Gegenstande*] (ibid., t.m.). But what is a form? A limitation, a *Begrenzung*. The without-form is, on the contrary, the without-limit, *Unbegrenzheit* (ibid.).

Thus the argument is the following: because the feeling of the beautiful results from a form, which is a limitation, its affinity lies with understanding. The affinity of sublime feeling, which. is or can be provided by the without-form, lies with reason. There is indeed a similarity between both cases in that the presentation of the given should be able to be thought by a concept but, in both cases, is not. This is why the concept of understanding, like that of reason, remains "indeterminate."

But this common trait must not allow one to forget the difference in nature between a concept of understanding and a concept of reason. The limitation of an intuitive given in a form does not in the least prevent a concept from being applied to it, from subsuming the given, and thus being determined by the intuition that corresponds to it. This limitation in form is, on the contrary, a condition of determination in the concept, and such is indeed the case when it is a matter of *knowing* the object through intuition. But when thinking must feel pleasure on the occasion of a given, such is not the case (in the feeling of the beautiful). In the case of sublime feeling, on the other hand, what prevents *a priori* any concept from applying to the given that provides this feeling in a determining way is that the given is unlimited or quasi-unlimited. The difference between the two aesthetic feelings in this regard can thus be correctly articulated. For taste, form arouses activity, only regulative and not determinant in effect, but this activity is the activity of understanding, the faculty of determining. This activity must not be able to succeed in determining the given, but, rather, must only make the attempt. If it were to succeed, the pleasure of taste would give way to the objectivity of knowledge. In the case of the sublime, the without-form immediately suggests a concept of speculative reason, for the object of such a concept is by definition forbidden presentation and there is no presentation without form.

This difference becomes clearer when we examine the passage in the "First Conflict of the Transcendental Ideas" expounded by the Dialectic of the first *Critique* (KRV, 396–402; *454–58*). The question is to know if the world is limited or unlimited in space and time. It cannot be unlimited because a spontaneous totality (space) or a successive totality (time) of states of things cannot be *given* in the forms of sensibility if totality is infinite. Nor can it be limited, for then one must presuppose an empty space beyond the extension of the finite world, or beyond the extension of an empty time before the beginning of the finite world, and no sensible intuition can provide objects that correspond to this supposition.

The critique concludes from this aporia that the question cannot be resolved in a determined way, that is, by understanding, for what is missing in the determination in both the thesis and the antithesis is the sensible intuition corresponding either to the unlimited or to what the limited leaves "outside" of itself (in space and time). Both claims are thus nonsuited, at least as theses of understanding. Nonetheless, the very concept of the limit persists, even when it can only be speculative. The limit is the object of an Idea of reason, a "being of reason."

Thus the difference between the beautiful and the sublime is linked to the difference between the limited character of the object and the without-limit of the object. The difference is not restricted to a difference between understanding, which would involve the limited character of the object, and reason, which would take charge of the unlimited. It is the limit itself that understanding cannot conceive of as its object. The limit is only conceivable with an outside and an inside. The limit, that is, immediately implies both the limited and the unlimited. However, there is no determinable concept of the unlimited. Moreover, the limit, the limited, and the unlimited, taken as objects, can only be objects of the Ideas of speculative reason. The limit is not an object for understanding. It is its method: all the categories of understanding are the operators of determination, that is, of limitation. Furthermore, the faculties of intuition or of presentation, sensibility and imagination, respectively, also proceed, in their order, by means of limitations: schemas when these limitations work for knowledge, and free forms when they work toward the pleasure of the beautiful. This is precisely what the Preliminary Remark to the deduction of pure concepts of understanding in the first *Critique* shows (KRV A, 131; *141*): understanding cannot be "deduced" in the critical sense, that is, legitimated in claiming to know the givens of intuition by determining them through concepts, if the concepts have not been delimited beforehand, that is, put into elementary form by the three syntheses of apprehension, reproduction, and recognition. This is where the limit first operates, making all presentation possible.

Thus we see that the difference between the sublime and the beautiful is not one of emphasis. It is a transcendental difference. The "transition" from one to the other signifies to imagination that its "facultary" partner will change. Thinking feels a sublime feeling when it comes up against the aporia expounded in the first antinomy, but in the order of presentation rather than of concepts. Yet it must still be pushed or attracted by an almost insane demand of reason.

The differentiation thus made explicit in the text modifies the apparent agreement between the feelings of the beautiful and the sublime as to the quality and quantity of the aesthetic judgments that are in play in these respective feelings. To this transcendental heterogeneity, Kant adds yet another difference that concerns the quality of delight in both feelings, but this time from the perspective of the "animation" that delight provides for thought.

Animation

What goes by this name in Kant's aesthetic has to do with a "dynamic," a theory of forces, in the almost Freudian sense of the term, or what came closest to it at the time, the Burkean psychology of tendencies. The dynamist interpretation is made explicit in the first paragraph, which attempts to identify the delight that a representation provides for thought: representation is then "referred wholly to the subject, and what is more to its feeling of life [*seines Lebensgefühl*]—under the name of the feeling of pleasure or of displeasure" (42; *40*). As in any doctrine (or metaphysics) of energy, pleasure is made a metaphor for the vital force of the "subject" and displeasure for the reduction of this force. The principle that increases the force is called *Geist*, which Philonenko translates as soul [*âme*: tr.] because its function is precisely to animate (175; *167*): the life vein of thinking.

The reader might be struck by this abrupt recourse to vitalism—along with the confusion in the use of the terms *Geist*, *Gemüt*, and *Seele* (ibid.), not to mention *Subjekt*. Does the critique not recognize that this is one of the metaphysical dogmas to which it is trying to put an end (KRV A, 7–16; *5–13*)? Does it need to put itself in the hands of a "vital principle" in order to explain the quality of aesthetic feeling? Is aesthetic feeling not an actual state of one of the faculties of the mind discerned by the critique, the faculty of feeling pleasure and displeasure, to be found with the two other faculties of the mind, knowing and desiring? Is aesthetic feeling not simply a transcendental name to designate the *a priori* condition discovered by critical reflection, on the basis of empirically observable aesthetic feelings, to deduce the possibility of these feelings? In making *Geist* the principle of growth of the vital force "in" the subject—the result of which is the pleasure that the subject feels—the critique seems to give in to the transcendental illusion that hypostasizes in a transcendental reality what is merely the condition of possibility of a judgment of taste from the point of view of its quality.

We must examine how the critical analysis of the feeling of the beautiful comes to invoke a vital force. At the end of the exposition of aesthetic reflective judgments and before proceeding to their deduction, Kant devotes two or three pages, as if parenthetically, to a discussion of Burke (130–32; *125–27*). He has no difficulty conceding to Burke the vitalism the *Enquiry* needs to explore the realm of psycho-physiological realities. "There is no denying... that as Epicurus maintained, gratification and pain... are always in the last resort [*zuletzt*] corporeal, since apart from any feeling of the bodily organ, life would be merely a consciousness of one's existence, and could not include any feeling of well-being or of the reverse, that is, of the furtherance or hindrance of the vital forces. For, of itself alone, the mind [*Gemüt*] is uniquely and completely life [*allein ganz Leben*] (the life principle itself)" (131, t.m.; *126*). Kant himself will not hesitate to make use of this vital principle in "empirical anthropology" (ibid.). It is even to be found in a text as late as the third "Conflict of the Faculties," which opposes philosophy to medicine. The critical refutation merely insists on the fact that vitalist realism prevents aesthetic pleasure from being distinguished from a delight with only *"egoistic"* validity (132; *127*). Vitalist realism ignores the demand, inscribed in singular taste, of being universally communicable without mediation. It encloses the feeling provided by the beautiful within a contingent idiolect, lacking the authority to be an "example" for others and the authority to "promise" a community of taste.

Thus the question of animation in Kant's text lies not so much in the presence of the vitalist motif derived from anthropology but in the way the critique draws the specifically transcendental trait of aesthetic pleasure from the metaphysical motif, that is, its immediate demand to be universally communicable. The paragraph devoted to genius (§49) shows the critique at work. More than any other passage in the third *Critique*, it begins by fully deploying the vitalist reading of genius in art: "'*Soul*' [Geist] in an aesthetic sense, signifies the animating principle [*das belebende Prinzip*] of the mind [*im Gemüt*]. But that whereby this principle animates [*belebt*] the psyche [*Seele*], the material [*Stoff*] which it employs for that purpose is that which sets the mental powers into a swing that is final [*was die Gemütskräfte zweckmäßig in Schwung versetzt*]" (175, t.m.; *167*).

However, this same paragraph, begun under the aegis of the dynamic, ends with the trait to which only the critique has access, in taste as in genius. Only the critique has access to the demand to be communicable inherent in the feeling of the beautiful. The text shows that the same demand is immediately inscribed in the creation of works of art because in genius the "production" rather than the "reception" of objects occasions this feeling. Genius is thus declared to consist in a "happy relation" (179; *172*)—happy in the sense that we speak of a *bonheur d'expression*, the joy of hitting on "the expression" (*der Ansdruck*) that is suited to "find out ideas [of the imagination] for a given concept" (ibid.), but above all an expression by means of which "the subjective mental condition [*die . . . subjektive Gemütsstimmung*] thus induced . . . may be communicated to others" (180, t.m.; *172*). I say "above all" because it is this "latter talent" (*das letztere Talent*) that is "properly" (*eigentlich*) termed "soul" (*Geist*). The soul is the power "to get an expression for what is indefinable in the mental state [*das Unnennbare in dem Gemütszustande*] accompanying a particular representation [*bei einer gewissen Vorstellung*] and to make it universally communicable [*allgemein mitteilbar*]" (180, t.m.; *172*).

This paragraph on genius is like a laboratory where the transmutation of elements, prejudged by dynamic anthropology, takes place. These elements are turned into the *a priori* conditions that result from the analysis of the critique. Yet the secret of this chemistry belongs to the heuristic power of reflection. The latter decomposes the "vital force" into its vectors and houses the components thus isolated with the "faculties of knowledge" (in the broad sense) that are in play in aesthetic pleasure.

How does the animating principle, the *Geist*, "animate" thinking? By supplying material, *Stoff*, as we have seen, to the faculties of knowledge—pure capacity to regulate, pure capacity to present. This throws them, swings them toward one another and against each other, in "play": "*in Schwung . . . d.i. in ein solches Spiel, welches sich von selbst erhält* [into a play that is self-maintaining]" (175; *167*). This play of the faculties is commanded by a "finality" (*zweckmäßig*: ibid.). The end pursued by this finality is not conceived, the finality is "perceived" in the object judged beautiful. This simple perception is what precisely characterizes the judgment of taste as it was characterized in the category of relation: "*finality* in an object . . . perceived in it [*an ihm*] apart from the representation of an end*" (80; *77*).

The faculties play with each other but are not guided by the concept of an end that would be the aim of their play: this explains the persistence of aesthetic pleasure. It is essential for it to "dwell" (*weilen*: 64; *61*), to "*preserve a continuance* [in demselben zu erhalten] of that state [of the subject]" (61; *58*), as this is essential to all pleasure. This is true to a such a degree that the *Verweilung*, the "way we linger"— a lingering that the play of the faculties imposes on thinking that judges aesthetically—puts thought into a state "analogous" to the passivity (*wobei das Gemüt passiv ist*: 64; *61*) it feels when it is attracted to an object. Analogous but not identical: the attraction paralyzes the faculties, the beautiful throws them into play.

In the passage to which I refer—the "Third Moment" of the "Analytic of the Beautiful," the moment that precedes the analysis of taste through the category of relation and that isolates the finality without end proper to aesthetic judgment (61–62; *58–59*)—the text marks the outlines, by no means comprehensive, of a temporality inherent in the feeling of the beautiful. The two important characteristics of cognitive time, which allowed one to "deduce" the "I think" in the first *Critique*—succession and the affection of the self by itself—are here suspended. As "the subjective" remains nothing other than its state almost passively, the "I think" forgets itself as the thought of the object turned toward experience by means of the forms of coexistence (space) and succession (time). The time of the aesthetic lingering is also the lingering, the pause of diachronic time. The sensation provided by the free play of the faculties institutes a manner of being for time that cannot involve an inner sense.

I return to the material, the *Stoff*, which the soul provides to the two faculties of knowledge, imagination and understanding, in such a way that they compete for it, one by thinking according to form, the other according to concept. This material—the word, for Kant, always connotes the manifold without order—is the aesthetic Ideas. The principle of "animation," the soul, that puts them forward in the play of the faculties thus finds its true name in the critique: it is "the faculty [*Vermögen*] of presentation of *aesthetic ideas*" (175, t.m.; *167*). Faculty of presentation is the name for imagination in the third *Critique* (76, 89; *73*, *86*). But imagination is said to present forms, and to present them by forming them. Here it seems it is responsible for presenting Ideas. Yet how could it present an Idea when the Idea is defined as having an object of which there is no possible presentation (KRV, 327–28; *368–69*)? But here we are speaking of aesthetic Ideas. Moreover, they are like the symmetrical reverse, the "counterpart (pendant)" (*Gegenstück*: 176; *168*), of the Ideas of reason, the negative property of which we are aware. The aesthetic Idea is a representation of an object such that there is no corresponding property in the *concept* of this object. The rational Idea is the concept of an unpresentable object; the aesthetic Idea is the presentation of an "object" that escapes the concept of this object, the presentation of what Kant calls *das Unnennbare*, the "indefinable" (180; *172*). It is the indefinable not of the object itself (the form) but of the state that the object provides for thinking.

Why call this presentation an Idea? Because it exceeds experience just as the Idea of reason exceeds experience. Furthermore, because reflection can find in experience an "analogous" presentation for the object of a rational Idea (221–23; *211–12*), the imagination can by "analogy" also "remodel" an object of experience and present an object that is not present in the latter (176; *168*) when, for example, experience is felt to be "too commonplace" (ibid.). With this characteristic excess or replacement, the aesthetic Idea ceases to be thought of negatively. It adds expression to the concept. It adds to the representation of the object the "material" that exceeds its determination by understanding, and that induces "solely on its own such a wealth of thought [*soviel zu denken veranlaßt*] as would never admit of comprehension [*zusammenfassen*] in a definite concept" (ibid., t.m.). This material is indeed provided by the imagination, that is, by one of the partners in play. It borrows from "actual nature," but it creates a "second nature" out of the material (ibid.).

This remodeling is achieved by an operation, constitutive of Kant's thought when it is seen as reflexive, the analogy. The analo-

gy transforms, commutes, a given by making it jump from one
realm of legislation or one territory of legitimacy to another. It
crosses the entire field of possible objects of thought, carrying a
relation of representations from one sector to the other, but the relation must be transposed according to the rules in effect in the
sector in which it arrives. The analogy allows the relation to emi-
grate, and then acculturates it.

The imagination that operates aesthetically is thus productive,
and not only "reproductive" (mnesic), as it had to be for the pur-
poses of theoretical knowledge. It takes liberties with the postulates
of empirical thought in general and in particular with the analogies
of experience, which are permanence, succession, and coexistence
(KRV B, 208–44; *229–72*), in a word with everything that Kant
refers to as "the law of association," which belongs to the empirical
employment of the imagination (176; *168*). The imagination creates another nature, which has to do not with thinking by concept
but with the derivatives connected with the concepts, the "secondary representations" (*Nebenvorstellungen*), the constituent elements of which are not attributed to it logically, but are nevertheless "(aesthetic) attributes" (177; *169*). It is not the logical determination of the concept of the all-powerful that contains the
representation of an eagle with lightning in its claws. This representation is an aesthetic Idea. It gives thought an "incentive to
spread its wings over a whole host of kindred representations" (177;
169), a host of representations that "provoke more thought [*mehr
denken lassen*] than admits of expression in a concept determined
by words" (ibid., t.m.). For the concept must be "definitely formulated in language" (*mithin in einem bestimmte Sprachausdrucke*:
178, t.m.; *170*). No language determinant of its object can remain
afloat before the tide of aesthetic Ideas. The tide carries away the
words of concepts. It should be understood that even in poetry or
literature where there are indeed words, these are the words of
analogy that engulf the words of definition. The latter, "opening
out" in "unbounded expansion" (177; *169*) are lost in "a field of
kindred representations [*ein unabsehliches Feld*] . . . stretching beyond its ken" (177–78; *169*). We are reminded here of Burke, who

argued that words themselves have, over other aesthetic materials, the privilege of engendering a limitlessness, a "horizon" resonant with Benjamin's *aura.*

This defiance offered by the free imagination controls the play in which understanding is taken. This play is in turn the reason for the "animation" in which the pleasure of the beautiful consists. A storm of Ideas suspends ordinary time in order to perpetuate itself. There is no need, in the end, for the vitalist metaphor, or for the metaphysics of energy, to understand that the letter, "language as a mere thing of the letter" (*mit der Sprache als bloßem Buchstaben*: 179; *171*), is in genius, and analogically in taste, exceeded by the soul (*Geist*), the life vein of thought. It is enough for the critique to introduce, as one of the *a priori* conditions of possibility for taste, a power of presentation that exceeds the power it has established as one of the *a priori* conditions of possibility for knowledge. The imagination, this power, can present givens, that is, synthesize them in forms beyond what understanding can know, i.e., beyond what it can synthesize in concepts. Because this capacity for a production that exceeds simple reproduction is an *a priori* condition for aesthetic judgment (as the capacity for reproduction is for determinant judgment), it must be universally communicable. This is why, when it is exercised even singularly, it is legitimate for it to require that the unlimited space it opens up for thought and the suspended time in which its play with understanding is sustained, be accessible to any thinking faced aesthetically with the same singular circumstance. This is something that the metaphysics of forces has great trouble establishing.

The Beautiful and the Sublime Compared in the Relation (Finality) and Modality of Judgment

Let us begin again with the comparison between sublime delight and the delight provided by the beautiful according to the categories of quality and quantity (90–91; *87–88*). The delight in the beautiful is felt "directly" as a "furtherance of life" like the delight arising from an "attraction" (although such is not the case because the delight in the beautiful is disinterested) (64–65, 68; *61–62, 65*). This delight participates in the play through imagination. The delight provided by the sublime on the other hand arises "indirectly" as a feeling with two conflicting moments: the "vital forces" experience a momentary check, *Hemmung*, an inhibition; they are held back, repressed. When they are released, they "discharge"—this is the *Ergießung*—all the more powerfully in the following moment (ibid.). Because of this transitory anguish, the sublime emotion is not like play. In it the imagination is seriously occupied. Contrary to taste, the sublime feeling is an emotion, a *Rührung*, that alternates between an affective "no" and "yes" (68; *65–66*). There is no analogy possible with attraction. Thought is not only "attracted" (*angezogen*) by the given circumstance, it is alternately "repelled" (*abgestoßen*) in an uncertain, incessant movement (91; *88*). Compared to the pleasure of the beautiful, the pleasure of the sublime is (so to speak) negative (this is why Burke distinguishes it as *delight*). It involves a recoil, as if thinking came up against what precisely attracts it. Kant's text anticipates the subsequent analyses by assimilating this negative pleasure to an "admiration" (*Bewunderung*) or to a "respect" (*Achtung*), which are also supposed to hold back before releasing and to hold back again (ibid.).

One might wonder what the "thing" is that arouses such ambivalence. Thus one progresses to the comparison of the beautiful and the sublime feelings according to the category of relation (finality). Beginning with Mallarmé, and perhaps even with Jean Paul, the aesthetic negatives, the thinking about writing, the reflection on modern art, have put forward the thing before which thinking retreats and toward which it races. What is certain is that with the sublime, the "happiness" with which creative imagination opens thinking to the unlimited field of aesthetic Ideas has disappeared. Gone is the superabundance, the supplement to naturalness that had come with an analogizing talent to extend "actual nature" and overwhelm the thinking of this nature.

However, the "transition" through finality sees this right away: taste presupposes the affinity of natural forms, even those enraptured by the free imagination, with the faculty of judging in its most elementary exercise—the aesthetic judgment of the feeling of the beautiful. If the stupor we have remarked upon does fall within sublime feeling, if in the object or the circumstance there is some "thing" that leaves thought dumbfounded even as it exalts thought, this object is not one of nature, or, rather, its nature is not that nature, the "writing" (*Chiffreschrift*: 160, t.m.; *153*) of whose forms is able to be immediately "read" by the feeling of the beautiful. The "thing" cannot belong to a nature that lets the imagination of genius search its "writing" for something further with which to present more forms than the writing presents, and with which to form another nature. Sublimity puts an end to the approval, the *Beifall* (92; *89*), that nature gives to thought through taste. No object of coded nature is sublime (91–92; *88–89*). A feeling is sublime insofar as "the thing" that arouses it goes against the affinity exhibited in taste and genius, insofar as it is felt to be "contra-final" (*zweckwidrig*: 91; *88*) to direct aesthetic judgment, "ill-adapted" (*unangemessen*) to the imagination, and an "outrage" (*gewälttätig*) to the latter (ibid.).

Thus as "the thing" does not belong to nature, it must be of "the mind." This, at least, is "all that we can say" (ibid.). Perhaps we can say a little more. If a sensible form cannot contain "the thing," then the latter has some relation to the Ideas of reason, for the objects of these Ideas precisely never give an adequate presentation of themselves in a form that would be adapted, *angemessen*, to them. However, even in the case of this unpresentability of principle, what remains presentable for the objects of rational Ideas is the inadequacy, the *Unangemessenheit*, the de-mensuration of all presentation. Presented in the sensible to and through the imagination, this "discrepancy" reminds the mind of the Ideas that are always absent to presentation and thus revives them. For example, the raging ocean is simply hideous, *gräßlich*, when taken perceptively. If it arouses a sublime emotion, it does so insofar as it refers thought negatively to a higher finality, that of an Idea (92; *89*).

This gesture of thought that averts the "horror," as Burke would say, the hideousness of the present, that subverts it and turns it into admiration and respect for an unpresentable Idea—this gesture is called "subreption" (*Subreption*: 106; *102*). In canon law *subreptio* refers to the act of obtaining a privilege or a favor by dissimulating a circumstance that would conflict with its attainment. It is an abuse of authority. What in the sublime is the favor obtained at the price of such an abuse? A glimpse of the Idea, the absolute of power, freedom. Why does thinking not have a right to it? Because in the given circumstance and by principle there is, strictly speaking, no presentation of the Idea in nature. What has been dissimulated in order to be granted this favor? The powerlessness of the imagination to present the object of reason. In what does the subreption consist? In obtaining or in extracting a quasi presentation of the object, which is not presentable, in the presence of a magnitude or a natural force that is "formless."

This is how thinking employs (*Gebrauch*) presentation (93; *90*). For Kant, let me repeat, there is in the word *Gebrauch* a sense of abuse, of crime, of sin almost, which is also present in *subreption*. It is the sin of modern man. Heidegger will say that with technique, Being gives itself as the "funds" that one has at hand, from which one can draw without having to understand it. Indeed, Kant's *Gebrauch* has a similar purpose: the denaturing of being that makes the poem obsolete and permits the means. I will not pursue this line of argument further, though it might lead one to an understanding of the affinity of aesthetic sublimes with an era of technique.

In conclusion, if nature contributes to sublime emotion it is certainly not through its forms, as in the feeling of the beautiful. It is, as we have seen, only when nature "gives signs of magnitude and power" (92, t.m.; *89*), of raw quantity, and in an inverted final relation. The quantitative is final for rational thought, but it is not final for the imagination. The differences between the beautiful and the sublime far exceed, it seems, their kinship as aesthetic feelings.

One last word on the "transition" from the beautiful to the sublime. There is a remarkable absence in the system of comparisons between the two feelings. Whether the comparison involves similarity or difference, it is not conducted under the category of modality. We know that in the "Fourth Moment" of the "Analytic of the Beautiful," judgment of the beautiful is always posited as necessary. We also know that this necessity of judgment is neither agreed upon nor "apodictic" but "exemplary" (*exemplarisch*: 81–83; 78–79). Is the same true for the sublime? The answer is not given until paragraph 29, which is devoted to the modality of the judgment in sublime feeling. Although there is still some confusion. Sublimity is said to be necessary, like beauty. But a slight difference persists as to the status of the necessity of sublime judgment. It is not certain that it is the same as in taste. This subtle difference will be of great significance when it comes time to determine the nature and the extension of the "communicability" of sublime feeling (see Chapter 9).

However, I have intentionally omitted the programmatic word used for the modality of sublime judgment in the exposition entitled "Subdivision of an Investigation," which treats this feeling to which paragraph 24 is devoted (93–94; *90–91*): "The delight in the sublime, just like [*ebensowohl als*] that in the beautiful, must . . . be made representable [*vorstellig machen*] . . . in its subjective finality, in its relation, and represent this finality as necessary in its modality" (93, t.m.; *90*; I do not take into account a "correction" made by Erdmann). The parallel between the two Analytics and their respective conclusions is thus strongly emphasized. But not without seeming a little forced. The difficulty comes from the expression *vorstellig machen*, to make representable, which applies both to the subjectivity of finality (which is a case of relation) and to the necessity of its assertion (which is a case of modality). That both should be "representable" is not self-evident. Let us recall, for example, the end of the "Third Moment" of the "Analytic of the Beautiful" where it was concluded that beauty is "the form of finality in an object, so far as it is perceived in it [*an ihm*] apart from the representation of an end [*ohne Vorstellung eines Zweckes*]" (80, t.m.; *77*). Without returning to the relation and modality of a judgment upon the beautiful, we will limit ourselves to examining how the necessary finality of sublime judgment (considering the latter according to the categories of both relation and modality) can be shown to be "represented."

Here we must defer to the nomenclature explicated in the section entitled "The Ideas in General" in Book I of the dialectic of the first *Critique* (KRV, 308–14; *348–55*). This section is responsible for the critique of the vague use that empiricism makes of the term "Idea" and for inscribing it within the legacy of a Platonic usage. The "serial arrangement" of representations comes to dispel all possible misunderstanding. Given that all thought is representation (I will not discuss this here, although the bias of Cartesian metaphysics should be recognized), one must be able to distinguish among perceptions, all of which are representations with consciousness, those that refer to the "subject" alone as modifications of its state without providing any knowledge of the object, and are called *Empfindungen*, sensations (KRV, 314; *354*). Insofar as sublime feeling is a subjective reflective judgment, the necessary finality that characterizes this judgment must belong to the family of subjective perceptions, that is, of sensations; in this respect the sublime feeling is similar to taste. But insofar as this sublime subjective state is necessarily related to the "presence" of a concept of reason, the absolute, sublime judgment must involve a representation from an entirely different family, which in the "serial arrangement" is precisely called an Idea (ibid.).

Would the finalization of sublime feeling by the absolute require the representation of the absolute by an Idea? Or else is the absolute in sublime feeling an object for thought that can also be represented by an Idea, in the use made of it by speculative reason, but that here is only felt, that is, "present" here only as the sensation of a necessary finality? Since we are referring to a reflective judgment, the second hypothesis must be correct. This is why I speak of the "presence" of a concept of reason: the object of this concept, the absolute, is felt without it being represented by an Idea. It is like sensation only in that it is present in sublime feeling and that it exerts its necessary finality. If the absolute were represented in sublime judgment by an Idea, the judgment would cease to be aesthetic and would become speculative: "If it is to be aesthetic and not to be tainted with any judgment of understanding or reason" "a pure judgment upon the sublime must . . . have no end belonging to the object [*gar keinen Zweck des Objekts*] as its determining ground [*zum Bestimmungsgrunde*]" (101, t.m.; *97*). Thus the absolute is not conceived of as an Idea but only felt. The nature of the representation implied in the sublime makes it a cousin of taste. But only a cousin, because it presupposes both a capacity to conceive of the absolute and a sensibility of the "presence" of the absolute—something of which the feeling of the beautiful is unaware.

Continuity and Discontinuity Between Beautiful and Sublime

The kinship between the two aesthetic feelings—which does not exclude a reading attentive to the differences, a reading of discontinuity, like the one that will be attempted here—permits a reading of continuity, which would emphasize the "tension" and the instability that characterize both feelings. One feels the beautiful, one feels the sublime, insofar as the relation between the power of presentation and the power of concepts relative to an object is not fixed by a rule.

Pleasure in the beautiful occurs when the powers of imagination and understanding engage with each other, according to a suitable "ratio" (83; *80*), in a kind of play. A play because they compete with each other, one with forms, the other with concepts, in an effort to grasp the object. But it is also play because they are accomplices in *not* determining the object, that is, in not grasping it by form and concept as they do in objective knowledge. The result is that the ratio suited to procuring the delight that is called pleasure in the beautiful is not itself determined; delight signals it. The tension between the two powers is also necessarily unstable (see Chapter 8).

We have seen that the imagination is the most responsible for this instability. It is employed in proliferating the *Nebenvorstellungen*, the "secondary representations" (177; *169*); it proliferates aesthetic Ideas. Yet when the imagination opens and reopens the field of "aesthetic attributes" (ibid.) it discovers around the object, is it possible that the object ceases to be recognizable by imagination's partner, understanding? One could even go so far as to imagine (so to speak) that the object thus elaborated escapes not only its identification by understanding but "recognition" in the strongest sense that the Deduction of pure concepts gives to this term in the first *Critique* (KRV A, 133–38; *149–60*). In the fullest sense because it is a matter of nothing less than the constitution of the "inner sense," that is, of the time implicated in all knowledge (ibid., 131–32; *142–43*). This constitution requires that three elementary syntheses be performed upon the pure diversity of givens in order to make the manifold representable (ibid.). The first consists in unifying the evanescent diversity in an intuitive "apprehension" (*Apprehension*), the second in repeating it in a "reproduction" (*Reproduktion*), that is, the work of the imagination (ibid., 131–33; *142–49*). "Recognition" (*Rekognition*) is the third synthesis of time, and the concept performs it: "If we were not conscious [*Bewußtsein*] that what we think is the same as what we thought a moment before, all reproduction in the series of representations would be useless" (ibid., 133; *149*). I will not pursue this demonstration further (see Chapter 4, pp. 102–9). It suffices to imagine, as a result of the productive imagination in taste and genius, a proliferation of representations grafted upon a single given such that the conceptual consciousness that is supposed to make these representations "recognizable," that is, to situate them in one singular series of apprehensions of reproductions of the manifold, is missing.

The hypothesis is as follows: in the excess of its productive play with forms or aesthetic Ideas, the imagination can go so far as to prevent the recognition by concept, to dis-concert the "consciousness" that is dependent upon understanding, the faculty of concepts. This fury evokes the "excesses" of the baroque, of mannerism or of surrealism, but is also always a potential disturbance in the "calm" contemplation of the beautiful. The *Geist*, the life vein of "animation," can always exceed the "letter," force it to give in, to resign, and the "happiness" of writing can thus turn into a delirium through an overabundance of "images."

We must remember, however, that this kind of disturbance (which Kant would certainly not see as providing the pleasure of the beautiful, lacking as it does a ratio suited to both powers) leads to the antipodes of sublime disturbance. And we readily give it the name of genius. However, genius is not in the least sublime for critical analysis; it is crazy with forms and crazy about forms, whereas sublimity originates from their "absence."

However, sublime feeling can be thought of as an extreme case of the beautiful. Thus it is through the faculty of concepts that the aesthetic feeling becomes unbound. One can imagine, in effect, that by dint of opposing the power of forms with concepts that are more and more "extreme" in order to put this power—the imagination—in difficulty, the power of concepts determinable by intuition, understanding, passes its "hand" (in this play) to the power of concepts of reason's unpresentable objects (see Chapter 4, pp. 109–15). The faculty of concepts no longer requires the imagination to give a rich and pleasant presentation to the concept of domination, in the traits of the master of Olympus, for example, to which it can add a thousand other "aesthetic attributes," but to the Idea of the all-powerful itself. But the object of this Idea is not presentable in intuition. The imagination cannot "create" a form that would be adapted to it, for all form is circumscription (76; 74) and the all-powerful is conceived of as an absolute that excludes all limitation.

The proliferation of forms by an imagination gone wild makes up for this powerlessness of principle, but then creativity is no longer in free play, pleasant, even fortuitous; it falls prey to a regime of anguish. This is what must be understood in the *Ernst,* the "seriousness," with which Kant qualifies the activity of the imagination in the sublime. It is the seriousness of melancholy, the suffering of an irreparable lack, an absolute nostalgia for form's only always being form, that is, limitation, *Begrenzung* (ibid.). Even as it deploys an unlimited field of proliferating forms before thought, the imagination remains a slave to its finitude, because each of the forms it invents and adds to the others remains limited by definition.

In genius the power of presentation strains its relation with understanding almost to the breaking point; their ratio ceases to provide a feeling of the beautiful, and the object, which occasions the feeling, seems in the end unrecognizable to the concept. In sublime feeling the tension works in the opposite direction. The concept places itself out of the reach of all presentation: the imagination founders, inanimate. All of its forms are inane before the absolute. The "object" that occasions sublime feeling disappears: "nature as sinking into insignificance before the Ideas of reason" (105; *101*).

Thus two aesthetics can be described on the basis of these two tensions, two aesthetics that are always possible, that always threaten art, periods, genres, and schools whatever they may be, a figural aesthetic of the "much too much" that defies the concept, and an abstract or minimal aesthetic of the "almost nothing" that defies form. To assimilate the two because both suppose a tension would be to abandon all critical rigor and to succumb to the transcendental illusion that confuses understanding with reason. Both are still aesthetics. Furthermore, one could not move into another family, nor could one localize them in another faculty's territory, in ethics, for example, save through another illusion. I say this because many readers of the "Analytic of the Sublime" think they discern in sublime feeling a kind of ethical atavism, a shadow cast by moral feeling on presentation (thus obliterating it). Kant himself invokes *Achtung*, respect, which is the result of moral law, to designate the relation that thinking has with "the thing" in sublime feeling. No doubt, but he also writes "admiration" (91; *88*), which is not a term that belongs to a moral terminology. We will explore this case further (see Chapter 7).

§3 Categorical Examination of the Sublime

Quantity and Magnitude

I come now to the subdivision of the "Analytic of the Sublime" discussed in paragraph 24. The analysis of this feeling proceeds according to the table of categories, like that of the beautiful. I will not go over this paradoxical but strictly critical procedure according to which reflective judgment is put to the test of its determination and called upon to exhibit its difference and even its resistance (see Chapter 1, pp. 43–49). Thus the sublime proceeds as does the beautiful. However, two additional provisions upset the parallel between the two Analytics.

The first seems relatively unimportant: in the sublime one must begin with the quantity of judgment rather than its quality as was done with the beautiful. Kant refers to the method followed in paragraph 23. The analysis of taste begins with the quality of judgment (it is a disinterested delight, not directed by an interest in the existence of the object) because what awakens the feeling of the beautiful is the form of the object alone, and thus this aesthetic pleasure is distinct from any other pleasure in its specific quality. Form, presented by the imagination, prevents thinking from giving any objective determination by concept, for the imagination is busy defying understanding by multiplying the number of associated forms. But above all the privileging of form protects thinking from any interest in the "material" of the object and consequently from any interest in its real presence. Desire or need does not linger over forms.

In the sublime, on the contrary (as we have seen in Chapter 2, pp. 56–60), form plays no role at all. In fact form conflicts with the purity of sublime delight. If one is still permitted to speak of "nature" in this feeling, one can speak only in terms of a "rude nature" (*die rohe Natur*: 100; *97*), "merely as involving magnitude" (*bloß sofern sie Größe enthält*: ibid.). This magnitude is rude and arouses sublime feeling precisely because it escapes form, because it is completely "wanting in form or figure" (*formlos oder ungestalt*: 134; *128*). It is this "formlessness" (*Formlosigkeit*) that Kant evokes to begin the analysis of the sublime by quantity (93; *90*).

However, the terms "magnitude" and "quantity" lead to a certain, overall confusion that reigns in the Analytic of the Sublime and renders its reading and interpretation challenging—the same confusion induced by the terms "mathematical" and "dynamical" (see pp. 89–96 and Chapters 4 and 5). For "magnitude" designates a property of the object, and "quantity" is a category of judgment. One has trouble seeing why the magnitude of nature, or what remains of it when it has been stripped of its forms, provides the aesthetic judgment that it occasions with any property whatsoever, whether universal or particular, in its logical quantity. Yet this is what is at stake: to show that when, in feeling the sublime, reflection judges that "this is great," the judgment, which is singular because its subject "this" is unique, is also universal in its quantity because the predicate "great" applies to the totality of the logical subject.

In the first *Critique*, Kant concedes that it is undoubtedly a property of singular judgments to be treated logically as universals for the reason that we have just stated (KRV, 107–8; *111*). But the difficulty does not lie here; it lies, rather, in the fact that sublime judgment, like taste, belongs to reflection. The logical categories that govern understanding or determinant judgment, must not be applied to sublime judgment. What must be applied to it instead, as we have already seen, are the "headings" of reflection (see Chapter 1, pp. 26–32), or "places" in a "state of mind" (KRV, 277; *310*). In reflection, a manner of comparing objects under the "heading" of identity/difference corresponds to the category of quantity in understanding. Referring as it does to the reflective judgment of sublime feeling, this manner can be glossed in the following way: when I judge "this" to be great, do I experience the sensation of one greatness among others (difference) or that of greatness plain and simple, of greatness itself (identity)? (I say "I" to facilitate the formulation. It is not the *Ich denke* that speaks, for reflection does not need it [see Chapter 1, pp. 15–19], but, rather, it is the "subjective" of sensation that speaks.) Tautegorically speaking, is "this" felt to be great, or more or less great? Answer: "this" is felt to be great, absolutely.

Thinking only reflexively compares "this" to other greatnesses under the "heading" of identity/difference, and it feels (this is the "quantity" of sensation) "this" to be great absolutely. It will not admit of any comparison with other greatnesses (difference). "If, however, we call anything not alone great but without qualification, absolutely [*schlechthin*], and in every respect (beyond all comparison) great, that is to say, sublime, we soon perceive that for this it is not permissible to seek an appropriate standard outside itself, but merely in itself. It is greatness comparable to itself alone" (97, t.m.; *93*).[¹⁵]

The formulation is clear. However, it requires a correction. For "the things of nature" are phenomena intuited in experience, and intuition constitutes them immediately as "aggregates" by synthesizing their parts. The axioms of intuition discussed in the first *Critique* (KRV A, B, 197–201; *217–20*) are the *a priori* conditions of the extensive magnitudes of phenomena. "I cannot represent a line, however small, without drawing it in thought, that is, generating from a point all its parts one after another. Only in this way can the intuition be obtained. Similarly with all times, however small" (ibid., 198; *218*). In the constitution of objects of experience the axioms of intuition thus seek "the synthesis of apprehension in intuition" necessary *a priori* to the constitution of the time of knowledge in general (KRV A, 131–32; *142–43*). The concept of extensive magnitude, or of *quantum*, adds to this immediate synthesis the consciousness of this synthesis. It is the "consciousness of the synthetic unity of the manifold [and] homogeneous in intuition in general, insofar as the representation of an object first becomes possible by means of it" (KRV B, 198; *217*).

"We may at once cognize from the thing itself" that the phenomenon is a *quantum*: "no comparison with other things is required" (95; *92*). One must simply be conscious of the unity of the manifold parts that compose it. But this "inner" synthesis of the thing cannot make one aware of "*how great* it is" (ibid.). For then the question is not to apprehend it as *quantum* but to measure its *quantitas*. Quantity is not magnitude (KRV, 198–99; *218*), but the number of times the same unit is contained in the extensive magnitude. It must be measured in relation to a unit, that is, by comparing it to another magnitude taken as a unit of measure. This unit is in turn chosen after being compared with other magnitudes (95; *92*). Unlike the *quantum*, the *quantitas* is thus not provided with an *a priori* synthesis in intuition. It requires a "numerical formula" (KRV A, 199; *218*) that works *a posteriori* on the given object. The *quantitas* does not involve an axiom of intuition, but the use of a concept of understanding: number.

Since the magnitude of the sublime thing is estimated as being absolute without possible comparison, it is therefore not measurable as a quantity. A new term must be introduced to designate its greatness, *magnitudo*: "to be great and to be a magnitude are entirely different concepts (*magnitudo* and *quantitas*)" (94; *91*). The sublime *magnitudo* is not the predicate of a "mathematically determinant" judgment but of "a mere reflective judgment upon its [the object's] representation" (96; *93*). A quantity cannot be absolute; on the contrary, it can be estimated as infinitely small or infinitely great according to the chosen unit of measure (96–97; *94*). In reality the absolute greatness attributed to the sublime object, its *magnitudo*, signals "the disposition of the mind evoked by [*durch*] a particular representation engaging [*beschäftigende*] the faculty of reflective judgment" (98, t.m.; *94*). We will see (see Chapter 4) in what this "occupation," given to the faculty by representation, consists.

Here we are speaking of *quantitas*. The sublime thing cannot have a measurable quantity because it does not admit of any comparison. But is the sublime thing at least a phenomenon? Is it the object, like any phenomenon, of an apprehensive synthesis in intuition that gives it an extensive magnitude, a *quantum*? That gives it an "aesthetic" and not "mathematical" magnitude, a magnitude "in mere intuition" (by the eye, *nach dem Augenmaße*), and not "by means of concepts of number" (*Zahlbegriffe*: 98; *94–95*)? The "measure" (of the eye) evoked here for estimating a magnitude is also made without comparison; it is the extension of the manifold that can be "apprehended" intuitively at once, in the same breath. This measure can be called "first" or "fundamental" (98; *95*) because its unit is that of the synthesis of apprehension.

We will return to this crucial question later on (see Chapters 4 and 5). The answer will be that sublime magnitude is absolute not because it coincides with this fundamental measure of apprehension but because it "almost" exceeds it; it is a little beyond its limit—let us say, at the limit. Consequently the sublime thing is not exactly a phenomenon: "Nothing . . . which can be an object of the senses is to be termed sublime when treated on this footing" (97, t.m.; *94*). The conclusion of this discussion adds the promised correction: "It is the use to which judgment naturally puts particular objects on behalf of this latter feeling, and not the object of sense, that is absolutely great [*schlechthin groß*], and every other contrasted employment small" (ibid., t.m.). Sublimity does not predicate the thing but the *Geistesstimmung*, the disposition of thinking that experiences or reflects on itself when it represents the thing to itself. Use, disposition: we recognize the two traits, heuristic and tautegorical, that characterize reflection. Tautegorical: this is judged absolutely great because the thought that judges this feels itself to be great absolutely. But what is the absolute magnitude of a state of thought? Heuristic: its absolute affinity with a finality in itself that it discovers on the occasion of this feeling (see Chapter 4, pp. 109–15).

From Quantity to Modality Through Relation

The analysis that I have outlined constitutes the essence of paragraph 25 entitled "Definition of the Term 'Sublime'" [Définition nominale du sublime: tr.] (94–98; *91–94*). In it the object is to un-

derstand the term "great," which is used to characterize the sublime. The elucidation is "nominal" in that it does not take the play
of the faculties of knowledge in the sublime judgment into consideration (or does so only very little). What it essentially does instead is to dispel the confusion of this "great" with a quantity of
extension in the object, which is conceptual, or with the "first"
measure of apprehension, which is intuitive. The true name of
sublime greatness is magnitude. Magnitude is a subjective evalua-
tion reserved for the faculty of reflective judgment.

In assigning the estimation of magnitude to reflection, the
analysis is already far along in one of the essential objectives of the
Analytic of Aesthetic Judgment. The analysis subtracts the aesthetic judgment from the aporia in which an anthropological description (like Burke's) cannot help confining it: left to its particularity, aesthetic judgment has no right to be universally communicable. On the contrary, "the judgments: 'That man is beautiful'
and 'He is tall' [this is an allusion to §17 devoted to the ideal of
beauty] do not purport to speak only for the judging subject, but,
like theoretical judgments, they demand the assent of everyone"
(95; *92*). The deduction of the legitimacy of this claim of aesthetic
judgment to be universally communicable is made in the "Analytic of the Beautiful" (in §§20 and 21; see also Chapter 8). The
quoted phrase puts the sublime on the same level as the beautiful
in this claim. We will see that things are not quite so simple (see
Chapter 9). Nonetheless, if aesthetic judgment can justifiably demand a universal agreement, it is because the reflective faculty is
universally communicable. In fact the reflective faculty is none
other than thinking itself insofar as it is affected by the fact of its
thinking. Whether the reflective faculty thinks theoretically or
practically, it always feels itself subjectively at the same time. We
say that the reflective faculty thinks aesthetically when it relates
the object that it thinks to the sensation (*aisthēsis*) with which the
object provides it. The "universality" and "necessity" of aesthetic
judgments are thus assured (the quotation marks remind us that
they do not refer to categories in the strict sense).

This said, there is a point that arrests one's attention in the definition of the term "sublime." One remarks that a slippage occurs, the same slippage as in the "Analytic of the Beautiful," by which universality and necessity are confused with each other in their function and even in their nature, as if the category of quantity to which universality belongs were not altogether distinct from that of modality to which necessity belongs. If one were to take the categories literally, the universality (or the singularity) of a judgment would signify that the predicate of magnitude was attributed to the totality of the subject of judgment "this" or, in the phrase quoted, to "that man." The necessity of the same judgment would signify that the judgment itself could not be "posed" otherwise than it is; the modality of a judgment, in effect, "contributes nothing to the content of the judgment . . . but concerns only the value of the copula in relation to thought in general" (KRV, 109; *113–14*). From these two logical values, the quantitative universal and the modal necessity, how does one draw the following consequence that one would be tempted to call "pragmatic" in the semiotic and linguistic sense—that every person should in effect judge "this (or that man) to be great"?

The economy of this slippage is expounded in paragraph 8 of the "Analytic of the Beautiful" (53–57; *51–54*). But before turning to the argument, let us first notice in this same paragraph a precious "note" relative to universality. The note provides proof of the slippage we are discussing. "First of all we have here to note that a universality that does not rest upon concepts of the object (even though these are only empirical) is in no way logical, but aesthetic, i.e., does not involve any objective quantity of the judgment, but only one that is subjective" (54, t.m.; *52*). Thus we must distinguish between an objective universal validity and a subjective universal validity. Subjective universal validity quantifies "the reference of a representation . . . to the feeling of pleasure or displeasure" while objective universal validity quantifies the reference of a representation "to the cognitive faculties" (ibid.). We will not create further difficulties for this last expression: following the general table of faculties that concludes the Introduction to our *Critique*, "cognitive faculties" refers to understanding. But one cannot help being surprised by the displacement imparted to universality. Instead of quantifying the relation of the predicate to the subject of judgment (the judgment is universal when the predicate applies to a subject in its totality, and particular when the attribution is valid only for a part of the subject of judgment), the quantity invoked by the note refers to the relation of the judgment itself to the faculty that judges, the understanding or feeling of pleasure and displeasure. But, as we know, this relation belongs to the category of modality.

Let us begin again with the opposition between objective and subjective. Universality, or, more precisely, universal validity, is called *Allgemeingültigkeit* in logic: the predicate is valid, *gültig*, for the whole, *gemein*, in its totality, *all*, of the subject of judgment. Playing with the composition of the term that designates objective universality, Kant proposes to call subjective universal validity *Gemeingültigkeit*, a validity for the whole. But the use of the word *gemein* implies a strong sense of community, of something that is put in common. The *Gemeinschaft* is opposed to the *Gesellschaft* as a spontaneous community of feelings, of practices, of mores that belong to a formally organized society, to an association by contract provided with rules and goals. In our *Critique*, the *Gemeingültigkeit* points to the *allgemeine Stimme* (56; *54*), the "universal voice," a universality of voices or suffrage, which is constitutively claimed by the singular judgment of taste. From this constitutive demand, the principle that founds it, *Gemeinsinn*, common sense, *sensus communis*, in Kant's Latin (82–83; *79–80*), will be deduced in paragraph 28. Owing to this play on the word "universality," the signification of universality leads us from the quantity in judgment to the modality of judgment. A subjective judgment is said to be universal when the duty to feel the same delight as the judging "subject" "is imputed to everyone" (*jedermann ansinne*: 53; *51*) given the same object. This is a modal and not quantitative characteristic: a different state of thinking is not deemed possible. One should say that the delight is thus not universal but necessary.

Let us return to the exposition that argues for this subjective "universality" in paragraph 8 (53–57; *51–54*). The argument begins by opposing aesthetic judgment as *Reflexionsgeschmack* (the taste of reflection) to the judgment associated with the empirical delight due to the senses, the *Sinnengeschmack* (the taste of sense), on the one hand, and to the determinant judgment by concept on the other. The latter can be universal in a strictly logical sense. Because of the aforementioned slippage, we will accept that everyone must necessarily accept it. The taste of sense, according to the same reasoning, refers to "judgments merely private" (*Privaturteile*: 54; 52) and does not demand the assent of others and cannot therefore claim universality. What this means, according to the same "confusion," is that it is not necessary for the delight I take in eating spinach, for example, to prevent others from not sharing in my delight.

The same is not true for the taste of reflection. Unlike a determinant judgment, this taste judges without concepts; and yet, unlike the taste of sense, it can be universal, or at least claim to be. What could the quantity of a subjective judgment, of a subjective quantity be? Neither the subject nor the predicate of this judgment being a concept, one has trouble seeing how one might quantify the application of one to the other. One barely dares speak of attribution in these conditions. One might risk saying that the object that provides the aesthetic delight is the subject of the judgment of taste and that its attribute is the delight itself. "This is beautiful" would then be glossed in the following way: "Given this, there is pleasure" (the conditions of which must be specified). Let us say: "This is pleasant." The equivalent of the universal quantity for a judgment of this kind would be that "pleasant" applies to the totality of "this" without remainder and without reserve: "This is entirely pleasant." The capacity to provide pleasure "saturates" the object.

However, if one were limited to this notion of subjective quantity, one would not be able to distinguish the pleasure of the senses, the agreeable, from aesthetic pleasure, the beautiful, nor would one be able to distinguish the delight related to "inclination" (*Neigung*) from that which is related to "favor" (*Gunst*: 49; 47). In other words (I would refer the reader to the discussion in paragraph 14) the pleasure provided by the "material" of sensation (supposing that it can ever be isolated from its form) or even the interested pleasure tied to a personal, "private" preference for a given form, can "saturate" the totality of the respective objects that arouse them, such that one would have to concede to the judgments implicated in these tastes of sense a universal validity. The exception made in this regard for the taste of reflection, for pure aesthetic pleasure, would no longer have a reason for being. It is precisely to avoid this consequence that reflective universality must be understood differently from the way in which we have just explained it and for this reason can be assimilated to a necessity that authorizes a principle of unanimity.

Once again, the transition from quantity to modality does not seem to be justified anywhere. Let me remind the reader that nothing prevents a particular judgment (from the point of view of quantity) from being posed as necessary (in its modality): that "some animals are quadrupeds" can be affirmed as necessary (in conclusion to a demonstration, for example). Conversely, a universal judgment can be posed "problematically," that is, as expressing a simple possibility (as when one establishes a hypothesis). The missing link between the modality of aesthetic judgment (its necessity that justifies its demand to be communicated) and its quantity (its universality, which would be the saturation of the pleasure-producing object) is the category of relation, which is the object of the "Third Moment" of the "Analytic of the Beautiful."

That an object that one is attached to because of an interest should provide pleasure when it is there (existent), a complete delight (one that is universal in the sense we have just read), indicates that there is an affinity between the object and thinking. For example, we say that the object satisfies a desire, a need, an inclination, a "taste." Thus the "capacity to desire" (to speak like Kant) was already determined by an end that the object satisfies. If the object satisfies these motives (whatever they may be), it is because it is "final" in relation to them. These motives saw the object as the means to their end; or the absence (the nonexistence) of the object was the (final) cause of these motives. This is what the psychologists call motivation: what puts in motion.

Yet what fills Kant with wonder, and what constitutes an essential point in the critique of aesthetic judgment, is that an affinity with the object, a final relation to the object, is felt by thought although thought is moved by the object in question according to no determinable motivation. "Finality . . . may exist apart from an end insofar as we do not locate the causes of this form in a will" (62; *59*). Of course, Kant adds, if one wanted to *explain* why the form of the object arouses delight in thought, one would have to find the will that conceived the form in such a way as to render it pleasant. This form would then be thought of "as an effect [that] is thought to be possible only through a concept of it," which is "to imagine an end" (61; *58*). "The representation of the effect is here the determining ground of its cause and takes the lead of it" (ibid.). Insofar as the faculty of desire is "determinable only through concepts, i.e., so as to act in conformity with the representation of an end," then it is precisely the will (61; *59*).

As we see, such an explanation of an object's aesthetic affinity with thinking would force this affinity out of the aesthetic territory, for the explanation would introduce both concept and will. Thus even though the critique must found this affinity on the action of a "supersensible" principle (see Chapter 8, pp. 215–18), the principle will remain an indeterminable concept, and its end, of which the affinity is one of the effects, will remain unknowable. There will be no question of will. As for the taste of reflection, one must recognize in it a "finality of form . . . without resting on its end (as the material of the *nexus finalis*)" (62; *59*). The sensation of pleasure that the judgment of the beautiful "predicates" on the object is "immediate," for it does not result from the mediation of a determinable end by a concept. One would not say that the object pleases because its form is "perfect" in relation to an "Ideal" of beauty—this is what is explained in paragraph 17 (75–80; *72–78*). No causality—and not simply no final causality—is applicable to taste. One could not even say that pleasure is the effect of the

beauty we attribute to the object. "To determine *a priori* the connection of the feeling of pleasure or displeasure as an effect, with
some representation or other (sensation or concept) as its cause, is
utterly impossible" (63; *60*). One must say that the consciousness
of the object's subjective affinity with thinking "constitutes" aesthetic pleasure (ibid.).

In referring back to the different "headings" that guide reflection
and that are called "concepts of reflection" (only by analogy with
understanding), we observe that in reflection the "comparison"
procedure of the "inner and the outer" corresponds to the category of relation (KRV, 277, 279–80, 284–85; *310, 313–14, 319–20;* see
Chapter 1, pp. 26–32). The subjective finality of aesthetic judgment, considered in the place of relation and replaced in the transcendental topology of reflection, is a pure inner finality. The pleasure of taste is altogether internal in that the sensation of finality
that constitutes it does not depend on any external cause, whether
final or not, subjective or objective.

This reflective finality is made accountable to the "faculty of the
mind" (*Gemütsvermögen*) that is the feeling of pleasure and displeasure. It is made more explicit when the critical analysis examines the play of the "faculties of knowledge" in taste. The imagination and understanding are in a relation of emulation with each
other in relation to the object, not in order to know it, but in such
a way as to arouse and perpetuate a happiness in thought: thinking
comes and goes from the presentation to the concept of the object.
We are better able to see how the "form of finality," which is that
of the judgment of the beautiful, consists in this play of coming
and going—all inner in effect—between the powers at the disposal of thinking, the power of showing and the power of concepts.
The object is but the occasion for play; it lends itself to it, through
its form. Yet this play, in turn, shows the affinity of the two powers with each other, a pure affinity, not subordinated to a specific
task, to tell the truth or to do right. This unity, which is never
stable and always indeterminate—the *Einstimmung* required and
promised by the judgment of the beautiful—is the unity of the
faculties before being the unison required of other individuals by

the individual who judges. The pleasure of this play reveals an affinity between the faculties that is transcendental and not originally empirical. It is the affinity of thought with itself despite the heterogeneity of its capacities. But the heterogeneity of thought's capacities reveals this affinity. We will explore this analysis further (see Chapters 8 and 9).

Thus we see why the judgment of the beautiful is posed as necessary. One certainly cannot demonstrate that all other aesthetic judgments upon the object are impossible: the argument on the subject of the beautiful is without conclusion, for lack of concepts. The judgment of the beautiful immediately attests to the inner finality of thinking in relation to thinking. The thought that presents is final with regard to the thought that conceives, and vice versa. Taste discovers the secret of the "art concealed in the depths of the human soul" (KRV, 183; *200*) that the schematism conceals and cannot reveal when the powers of thought are absorbed in the "serious" matters of knowledge. Taste, on the other hand, allows the powers of thought free range and thinking feels that it is happy. The form of this inner finality, thus linked to the *a priori* conditions of all thought (its faculties, heterogeneous, but capable of unity), suffices to legitimate the demand that the happiness of the beautiful be accessible to all thinking, given the same object. Thus the transition from the universal quantity of the judgment upon the beautiful to its necessary modality is made possible by the final relation.

Mathematical and Dynamical

At the end of paragraph 24 the text introduces the second original provision of the sublime that disrupts the categorical order followed by the Analytic of the Beautiful. Disrupts or, rather, complicates or, better yet: overdetermines. The examination of the sublime according to the four categories will be divided between the two "families" of the mathematical and the dynamical, which respectively regroup the first two categories, quality and quantity, and the second two, relation and modality.

I have said that these terms may be confusing. They do not signify that there are two kinds of sublime, the one mathematical and the other dynamical, as the French translation of the section titles might suggest: "Du sublime mathématique" (The mathematically sublime), "Du sublime dynamique de la nature" (The dynamically sublime in nature). The German is less equivocal: the expressions *vom Mathematisch-Erhabenen* and *vom Dynamisch-Erhabenen der Natur* indicate that the sublime (of nature) is on the one hand considered "mathematically" and on the other "dynamically" (or according to the order of the categories already mentioned). However, the insistence on regrouping the categories in mathematical and dynamical "families" deserves attention. The Analytic of the Beautiful did not require this additional classification.

The division into dynamical and mathematical is introduced in the text by an addition in the second edition to the commentary on the table of categories explained in the *Critique of Pure Reason* (KRV B, 115–18; *121–22*). But the division is already made in the first edition of this same *Critique*, a little later, on the subject of the synthetic principles of pure understanding (KRV, 196–97; *216*). These principles are the *a priori* rules that understanding observes in constituting not experience in general but the objects of experience or in experience. Like forms of intuition, the categories of understanding are the conditions of the possibility of experience in general. Following this, one must establish the conditions of the possibility of objects as they are found in experience. If these objects did not satisfy principles of constitution that were compatible with the *a priori* syntheses, which are the forms of space and time and the categories, the objects would remain unknowable. There could be no real knowledge of the objects, but only a possible knowledge of possible objects.

By dividing the four principles (axioms of intuition, anticipations of perception, analogies of experience, postulates of empirical thought in general) into mathematical and dynamical, Kant explains that he does not intend to present the first two as "principles of mathematics" and the other two as "principles of general physical dynamics" (ibid.). In both cases he is concerned with the "*a*

priori determination of appearances according to the categories"
(and I will permit myself to add: according to the forms of intuition. Kant himself observes that the principles regulate the relation of understanding to "inner sense," which is time, the universal form of intuition). But the division into mathematical and dynamical merely involves a difference in the "certainty" (*Gewißheit*)
provided by the principles. All the principles provide thought with
a "complete" (*völlig*) certainty as regards the result (the object of
experience) obtained by the syntheses performed according to
these principles. However, the certainty provided by the first two,
the axioms and the anticipations, is "intuitive," whereas the certainty resulting from the other two, the analogies and the postulates, is "merely discursive" (ibid.).

What this means is that thinking can be intuitively certain that
any phenomenon is an extensive magnitude (through the axioms
of intuition), and that all sensation that makes thought aware of a
phenomenon has an intensive magnitude, a degree (through the
anticipations of perception). However, thinking is only certain
"discursively" and not through an immediate intuition of a phenomenon's being necessarily linked to another phenomenon in
time, whether it be according to the principle of permanence, of
succession, or of coexistence (that is to say, according to the anticipations of perception). The same is true for the postulates of empirical thought.

This difference in certainty, which authorizes the cleavage between the mathematical and the dynamical, nonetheless remains
difficult to grasp. What "discourse" does an analogy of experience
need for it to be accepted as certain (altogether certain, in every
case) that a phenomenon either persists as such in time or else succeeds another, or else coexists with it? A note from the second edition added to the passage I am discussing here makes things clearer by specifying the nature of the syntheses—rather than the kind
of certainty with which they provide thought—in play in the
mathematical and dynamical principles (KRV B, 197–98; *216*).

The mathematical synthesis is called *compositio, Zusammensetzung*, a term that will play a role in the analysis of the sublime (see

Chapter 4, pp. 102–9). It consists in unifying several elements that "do not necessarily belong to one another" on the one hand and are "homogeneous" on the other, that is, they involve the same faculty of knowledge. Thus the two triangles into which a square is divided when one draws its diagonal are united by a "composition" of a mathematical nature: they are homogeneous because they are both given according to the axioms of intuition but do not necessarily belong to the same unity, for they must be enumerated in order to produce this unity (the number two). The "numerical formula" is not an axiom of intuition, but consists in the *a posteriori* "aggregation" of extensive magnitudes (here, the triangles: KRV, 198–200; *218–19*). The same would be true for intensive magnitudes, i.e., phenomena considered according to the quality of sensation they provide. Understanding regulates their appearance in existence by the *a priori* principle called anticipation of perception, but the unification of their respective intensities that are homogeneous consists here again in a mathematical "composition" *a posteriori*, which Kant distinguishes from the "aggregation" of their extensive magnitudes under the name coalition of intensities (KRV B, 197–98; *216*).

If we relate this definition of the "mathematical" synthesis to the Analytic of the Sublime, we find in paragraph 26, which will be studied further (see Chapter 4), that the tension and even the displeasure inherent in the sublime feeling come precisely and foremost from the mathematical "composition" required by the magnitude of the object called sublime. This is not of course to say that the *Zusammensetzung* (102; *98*) presents a difficulty in itself for understanding or for the faculty of presentation, for it is a principle of composition of phenomena as extensive magnitudes; it is an axiom of intuition. But the *result* of composition becomes unpresentable for the faculty of presentation, the imagination; the result cannot be "comprehended" at once as a whole, according to the fundamental (aesthetic) measure of imagination. This occurs when the mathematical composition of the units that make up the object achieves very great magnitudes, and the imagination is still

required (for a "reason" that remains to be determined) to provide
an immediate intuitive apprehension of it. The mathematical synthesis thus creates a problem, not in itself once again, but because
it is supposed to be doubled by an "aesthetic" synthesis: the presentation of the infinite. If we were to ask why such a challenge is
put to the imagination's capacity of apprehension, we will discover a finality in the judgment of the sublime that is very different
from that of the beautiful.

Let us return to the note added to the presentation of the synthetic principles of pure understanding in the second edition of
the first *Critique*. The dynamical synthesis is not a composition
but a *nexus*, a *Verknüpfung*, the "connection" of elements, which
are thus linked *a priori* and not "arbitrarily" (as the triangles were,
by the tracing of the diagonal) but which are heterogeneous, that
is, they do not involve the same faculty of knowledge. The necessary synthesis of what is heterogeneous is thus dynamical. For example, an accident cannot be conceived of without the substance
it affects, nor can the effect without the cause of which it is the
result: their unity is necessary *a priori*. However, the accident and
the effect are phenomena given in experience by intuition and the
principles of understanding, whereas substance and cause are the
object of pure concepts and have no possible intuitive presentation in experience. They are heterogeneous according to the terms
by which they are necessarily united (KRV B, 198; *217*).

In the sublime considered dynamically we will find the same
heterogeneity of elements united by the synthesis and the necessity of the synthesis. The elements are on the one hand the object
that provides the imagination with difficulty in presentation, the
"colossal," "rude" object (100; *97*), "devoid of form" (90; *87*), and
on the other the Idea of the infinite, of the absolute whole or absolute cause (105–6, 109–11; *102, 106–7*). The Idea has no corresponding object presentable in intuition (except by analogy). The
faculty of presentation cannot apprehend an extensive magnitude
that exceeds its "first" measure. The synthesis of these heterogeneous elements, their *nexus*, consists in bringing the without-form,

barely apprehended in nature, to the "presence" of the Idea of reason. Thus the powerlessness of the imagination becomes the *sign* of the omnipotence of reason.

This synthesis is necessary *a priori*, for the two terms that it unites could not be united by an arbitrary decision (such as drawing the diagonal of a square). Paragraph 29 explains this necessity: the "colossal" is only felt to be sublime if thinking can represent the absolute to itself at the same time, if it is "susceptible" (115; *111*) to the Ideas, if it has an *Empfänglichkeit* for them.

This mathematical/dynamical operator, or meta-operator, is useful for critical thought as a whole, in particular for unifying the results of the first *Critique* with those of the second, i.e., in resolving the antinomies that speculative reason comes up against when it seeks to form the concept of the world or of the cosmos (KRV, 384–484; *437–548*). It appears to be demonstrable that the world should have a limit in time (a beginning) and space, but that it does not is also demonstrable. Similarly one can demonstrate that in the world composite substances are formed of simple substances, and that they are not. One can demonstrate that the series of conditions that unite the phenomena of the world need a first cause (which is not conditioned), but also that such a cause cannot be admitted. Or, finally, one can demonstrate that the existence of the world requires the existence of a necessary being (in the world or outside of it) to be its reason, but also that the existence of this being can never be deduced from the existence of the world.

How can reason escape these aporias? This is where the mathematical/dynamical meta-operator becomes crucial. One recognizes in the syntheses in play in the first two antinomies the very syntheses that were operative in the first two principles of understanding. They serve in forming the series that unite the phenomena in experience, which are seen as either extensive magnitudes (axioms of intuition) or intensive magnitudes (anticipations of perception). These syntheses are mathematical; they unite in a non-necessary way a multiplicity of homogeneous elements. Speculative reason asks whether or not the series formed by these syntheses should be arrested (at a beginning in extension, at the simple in "intension"). The conclusion is easy to give: they cannot be. Any object of experience is constituted according to these principles. Furthermore, the only knowledge that understanding can give (with the help of sensible intuition) consists in discovering how a phenomenon is conditioned by other phenomena in its extension and intension. These other phenomena, the conditions, are subject in turn to the same constitutive principles and to the same explication. Should one therefore conclude that the world is indeterminate in extensive magnitude and infinite in intensive magnitude, that there is neither an outer nor an inner limit? No, not this either. The indeterminate in extensive magnitude and the infinite in intensive magnitude are not phenomena. What is indeterminate is the regression in the series of conditions, and what is infinite is the progression in the decomposition into parts (KRV, 449–54; 504–10). This property results from a regulative principle imposed on knowledge by reason; this property does not provide any knowledge of magnitude of the world, either extensive or intensive.

In the third and fourth antinomies (if the world admits of a first causality in relation, and if its existence should be posed necessarily in modality), the recourse to the dynamical synthesis allows for a very different solution. This recourse is possible because causality, or the relation of an effect to its cause, does not unite two homogeneous elements: the effect is a phenomenon, the cause a concept, whose object cannot have an intuition. The elements are heterogeneous, but their union is necessary: one cannot think one without the other. Nothing, moreover, prevents the same phenomenon, which is the object of a mathematical synthesis (when it is placed in a contingent series of conditions that are homogeneous to it as extensive and intensive magnitudes), from "also" (*auch*: KRV, 463; 521) being considered, with regard to its existence, the effect of a cause that is by definition unconditioned—freedom— and also from being combined with an element that is heterogeneous to it in a dynamical synthesis.

From this solution we will conclude that mathematical synthesis and dynamical synthesis do not exclude one another, and we must remember this when we read the "Analytic of the Sublime." Indeed the problem is displaced, for here it is not a question of determinant judgments as in the antinomies, but of an aesthetic judgment, which is reflective and subjective. However, *mutatis mutandis*, it is conceivable on the one hand that sublime "magnitude" does not completely escape the axioms of intuition and the anticipations of perception, or even the most elementary syntheses—those of apprehension and reproduction of the manifold in an intuition—(there is an "object" given in sublime feeling) and on the other hand that this same magnitude will be taken as the (negative) effect in presentation of a pure Idea of reason.

Quality, Once Again

What motivates the union of the two syntheses, mathematical and dynamical, in the critical analysis of the sublime is the very quality of feeling as it is observed in empirical reality. There is no need for a meta-operator to analyze taste. This is because the nature of delight is very different in each of the two aesthetic feelings. Paragraph 24 very quickly places the sublime on the side of taste from the point of view of their quality: both are devoid of interest. But the qualification is a negative one. The preceding paragraph, in which both feelings are compared, is more articulate. But it also recalls their difference, as we have already seen (see Chapter 2, pp. 56–67). Qualitatively, sublime feeling seems "contradictory." We know that the quality of a subjective judgment consists in delight or displeasure. In this regard the judgment of sublimity is qualitatively different from the judgment of beauty because it associates displeasure with pleasure.

As a category of understanding, quality requires that a judgment be either affirmative, negative, or "infinite" (*unendlich*: KRV, 107; *110*). In the first case, the judgment truly attributes the predicate to the subject, in the second it denies it, in the third it limits it. Whence the three categories of the "class" quality: *Realität, Negation, Limitation* (ibid., 113; *118*). The third category in each class "always arises from the combination of the second category with the first" (KRV B, 116, t.m.; *122*). Thus for quality "limitation [*Einschänkung*] is simply reality combined with negation" (ibid.).

Because a subjective judgment related only to the faculty of feeling pleasure and displeasure is involved here, its quality is expressed as pleasure when it is real or affirmative, displeasure when it is negative, or pleasure linked to displeasure when it is limited or infinite. This last case is that of sublime feeling with regard to its quality: in the sublime pleasure is limited by displeasure, which makes this feeling an infinite [*indéfini*: tr.] subjective judgment. This infinite [*indéfinité*] quality is what forces the critique to have recourse to the two syntheses I have discussed. The dynamical synthesis accounts for the component of pleasure, and the mathematical synthesis for the component of displeasure. As an aesthetic reflective judgment, the co-presence of these syntheses is only felt. This co-presence consists entirely in the violent and ambivalent emotion that thinking feels on the occasion of the "formless."

§4 The Sublime as Mathematical Synthesis

"Comprehension" Is "Measured"

The "drama" that goes by the name of the sublime considered "mathematically" (*das Mathematisch-Erhabene*), which is not the mathematical sublime, is undoubtedly similar to the conflict that gives rise to the first two antinomies in the Dialectic of the first *Critique*. This conflict insists on the fact that the syntheses invoked by both parties in order to come to a decision about quantity (beginning or not) or about quality (simplicity or not) of the world in its totality are only mathematical and unite homogeneous elements—the phenomena in the world. However, an absolute limit, a beginning, a border without exteriority, a simple element that is not subject to a possible decomposition into parts, cannot be a phenomenon, because it is always supposed to be unconditioned. We will also find this aporia in the "mathematical" analysis of sublime judgment. However, we will find it transposed.

To localize the change of scene required by the analysis of the sublime more precisely, one could situate it not only in relation to the scene of the Antithetic of speculative reason but also in relation to the Analytic of the Beautiful. The judgment upon the sublime is a reflective judgment, like the judgment upon the beautiful, and not determinant, like those that enter into conflict in the antinomies. But in the constitution of sublime feeling, reason is substituted for understanding as imagination's partner; this is why the latter experiences a failure unknown to it in taste, which is analogous to the aporia expounded in the first two antinomies.

It follows from the fact that sublime judgment is reflective, as is the judgment upon the beautiful, that what is at stake is not the knowledge of the object, but the subjective sensation accompanying the presentation of the object. This is true for the aspect of reflection I have called tautegorical (see Chapter 1, pp. 8–15). As for the heuristic aspect (see Chapter 1, pp. 26–32), one could say at first glance that what is true for the beautiful is also true for the sublime: the rule for the synthesis of (reflective) judgment is not given by a category or a principle of pure understanding, as is the case for an objective determinant judgment. The rule remains to be found, and it must remain so. Thus "the sublime pleases" (*das Erhabene gefällt*: 94; *91*) like the beautiful "simply pleases" (*bloß gefällt*: 49; *47*). In both cases the pleasure is due to a subjective finality. But this finality is altogether different in the sublime from what it was in taste. "The object is grasped [*aufgenommen*] as sublime with a pleasure that is only possible through the mediation [*vermittelst*] of a displeasure" (109, t.m.; *105*). One must look for the source of this "happiness" crossed with unhappiness elsewhere than in the affinity of the faculty of presentation with the thinking of concepts. Rather, it is to be found, paradoxically, in their heterogeneity. The resolution of the conflict constitutive of sublime judgment requires a "dynamical" synthesis because of the heterogeneity of the imagination and reason. In this conflict, the imagination does not contribute to pleasure through a free production of forms and aesthetic Ideas, but in its powerlessness to give form to the object. The rule of the synthesis of judgment is lacking here not for want of profusion but for want of presentation.

In this respect, the situation is similar to that of the antinomies of the first *Critique*. The imagination (matched, however, with understanding in order to produce knowledge; this is the difference with imagination's situation in the sublime) was supposed to present a beginning or a limit (a temporal or spatial zero), the simple (a zero in intensity), an absolute in causality or in the existence of the world. It was shown that the imagination was incapable of doing so in all of the above cases, for the imagination can only present phenomena, and the absolute is not a phenomenon. In the reflective judgment of taste, the issue is no longer to know the objects but to experience pleasure on the occasion of objects. For this pleasure to be aesthetic, it must be independent of all interest in the material of the phenomenon; it must be due only to objects' form insofar as the form can affect the "state" of thought. The imagination is precisely in charge of these forms. Indeed, this putting into form is no longer subordinated here to the rules and principles of understanding, for it is not a matter of making the phenomenon knowable. The "schematism" (which is this putting into form: KRV, 180–87; *196–205*) leaves room for the free production of forms whose end is, on the contrary, to prevent understanding from placing these forms under its rules and principles. However, understanding continues its game in the face of this challenge, to which it tries to respond, but to no avail. Thus a union is established between understanding and the imagination, which is very different from that required by knowledge. There is a competition of sorts between the two powers in this union where each feels its force, yet is unable to overpower the other. It must be remembered that in this free play, however numerous and profuse the forms presented by the imagination may be, each of them is effectively "presented" or presentable within the limits of the "comprehensive" synthesis, which is the affair of the imagination.

When reason is imposed upon imagination as its partner in sublime feeling (when understanding is no longer its partner), things change radically. Reason is also the power of concepts, whose objects (of thought) have no possible presentation in experience. Thus reason opposes the imagination not with categorical rules and principles, which would be applicable *a priori* to what the imagination can present, but with Ideas that are inapplicable *a priori* to any presentation, because the objects of these Ideas are absolute or limitless, whereas the "comprehension" (*Zusammenfassung*) that allows for the presentation of sensations in a unity has what one calls "limits." Comprehension has a limit or, rather, is limitation itself before any conceptual rule, for it consists in a putting into form, and form is a limitation. To say that the givens are shaped together, *zusammengefassen*, means that their relations are arrested by and in the form that results from their shaping.

The aesthetic "estimation" (*Schätzung*) of magnitude in a single intuition is like that of a visual field. It is measured by "comprehension" just as the visual field is measured "by the eye" (*nach dem Augenmaße*: 98, t.m.; *95*). The visual field is limited; the magnitude that the faculty of presentation can embrace at one time has a maximum measurement. This maximum is "subjectively ... determined" (ibid.). The faculty of presentation experiences, feels that it is held back by an insurmountable limit in the extension of its actual intuition. This limit is the absolute, felt subjectively or aesthetically, of what the faculty of presentation can grasp in terms of presentable magnitude. It is enough for thought to feel this measure as insurmountable, as subjectively absolute, for this aesthetic maximum to convey "the idea of the sublime" (*es die Idee des Erhabenen bei sich führe*) and to call forth the "emotion" (*diejenige Rührung*: 99; *95*) that characterizes this feeling. A mathematical estimation of very great magnitudes by means of numerical concepts (98; *95*) cannot engender this emotion, and we will see why it cannot.

Kant takes the opportunity provided by the examination of this aesthetic measure to make an observation that anticipates some of Husserl's analyses. The very notion of magnitude in general, including its mathematical sense, is grounded in the measure of imagination's "comprehension." Mathematical magnitude cannot be constituted mathematically. It can be measured. But the measure is itself a magnitude. It must be measured in turn. The mathematician would say that the unit of measure is chosen arbitrarily. Kant agrees with this (108–9; *104–5*). But the very notion of measure does not result from this choice of unit. It proceeds from the "aesthetic" limitation of the comprehension of the manifold in a single presentation. This is the "first or fundamental measure" (*Grundmaß*) by which all mathematical measure is made possible as numerical determination (98; *95*). The "horizon" of comprehension is the magnitude of the measure that makes the measure of magnitudes possible. A great "evaluator," so to speak, a measuring measure for all measured magnitudes. From the aesthetic to the mathematical the word "measure" thus changes meaning. For the imagination, measure is the maximum magnitude that is presentable at once. For understanding, there is no maximum numerical magnitude. Understanding can measure magnitudes with very small or very large numerical units without encountering any obstacle.

"Composition" Is Infinite

The sublime drama thus appears to result from this "fundamental" threshold that the faculty of presentation itself opposes to all aesthetic estimation of magnitude: "When the apprehension [*Auffassung*] has reached a point beyond which the representations of sensuous intuition in the case of the parts first apprehended begin to disappear from the imagination as this advances to the apprehension of yet others, as much, then, is lost at one end as is gained at the other, and for comprehension [*Zusammenfassung*] we get a maximum that the imagination cannot exceed" (99, t.m.; 96). In short the case seems to be rather classical. Does it not resonate with Descartes' chiliadic polygon that can be conceived but not imagined?

However, a difference separates the Cartesian example from the Kantian description that we have just read. The thousand-sided polygon is a figure constructed by understanding by means of numerical concepts. The analysis here, on the other hand, involves the confrontation of imagination's comprehension, limited to its "first measure," with "magnitude" as it is to be found "in rude nature" (*an der rohe Natur*: 100; 97). Kant's appeal to the example of the tiers of an Egyptian pyramid or to the interior volume of the Basilica of St. Peter in Rome should not be a source of error. It is only a question of showing that from a "proper" distance (proper to sublime emotion) these magnitudes, which are indeed mathematically measurable, can nonetheless exceed the measure "by the eye" to which the measure of imagination's comprehension is once again compared; natural magnitudes can also exceed the measure of imagination's comprehension spontaneously, in a "rude" way.

The catastrophe that the imagination experiences in the sublime (from a "mathematical" point of view) has not at all to do with the incommensurability of the "fundamental measure" of imagination's comprehension with the very great measures that understanding can conceive of by the recurrent addition of a unit to itself and by the choice of larger and larger units of measure. The unit chosen by understanding to measure magnitudes, even if it is very large (in the series of numbers)—the earth's diameter counted in miles, for example, and then taken as the unit with which to measure interplanetary distances (102, 105; *98, 101*)—would not pose an insurmountable obstacle to the cooperation that imagination gives understanding when the latter wants to obtain a determinant knowledge of the magnitudes it measures. One could even say that the extension of knowledge requires the use of larger and larger units—or smaller and smaller ones, for there is also an infinite number of possible units in decreasing order to measure the microscopic, and microscopes give us as great an "abundance of material" as telescopes do in this regard (97; *94*). The only condition, which is that of knowledge, is that the imagination always be able to present by apprehension, unit after unit, the partial magnitudes that understanding measures and adds to each other. The following clearly expresses this: "In the successive aggregation of units requisite for the representation of magnitudes the imagination of itself advances *ad infinitum* without let or hindrance—understanding, however, conducting it [*leitet sie*] by means of concepts of number for which the former must supply the schema" (101; *98*).

This cooperation of the imagination and understanding in the representation, *Vorstellung*, of magnitude might appear to be paradoxical if one thinks that the imagination contributes with its "comprehension" (*Zusammenfassung*). This is the word one finds in the German text, but following a correction made by Erdmann. Kant had written *Zusammensetzung*, "composition." And composition is not comprehension. The former *Zusammensetzung* (*com-*

positio) is defined, I will remind the reader (see Chapter 3, pp. 89–96), in a note to the "Systematic Representation of all the Synthetic Principles of Pure Understanding," added in the second edition of the first *Critique* (KRV B, 197–98; *216*): it is the "synthesis of the manifold where its constituents do not *necessarily belong to one another*," "the synthesis of the *homogeneous* in everything that can be *mathematically* treated" (ibid., t.m.). The example given to illustrate composition is, I will remind the reader again, the relation between the two triangles that one obtains when one draws the diagonal of a square. They are homogeneous to each other, but their combination is not necessary, for each can be conceived of without the help of the other. On the contrary, one cannot think the effect without the cause; their synthesis is necessary, although they are heterogeneous in nature (the cause, unlike the effect, is not a phenomenon).

Yet the first principle according to which understanding constitutes the objects of experience, according to which it constitutes the phenomena as knowable, requires that they be intuited in space and time as extensive magnitudes. This principle is called the axiom of intuition. It states that phenomena "cannot be apprehended [*apprehendiert*], that is, taken up into empirical consciousness, save through that synthesis of the manifold . . . that is, through composition [*Zusammensetzung*] of the homogeneous manifold and consciousness of its synthetic unity" (KRV B, 198; *217*). As for this consciousness, it is constituted by "the concept of a magnitude (*quantum*)" (ibid.). This concept, which is the consciousness of "the unity of the composition of the manifold [and] homogeneous" (ibid., 198, t.m.; *217*), is an act of understanding. But the unity of the *Zusammensetzung* itself is the schema that corresponds to the concept of magnitude, and it is the act of the imagination preparing the manifold for knowledge through understanding by means of the concept of magnitude (and later of number).

One must see that composition is an operation which consists in the successive addition of one part to another, the parts being homogeneous. One only represents a line to oneself in space or a duration in time by "generating [*zu erzeugen*] . . . all its parts one after another" (ibid., 198; *218*). This successive synthesis is the *a priori* condition of "apprehension" even of phenomena, as we have seen. The text insists: only "through successive synthesis of part to part in [the process of] its apprehension [*in der Apprehension*]" can the phenomenon "come to be known" (ibid.). Thus one could say that apprehension needs composition, or even that it is composition, at least in regard to the magnitude of phenomena.

However, a first difficulty must be resolved here if we do not want to misunderstand the "comprehension" evoked in paragraphs 26 and 27 of the third *Critique*. Let us try to situate the axiom of composition in apprehension in relation to the syntheses discussed in the Preliminary Remark to the Deduction of the categories in the first *Critique* (KRV A, 131; *141*). One must be aware that these syntheses are constitutive of the possibility of experience in general, and not of the possibility of the objects of experience, as is the axiom of composition. Thus they are even more fundamental (ibid., 131–32; *144*); the axiom itself presupposes them. Yet, with this reservation in mind, it seems that the "composition in apprehension" required by the axiom corresponds to the first *two* syntheses, that of "Apprehension [*Apprehension*] in Intuition" and that of "Reproduction [*Reproduktion*] in Imagination." The third, that of "Recognition [*Rekognition*] in a Concept," appears to correspond to what the axiom calls the "consciousness of unity" already obtained by composition, because this consciousness of unity is nothing other than the concept of magnitude.

Let us see how the successive composition of the apprehension of the phenomenon as extensive magnitude demands syntheses of apprehension and reproduction. The first consists in containing (*erhalten*) the manifold "in a single moment" (*als in einem Augenblick*) in such a way that the "run-through" [*par-cours*: tr.] or the "trans-currence" (*das Durchlaufen*) is "held together" by a single take, so to speak, the *Zusammennehmung* (ibid., 131–32; *143*). Obviously there is only a flux, a passage of the manifold, if there is succession, and the latter requires the simultaneous for its constitution. The current flows only in the "hold" of what does not flow.

No movement without rest. And vice versa. Composition by succession, *Zusammensetzung*, requires this more originary "support," the *Zusammennehmung*, which provides the composition by succession with the units to compose.

But composition also requires that these units be placed one after the other and that each not disappear when the other appears, for otherwise there would be no succession to make up the magnitude of the phenomenon. This is the synthesis that the imagination performs as "reproduction." "When I seek to draw a line in thought, or to think of the time from one noon to another, or even to represent to myself some particular number, obviously the various manifold representations that are involved [which are the parts of the line, of the duration, or of the number] must be apprehended by me in thought one after the other" (ibid., 133; *148*). Moreover, in order to show the necessity of reproduction, Kant adds the following, which seems to echo the text of paragraph 26 of the third *Critique* explaining the limit of "aesthetic comprehension" (the imagination loses "as much . . . at one end as is gained at the other": 99; *96*): "If I were always to drop out of thought the preceding representations (the first parts of the line, the antecedent parts of the time period, or the units in the order represented), and did not reproduce them while advancing to those that follow, then a complete representation would never . . . arise" (KRV A, 133, t.m.; *148*). Reproduction allows a unit apprehended earlier, thus actually absent, to be kept present in thought. This synthesis of retention is the doing of imagination. And "composition" necessarily includes it.

Now we can return to the text of paragraph 26 of the "Analytic of the Sublime" cited earlier. The "composition"—the *Zusammensetzung*, as Kant wrote it, and not the "comprehension," the *Zusammenfassung*, as Erdmann mistakenly corrects it—"requisite for the representation of magnitudes" is a synthesis that the imagination can advance "itself . . . *ad infinitum*" (101; *98*). This synthesis is in fact nothing other than the apprehension and reproduction necessary to the constitution of the time of knowledge (and of space secondarily), but applied to the constitution of objects of knowledge according to their extensive magnitude. In this composition, the imagination is able to let itself be "guided" by the concept, which is in short the "consciousness" of the unity produced by the imagination's synthesis. Furthermore, the magnitudes conceived of by understanding can be very large (numerically) without the imagination being prevented from supplying the corresponding "schema" (ibid.). As large as it may be, a magnitude is apprehended intuitively by parts, and every apprehension is "maintained" or "reproduced" (in its absence) in the following apprehension (which is only "following" because the preceding is maintained). In other words the *ambitus* of the *Zusammennehmung* always remains the same. The recurrence of the preceding apprehension in the current one does not at all enlarge its *ambitus*, no more than a gesture is a hundred times larger when it is repeated for the hundredth time. As for the concept, it determines the number of "times" (of apprehensions supplied by the imagination), thus allowing for the recognition of the magnitude of the object.

Thus one can understand why the imagination and understanding are in perfect affinity when proceeding by recurrence. Recurrence is a synthesis of the homogeneous of which both are capable without particular effort, each according to its order (respectively, schema and concept). This is why "this procedure insofar as it belongs to the logical estimation of magnitude . . . is doubtless something objectively final according to the concept of an end (as all measurement is)" (101, t.m.; *98*). "Objectively final" because the combination of the two faculties is finalized upon the determination of the magnitude of the object: its measurement. However, because this finality is subordinated to the "concept of an end," which is this cognitive determination, it is not at all aesthetic; it brings to the thought that proceeds to this recurrence no immediate pleasure, "not anything which for the aesthetic judgment is final or pleasing" [*Gefallendes*] (ibid.).

This negative remark in the text of paragraph 26 brings us back to the examination of aesthetic feeling. The remark evokes the pleasure of the beautiful. The remark following it addresses sublime feeling. In the "intentional finality" (*in dieser absichtlichen Zweckmäßigkeit*) implied by composition, "there is nothing compelling us to tax the utmost powers of the imagination, and drive it as far as ever it can reach [*reichen*] . . . so as to push [*treiben*] the size of the measure, and thus make the single intuition holding the many in one (the comprehension [*Zusammenfassung*]) as great as possible" (ibid., t.m.). Composition, even *ad infinitum*, has no effect of tension on comprehension and its "first measure," of pushing the limit. Let me explain the argument following this sentence: the *Zusammenfassung*, the comprehension of units by the imagination, can be "pushed" by understanding to ten or four; in any case the magnitude will be produced in a successive fashion (according to the decimal or quaternary principle that one has accepted). Magnitude will be produced by composition, *Zusammensetzung*, and also by apprehension, *Auffassung*, if the *quantum* is graspable in a single intuition. The imagination can choose for its unit a magnitude that it can take in "at a glance" (*in einem Blick fassen*) a foot or a rod, for example. The imagination can also take a "German mile" or "the earth's diameter." Understanding will in both cases be "as well served and as satisfied." And yet in the second case (the mile, the diameter), the imagination will only have the "apprehension" (*Auffassung*) of the magnitude taken as unit, but not the *Zusammenfassung*, the (*comprehensio aesthetica*) of it. But this does not prevent the understanding from having a (*comprehensio logica*) of the magnitude by means of numerical concepts (ibid.). And I would add: this does not in the least prevent the imagination from effectuating the "composition" of the magnitude, which is the twin of this logical comprehension—the composition or the recurrence by "reproduction" of the parts of a German mile or of the earth's diameter, for the imagination has an *Auffassung*, an apprehension, of each of the parts.

We can clearly see where and when the sublime feeling has a chance of arising: it is when the imagination is asked to have an aesthetic comprehension of all the units included by composition in the progression. For then, if all the parts composed successively cannot be comprehended in a single moment (which is necessarily the case as the series increases by composition) because the imagination is limited to its "fundamental measure," then the power of presentation, *das Darstellungsvermögen*, of the imagination finds itself literally overwhelmed. The eye beholding the tiers of the pyramid or the interior of St. Peter's in Rome can be overwhelmed if one is a distance such that the eye cannot "comprehend" in a glance what it can "compose" successively.

The Infinite Is Not "Comprehensible" as a Whole: Fear

This aesthetic comprehension of the whole (at one time) of a very large or infinite series is what reason demands of the imagination and what provokes the sublime emotion. Thus one of the protagonists in aesthetic judgment changes. The partners are no longer imagination and understanding, whose agreement is possible and necessary to make an objective determinant judgment, and whose subjectively final harmony provides the pleasure of taste in aesthetic reflective judgment. Instead we have imagination and reason, or, more precisely, because it is an aesthetic reflective judgment, we have the subjective sensation that accompanies the exercise of the imagination and the subjective sensation that accompanies the exercise of reason.

One might ask the following question, Why are there two sensations when there is just one feeling, the sublime? It is because this feeling consists of two contradictory sensations, pleasure and displeasure, "attraction" and "repulsion." Thinking feels itself *angezogen* and *abgestoßen*, as we have read in paragraph 23 (91; *88*). Yet is it not, in the end, a pleasure because it is an aesthetic judgment? One might be tempted to say this, but one must concede that it is a "negative pleasure" (*negative Lust*: ibid.). The fact remains that these observations are still merely descriptive. The properly critical question asks how this negative pleasure is possible. Or in other words, to put it in the form of a problem: given that there is a sublime aesthetic feeling, how does one find the subjective finality that unites the two kinds of sensations condensed by sublime aes-

thetic feeling in such a way as to make this feeling a negative pleasure?

From the mathematical syntheses that have occupied us in this
chapter, where the sublime judgment was considered under the
reflexive "headings" that correspond to the categories of quality
and quantity, one gets a sense of the direction one needs to follow
in order to find a solution to this problem. The imagination cannot "actually" synthesize the magnitudes into an apprehension unless the magnitudes do not exceed the "first measure" of its "comprehension." One could call this measure subjectively absolute.
The maximum that the aesthetic "estimate" of magnitude is permitted by the imagination can itself be "considered [*beurteilt*] an
absolute measure [*als absolute Maß*]" (99; *95*). Thus there is a subjective absolute in the presentation of a magnitude. As we have
said, the proliferation of forms and aesthetic Ideas in the imagination of the amateur or the artist does not strike a blow to this measure; this measure applies in turn to each form or actual "Idea."
Furthermore, the quality (the other mathematical synthesis) of aesthetic judgment is reinforced by this measure, and the pleasure in-
creased. However, at the moment of passing beyond this absolute
limit, the comprehensive synthesis of magnitude becomes impossible, and the quality of the state, in which the thought that imagines finds itself, is reversed: it is afraid of this *Überschwengliche*, of
this transcendent, this movable and confused (*schwingen*) beyond
(*über*) "like an abyss [*Abgrund*] in which it fears to lose itself"
(107; *103*). Beyond its absolute of presentation, thinking encounters
the unpresentable, the unthinkable in the here and now, and what
Burke calls horror takes hold of it. But why does thinking need to
go this far?

In this demand to reach the limit we recognize a characteristic of
reason. From the point of view of quantity, reason pursues the series of magnitudes conceivable *ad infinitum*. One might remon-
strate that nothing can stop understanding in the composition of
larger and larger units by means of numerical concepts. Is the
quantitative infinite produced by the unlimited recurrence of one
unit added to itself (which the imagination can easily follow by

way of "composition") not already the object of a concept of understanding? But "in comparison with this [the infinite] all else (in the way of magnitudes of the same order) is small." This is why we say that "the infinite is absolutely (not merely comparatively) great" (*das Unendliche . . . ist schlechthin [nicht bloß komparativ] groß*: 102; *99*).

The next part of the argument asserts that the concept of the infinite formed by understanding or the horizon of a progression *ad infinitum* is not "of capital importance" (ibid.). But before taking the next step necessary for an understanding of what the infinite of reason is about and how it affects thought, let us stop for a moment at the infinite of understanding, of progression, insofar as it produces in thought a kind of sublime feeling. I am referring here to the end of paragraph 26 (105; *101*).

There are "examples of the mathematically sublime [*Mathematisch-Erhabenen*] in nature [*der Natur*]." They are provided "in mere intuition" (*in der bloßes Anschauung liefern uns*), which I take to mean: in a simple, intuitive way. On the side of intuition, the very concept of understanding could contribute, as we will see, to this sublime feeling. The concept of understanding would be "direct" in that it would not be mediated by an Idea of reason and would owe nothing to the way reason conceives of the infinite. Thus these examples of the sublime are "mathematical" in which intuition can follow understanding in its progression toward the infinite. The case may seem unexpected after what has been said about the measure of subjective comprehension permitted to the faculty of presentation. So what are we to make of the following: "Our imagination is afforded, not so much a greater numerical concept as a large unit [*großes Einheit*] as measure [*als Maß*] (for shortening the numerical series)" (105; *101*)? This is not clear. This even seems to contradict everything that one understood of imagination's "first measure." Does the "large unit" not exceed this measure, can it be present to the imagination otherwise than by composition? If the "large unit" exceeds the measure, then the case is the same as with a conflict with reason. If indeed it is a matter of the relation of the imagination to understanding, as the parentheses suggest ("shortening the numerical series" is for understanding to change the unit of measure as it progresses toward great magnitudes), it is difficult to see how the instance may be sublime: the imagination follows the progression of understanding by composition without encountering any obstacles.

By giving examples meant to shed light on this obscure affair, the text in fact displaces the notion of this sublime of "mere intuition." Thus in view of abridging the numerical series while it progresses in magnitudes to be measured, understanding changes its unit of measure. Understanding can estimate the magnitude of a tree by the height of a man, that of mountains in tree units, of the earth's diameter in "mountains," of the planetary system in terrestrial diameters, of a galaxy in "planetary systems," of a nebula in galaxies (105; *101*). There is no limit to cross in this progression. There is nothing that could "hold out" (*erwarten*) against the process of these substitutions of units (ibid.).

However, the estimation of "an immeasurable whole" (*eines so unermeßlichen Ganzen*: ibid.) reflexively produces a feeling of sublimity. Indeed, the matter is one of "aesthetic" estimation, that is, of the state of pleasure or displeasure in which the "object," the "immeasurable" whole, puts thought. Is this a thinking of concepts, of understanding, or, as was stated under the name of mere intuition, of presentation, of imagination? And is it indeed the thought of a "large unit"?

Here Kant specifies and corrects himself: the sublime sensation "does not lie so much in the greatness of the number, as in the fact that in our onward advance [*im Fortschritte*] we always arrive at proportionately greater units" (ibid.). Thus it is the thought not of a "large unit" but of the progression toward the always "greater" which is felt as sublime. As for knowing whether thinking feels this feeling in conceiving of the progression, in imagining it, or in intuiting it, the text seems to bring the discussion to a close: "The systematic division of the cosmos [*des Weltgebäudes*] conduces to this result [to this feeling]. For it represents all that is great in nature as constantly [*immer wiederum*] becoming little" (105, t.m.; *101*). This "systematic division" is the part left to understanding in the formation of this feeling. The progression is due to this systematic division and so is the "conversion" of the estimation of magnitudes that accompanies the change of the unit of measure to which understanding proceeds when "shortening" the numbers. However, Kant adds, "strictly speaking" (*eigentlich*: 105, t.m.; 101), what this systematic division of the universe by understanding "represents" to us when it changes the scale of measure, what it represents to thought, is "our imagination in all its boundlessness [*in ihrer ganzen Grenzenlosigkeit*], and with it nature as sinking into insignificance [*verschwindend*] before the Ideas of reason once their adequate presentation [*Darstellung*] is attempted" (ibid.).

What seems to have been decided in favor of the concept of understanding in the production of this sublime feeling is thus taken away [*retranché*, also to be understood as *re-tranché*, decided again: tr.] from it in the end. Moreover, this is what happens to the thought that imagines: it is blocked, which is a sign that the situation is different from the transcendental situation of the progression. The imagination can follow understanding in its progression toward very large units. It can continue to present magnitudes of even a cosmic order: it composes the apprehension of a presentable magnitude by reproductive synthesis, many times. Thus it can continue to supply the "schema" for large numerical concepts.

However, a mutation occurs on the part of concepts. The recurrence *ad infinitum* of the "and so on" brings thinking to conceive not only the next "time" but "the most times" at the same time, all at once, in a single moment. The infinite maximization of magnitudes leads to the Idea of an infinite magnitude, always already larger than any measurable magnitude. This magnitude is not numerable by recurrent addition of a unit to itself, however large it may be. It is off-limits for understanding. As we have said, the understanding cannot conceive of the unlimited, or even of the limit. These are concepts whose object is not presentable in intuition. However, knowledge requires that in the schema the concept be combined with the presentation of its object. The infinite of magnitude, conceived as the whole (at one time), is not a possible object of experience; there is no intuition of it. It is simply an object of thought, the object of a concept that remains undetermined for want of adequate presentation. The thought that conceives of such an object is thus no longer understanding but reason.

What our text analyzes is, in short, the change of imagination's partner in the course of the progression *ad infinitum* of measures of magnitude. This change can be recognized by the change of the subjective "state" in the thought that imagines. A kind of dizziness, which is nonetheless euphoric, takes hold of it while it follows the faculty of concepts in its progression toward very great measures. This is a kind of "mathematical" sublime due solely to the composition *ad infinitum*. Why "sublime"? Because the progression shows that every magnitude of nature will appear small in the end, and that every composition of a great magnitude by the reproductive imagination can be followed by a superior composition in which the former magnitude will be but a part of the magnitude apprehended in the future. Thus the progression in a series provides this quasi-sublime feeling. I say "quasi" because it does not yet involve the breaking of imagination's "first measure," but simply its "boundlessness" in the recurrence of the synthesis of reproduction; it only involves the faculty of composition (*Zusammensetzung*).

But when the concept of the large number is transformed into the Idea of an absolute or actual infinite, the mathematical synthesis by composition is powerless to give a presentation of it. Before this Idea, the dizziness of the thought that presents is transformed into a mortal anguish. The imagination sinks to a zero of presentation, which is the correlate of the absolute infinite. Nature founders with it, for nothing of it is presentable as an object of this Idea.

Here we return to what is "of capital importance." What is of capital importance is not only the progression *ad infinitum* by association of understanding and imagination, it is "also [*auch*] the mere ability even to think [*nur denken*] it [the infinite] as *a whole*" (102 t.m.; *99*). This indicates that the mind (thought) has the power to "transcend" (*übertrifft*) everything that sense can measure (ibid.). It is no longer a question of the infinite as the horizon of a recurrent composition, but of the "given infinite" (*das gegebene Unendliche*: 103; *99*), given actually as an object of thought. Furthermore, if a presentation had to be provided, one would need a "comprehension" (*Zusammenfassung*) to provide in a single moment, as a single unit, a standard of measure that would be in a determined relation with this infinite, and would even be expressible in numbers (ibid.). Something that the "first measure" of imagination's comprehension precludes.

One must go further still, and this further step proves that the faculty that conceives of the infinite as a whole cannot be understanding. The infinite as a whole is to the infinite of the sensible world what a "noumenal" object (KRV, 257–75; *287–308*), the object of thought alone, is to a single phenomenon, the object of knowledge. However, if understanding can advance to the infinite through the regressive series of the conditions of phenomena in the world, it is because it is supported by the Idea of the infinite as a whole, which only "a faculty that is itself supersensible" can form (103; *99*). The notion of the serial infinite proceeds from the notion of the actual infinite. What this means is that even in "the pure intellectual estimation of magnitude" (*in der reinen intellektuellen Größenschätzung*) made by understanding, "the infinite of the world of sense," which is at the horizon of this estimation, must be "*completely* comprehended *under* a concept" (unter *einem Begriffe* ganz *zusammengefaßt*: ibid.). This concept belongs so little to understanding that mathematical estimation never succeeds in thinking the infinite of the world of sense "by means of numerical concepts"—the only ones it has at its disposal (ibid.). The object of the concept in question, the infinite as totality actually given in thought, does not belong to the world; it is the "substrate" (*Substrat*: ibid.) underlying it. Moreover, the thought that conceives of this object is called reason. Such is the impossible partner with which the imagination is provided (and annihilated) in order to produce the aesthetic reflective judgment called sublime.

The Infinite Is Thinkable as a Whole: Exaltation

The aesthetic reflective judgment is a feeling made up of two sensations, as we have said. The moment has come for us to ask ourselves about the sensation that affects thought when it thinks the infinite as a whole, or, as it is called a little later, *das Absolut-Ganz*, the whole as absolute, the absolute whole (105; *102*). The answer to this question does not allow one to determine the quantity of sublime feeling as such, in its essential complexity, but only the quantity of one of its components, the affection produced in reasoning thought to which the noumenal object is present. This affection is analyzed in paragraph 27 under the mathematical category of quality, and in paragraph 28 in the section devoted to the sublime, the affection is considered dynamically under the category of relation. Let me remind the reader that the reflexive "heading" that corresponds to the first category is identity/difference (KRV, 278–79, 283–84; *312–13, 318–19*) and that the "heading" that corresponds to the second category is that of inner/outer (KRV, 279–80, 284–85; *313–14, 319–20*). Here, just as with taste, we are concerned with reflective judgment.

The greater part of paragraph 27, devoted to the quality of sublime judgment, consists in deriving this quality from the analysis of quantity using the category of relation. It derives this quality in such a way that the whole of sublime feeling is exposed in its inner heterogeneity. I therefore reserve this examination for the next chapter, which concerns the synthesis of the heterogeneous affections that constitute sublime feeling—a dynamical synthesis. Let us go to paragraph 28. It first examines the emotion felt by the thought that imagines when it is given the object said to be sublime: this emotion is fear. It is said that the fearfulness is not effectively determined by a presentable, formidable object (as it is in Burke's analysis, to which this discussion is implicitly addressed). We know that the faculty of presentation feels displeasure, and even anguish, at the thought of having to provide a phenomenon corresponding to the Idea of the infinite whole through "aesthetic comprehension." This subjective component comes from the imagination. Where, then, is the component corresponding to the Idea of the whole that comes from reason?

One is tempted to return to the beginning of paragraph 27, which introduces "respect" as being the feeling aroused by the presence in thought of an Idea of reason. But we will see that this is not yet the sensation we seek. The text reads as follows (I have taken the liberty of translating it a little more "freely" than one usually does; I do this in order to convey the argument more clearly): "The feeling, namely, that our power is not what it should be [*Unangemessenheit*] to attain to an Idea that is a law for us—this feeling is RESPECT [*Achtung*, which might be more accurately rendered as "regard"]. Now the Idea to be comprehended [*die Idee der Zusammenfassung*] in the intuition of a whole, any phenomenon whatsoever that may be given us is of this sort [*solche*]: it is imposed upon us [*auferlegt ist*] by a law of reason, which knows no definite, universally valid and unchangeable measure except the absolute whole [*das Absolut-Ganz*]" (105, t.m.; *102*). One is tempted to conclude that respect is the sensation that we are looking for, the sensation which in the sublime results for thought from the presence of the Idea of reason. However, when one takes a closer look, this is not the case. "Respect" is explicitly (and strangely) described here as the affect provoked in thought not by grasping the absolute whole; rather, it is provoked by the incommensurability, the *Unangemessenheit*, of our "power" (*unseres Vermögens*), of our faculty to grasp, *zur Erreichung*, at this moment (ibid.).

What is the power or the faculty in question? The text cited does not qualify it, but what follows leaves no room for doubt: "But our imagination, even when taxing itself to the uttermost [*Anstrengung*] on the score of this required comprehension [*Zusammenfassung*] of a given object in a whole of intuition (and so with a view to the presentation [*Darstellung*] of the Idea of reason), betrays [*beweist*] its limits [*ihre Schranken*] and its inadequacy [*Unangemessenheit*]" (106; *102*). Thus it is indeed a question of the power of presentation, and of the distress experienced by the thought that imagines when it must "comprehend" an object in a single intuition, or when it must comprehend the form of an object that corresponds to the absolute whole conceived by reason. Respect can provoke this distress or accompany it, when thinking compares its finitude in matters of presentation (or will) with its infinitude in matters of concepts (or with freedom). But respect in the strict sense could not result from this comparison. Nor can it be a *delight* immediately provided by this infinitude. Respect is barely a feeling; it is a "blank" feeling to which we will return (see Chapter 7 and Chapter 9, pp. 234–39). Respect is above all *the* moral feeling, the way in which the Idea of the law affects thought. The thought that feels respect is the thought that wants, the thought that desires, and not the thought that presents or imagines, to which our text seems exclusively to refer. The faculty of desire must be added—along with the imagination—to the agreement or conflict of the faculties necessary to the formation of sublime aesthetic judgment, in order that the allusion to moral feeling acquire its full force and that its foundation be properly understood. This is done in the "dynamical" examination of the sublime in paragraphs 28 and 29, but in a way that still remains somewhat implicit (as it is in the preceding paragraphs).

There is a kind of persistent timidity to grant moral feeling its place in the sublime; the recurrence of parentheses when moral feeling is mentioned is a sign of this. Capable of transcending "every standard of sensibility . . . from another point of view (the practical)": this is said of the thought that finds matter for its "broadening" in the conflict of the sublime (103, t.m.; *99*). The sublime "temper of mind" is conformable to that temper "which the influence of definite (practical) ideas would produce upon feeling" (104; *100*). I am speaking of the "mathematical" approach. Even in the dynamical examination one finds parentheses to refer to morality: reason does violence to sensibility "with a view to extending it to the requirements of its own realm (the practical)" (115; *111*). The judgment upon the sublime has its foundation in "a native capacity for the feeling for (practical) ideas, i.e. for moral feeling" (116; *112*).

However, the parentheses are not constant, and they also serve to remind the reader of the principle established in the *Critique of Practical Reason*: reason is pure practical will, and it legislates over the realm of will with an Idea, that of absolute causality or freedom, which founds moral law. However, if the reference to this principle is not developed further in the "Analytic of the Sublime," it is because sublime feeling cannot be identified with moral feeling. Very simply because the moral feeling, respect, is not an aesthetic feeling (see Chapter 7).

The delight that the Idea of reason provides, the absolute whole (or the absolutely powerful) in the case of sublime feeling, is undoubtedly more accurately named when in paragraph 28, following the discussion of the nature of fear and the importance to give it in this feeling, Kant observes that even if fear is not real or realistic—even, that is, if the amateur of the sublime is not really in danger—the "soul-stirring delight" (*dieses begeisternde Wohlgefallen*: 112; *108*) that he feels when he is given the object called sublime loses none of its "seriousness" (*Ernst*: ibid.). *Begeisternde*, soul-stirring in that it revives the *Geist*, the mind—the life vein of thought (see Chapter 2, pp. 60–67). If nature can be judged sublime, it is not because nature "excites fear, but rather because it appeals [*aufruft*] to a force in us that is our own (one not of nature) . . . to regard as small those things of which we are wont to be solicitous (worldly goods, health, and life)" (111, t.m.; *107*).

The description here is made in the language of the dynamical (in the physical sense), as is the entire passage that begins with an almost mechanical reflection on the notion of "resistance" (*Widerstand*: 109; *105*). As if Kant himself were mistaking the sense of the term "dynamical." He makes no mistake. We will see (see Chapter 5) that if the contradiction in the sublime can be resolved dynamically, it is in the same way that the third antinomy of speculative reason could be. First causality or freedom is accepted as is the conditioning of phenomena because freedom is of a noumenal order, whereas the conditioning of phenomena rules the phenomenal world. It is this first causality or freedom in the Idea of the all-powerful that allows our weakness, as phenomenon, to resist the frenzy of the forces of nature. And once again, because it is a question here of the Ideas of freedom, the critical analysis has passed to an examination of the faculty of desire, which justifies the use of a vocabulary of forces.

Thus in sublime feeling thought feels sensation as an "appeal" made to a "force" in it that is not "one of nature." This sensation is a soul-stirring delight, a sharp pleasure. Why is this? Because this appeal actualizes the *destination* (*Bestimmung*) of our *Geistesvermögen*, of our spiritual faculty—of the power of thought at its strongest—as it discovers this destination. One hears the *Stimme* in the vocation of the *Bestimmung*, the destination. This voice calls to thought in the sublime situation offered by nature. If the appeal exalts thought it is because it comes from the very "place," the transcendental place toward which it is already turned, toward which (to which?) it "is going and giving itself"—*se rend*, as we say in French.

What is the nature of this voice that calls? The answer is already given in paragraph 26 concerning not forces but magnitudes: *Nun aber hört das Gemüt in sich auf die Stimme der Vernunft* (the mind, however, hearkens now to the voice of reason: 102, t.m.; *98*). This voice "requires" (*fordert*): "for all given magnitudes ... those which can never be completely apprehended [*ganz aufgefaßt*], though (in sensuous representation) estimated as completely given [one recognizes magnitudes obtained by composition], [the voice of reason] requires totality [*Totalität fordert*]" (102, t.m.; *98–99*). "Totality," that is to say, their "comprehension [*Zusammenfassung*] in *one* intuition" (102; *99*). This needs to be made clearer still, for thought could be mistaken about the extension of totality demanded of it by the voice. The latter "calls for a *presentation* answering to all the above members of a progressively increasing numerical series, and does not exempt even the infinite from this requirement, but, rather, renders it inevitable for us to regard this infinite (in the judgment of common reason) as *completely given* (i.e., given in its totality)" (102; *99*).

This is what the voice says to thought with regard to magnitude. There is no doubt that it says the same thing with regard to force. Here, too, thought is required, called on to accomplish its destination, the absolute whole, the infinite of will. Furthermore, this intransigent, inevitable (*unvermeidlich*) requisition is reflexively felt as a soul-stirring delight. Why is this? As we have said, thought recognizes in it, in this requisition, its destination, its vocation. Thought is destined for the absolute. It is no accident that this "discovery" is made by the critique when it analyzes the sublime aesthetic judgment under the category of relation. For the object that arouses soul-stirring delight, the "rude" magnitude or force that one thinks one finds in nature, should be predicated, in the good logic of determinant judgments, under the relation of inherence and subsistence. Moreover, the judgment that attributes the predicate of absolute should be declared "categorical" (KRV, 113, 107; *118, 110*). However, sublime judgment is not determinant in relation to the object. It is reflective with regard to the state of thought when it thinks the object (tautegorical). It is fitting to apply not the category of relation to it, but rather the corresponding reflexive "heading" of inner/outer (KRV, 276–97; *309–33*).

I will try to elucidate this difficult point. We have already said (see Chapter 2, pp. 60–67) that the Idea of the absolute is not present in sublime judgment as such, that is, as a concept of reason, because then the sublime judgment would be a determinant judgment. Because it is a reflective judgment, the Idea of the absolute is only "present" and this presence is that of the "soul-stirring delight" that thinking feels on the occasion of the object it judges sublime. This sensation, and this sensation alone, signals the call of reason that the critique makes explicit. Thus for reflective judgment it matters less that the object of this Idea is absolute (although reflective judgment is led to discover the absolute in its heuristic capacity, which is what the critique does, being itself reflective). What matters is that the delight is felt to be absolute. The reflective absolute predicates not an object, but a state of thought. Moreover, for thought to feel called on or requisitioned by the voice of reason is an absolute delight, because it is the absolute vocation of thought to think the absolute. The absolute, from the point of view of the category of relation, is indeed pure inherence, that is to say, an "object" judged as having nothing outside of itself, i.e., having nothing in relation to it. This object is the paralogism of an entity that, from the point of view of relation, is without relation. However, transposed onto the reflective judgment of the sublime, the category of relation becomes a reflexive "heading," and pure inherence is referred to as a "pure inner." If the shadow (or the glare) of the absolute Idea projected on the state of thought, or, rather, projected *in* the state of thought, provides thought with such delight, it is because thought recognizes in this shadow or in this light the truth of what it is in itself "before" all determination. By itself, I am speaking absolutely, "before" it was opposed by givens that had to be grasped by forms of sensibility, assembled in schemas, known by concepts, or estimated according to the good (although in this the critique declares thought to be autonomous; but this autonomy is exercised under an obligation that transcends it)—"before" all of this, thinking is the power to think, *Geistesvermögen,* irrelative, "raw," that comes from nothing other than itself, and is thus in this sense "inner." Limitations, forms, schemas, rules of concept, illegitimacies, illusions that the critique constantly opposes to this power make no sense if one does not first accept the presupposition of Kantian thought—which is no secret—that "there is thought," and this is absolute. This is what "the voice of reason" says in sublime feeling, and this is what is truly exalting.

§5 The Sublime as
Dynamical Synthesis

Attempt to Resolve the Differend
Through Ethical Mediation

Reason thus enters "the scene" in the place of understanding. It challenges the thought that imagines: "make the absolute that I conceive present with your forms." Yet form is limitation. Form divides space and time into an "inside," what it "comprehends," and an "outside," what it puts at a distance. It cannot present the absolute. But there is something more serious still. The limitation constituted by the "comprehension," the *Zusammenfassung*, of givens in a form is also limited. Presentation cannot grasp an infinite of givens at one time and in a single form. If it is asked to present more, it comes up against its maximum, its "measure," which is the subjective foundation of all magnitude. This measure is the absolute of the thought that presents (98; *95*), the absolute "aesthetic" magnitude that is possible.

This differend is to be found at the heart of sublime feeling: at the encounter of the two "absolutes" equally "present" to thought, the absolute whole when it conceives, the absolutely measured when it presents. "Meeting" conveys very little; it is more of a confrontation, for, in accordance with its destination, which is to be whole, the absolute of concepts demands to be presented. A situation to be qualified as tragic if one is attentive to the "sensation" that results from it (aesthetically) for thought, or absurd if one wished to characterize it logically. In this latter aspect, it is contradictory that the absolute should be put into relation with something other than itself, for it is the without-relation. All the more so if that something is also an absolute. Their being put into relation abolishes each of them as absolute. But if each must remain the absolute it continues to be its own sole recourse, its court of appeal, unaware of the other. This conflict is not an ordinary dispute, which a third instance could grasp and put an end to, but a "differend," a *Widerstreit* (107; *103*).

We have seen (see Chapter 3, pp. 89–96) that the function of the dynamical synthesis (linked to the categories of relation and modality) is to place two heterogeneous elements in a necessary unity. The critique here is concerned with elaborating such a synthesis: we have just seen that the elements to be united are in effect heterogeneous. One could say absolutely heterogeneous, the absolute of the infinite and the absolute of the finite, and their synthesis is necessary *a priori* as the condition of possibility of sublime feeling, which is an empirical reality. However, in spite of the nature of the conflict, which should not allow for this solution, a transaction is outlined, here and there, to reconcile the two powers of thought—that of presenting forms, and that of conceiving Ideas—according to the model of the agreement between understanding and imagination that the critique elaborates on the subject of taste.

Here are two passages in which this parallel is suggested, not without some reservation, but in both cases according to the explicit figure of "the same . . . , the same":

> Therefore, just as [*gleichwie*] the aesthetic faculty of judgment in its estimate of the beautiful [*in Beurteilung des Schönen*] refers the imagination in its free play to the *understanding* to bring out its agreement [*zusammenzustimmen*] with the *concepts* of the latter in general (apart from their determination): so [*so*] in its [the faculty of judgment's] estimate of a thing as sublime it refers that faculty [the imagination] to *reason* to bring out its subjective accord with *Ideas* of reason (indeterminately indicated), i.e. to induce a temper of mind [*eine Gemüts-*

stimmung] conformable to [*gemäß*] that which the influence of definite (practical) Ideas would produce upon feeling, and in common
accord with [*verträglich*] it. (104, t.m.; *100*)

With a slight nuance, the same parallel is to be found a little
farther on: "For just as [*sowie*] in the estimate of the beautiful
imagination and *understanding* by their concert [*Einhelligkeit*] gen-
erate subjective finality of the mental faculties, so [*so*] imagination
and *reason* do so here by their conflict [differend]" (107; *103*), in
the estimation of the sublime. The text also immediately adds that
in the latter case, the finality that thinking subjectively feels is the
finality that destines it to think the absolute of magnitude as Idea,
and thus the finality of reason itself, the "preeminence" (*Vorzü-
glichkeit*) which can only be made "intuitively evident" (*anschaulich*) by the "inadequacy" (*Unzulänglichkeit*) of the imagination. (One may find surprising the way in which the latter is qualified: a "faculty which in the presentation of magnitudes [of objects
of sense] is itself unbounded [*unbegrenzt*]" [107; *104*]. This boundlessness can only be that of the *Zusammensetzung*, accorded to understanding in its progression, but without value for reason.)

By forcing the parallel between the beautiful and the sublime, by
having recourse to the principle of a finality in both cases, the confrontation of reason and imagination in the sublime, it seems, can
be brought back to the measure of a dispute, of the gentle dispute
between understanding and imagination that gives taste its value of
emulation for thought. The ultimatum put to the faculty of presentation by reason can also be understood as a proposal of alliance, and the war can be understood as being motivated by the
project of a pact. We have noted that reason's claim to a presentation of the absolute is (in the preceding set-off quotation) lessened
by the introduction of an analogy to the unreal: it would be
enough for the imagination to present something that could affect thought (provide it a sensation of itself) in a way similar to the
way thought would be affected if thinking thought (without presentation) the Idea of practical reason, that is, the law and its foundation, freedom.

This of course can be only an analogy. For when thinking feels moral law subjectively, the feeling that corresponds to this "state" is called respect (KPV, 74–110; *84–123*). And respect "under the name of moral feeling is . . . produced solely by reason" (ibid., 79; *89*). Respect does not "serve" for anything except as "an incentive [*Triebfeder*] thanks to which the law makes itself a maxim" (ibid., t.m.). Which means that respect is the subjective sensation that thinking feels when it is grasped by practical law, that is, not as an object of possible (or impossible) knowledge but as an incentive to act, what is called a maxim. Respect is the sensation of thought that is obliged, thought that is purely and immediately obliged by practical reason. An obligation that is not *pflichtmäßig* (according to duty) but directly *aus Pflicht* (from duty: ibid., 84; *95*). This altogether "singular" (*etwas Besonderes*: ibid., 82; *93*) temper has no reference to any objects that could affect thought or make thought dependent on them by the feeling they provide for it. This latter feeling is called "pathological" (*pathologisch*: ibid.) because thinking is subject to its state as if it had come from outside itself. Thus respect cannot be "reckoned either as enjoyment [*Vergnügen*] or as pain [*Schmerz*]" (ibid., 83; *94*), which are the witnesses to thought's liability. This seems strange: a feeling that does not involve the faculty of pleasure and displeasure—a "blank" feeling. It is only an extrinsic or secondary effect that this feeling is accompanied by displeasure, and that pure obligation resolutely opposes the attachment of the will to its favorite object, the ego (ibid., 81; *92*); the ensuing pain comes from the faculty of desire's attraction to or preoccupation with an object. But this object is not the law. Thought oriented practically, the thought that looks to act and judges action either good or bad, does not initially feel any "passion." It does not suffer in the least. The "soul-stirring delight," which is thought's temper or its "state" when the "presence" of the absolute makes itself felt in the sublime, is perfectly foreign to it (see Chapter 7).

This is why the analogy of the temper required of thought in sublime reason with the temper in which thought is to be found in practical reason must remain merely an analogy. The substitution of one for the other is not possible. What properly defines reason as an absolute practical causality is that it wants the presentation of its Idea in the phenomenal world. Subject to this obligation, the thought that presents tries to force itself (106; *103*) to provide the most adequate presentation corresponding to the absolute of reason. The thought that presents thus advances toward what is impossible for it. The mountain masses, the pyramids of ice, the overhanging, threatening rocks, thunderclouds, oceans rising with rebellious force, volcanoes (104, 110; *101, 107*), everything "rude" to be found in nature is sublime in presentation because it is at the limit of what can be grasped in a single intuition: *beinahe zu groß ist*, it is "almost too great" (101; *97*), and too great even for our faculty of apprehension, *Auffassungsvermögen* (ibid.). This effort is in fact similar to the effort of the will that aims for virtue. This effort is indeed similar, but with the difference that the imagination belongs to the capacity to know, whereas the will is the faculty of desire; furthermore, the result of the violence that virtue does to itself is moral, whereas the result of the violence that the sublime does to itself is aesthetic. The admixture of fear and exaltation that constitutes sublime feeling is insoluble, irreducible to moral feeling (see Chapter 7).

Attempt to Resolve the Differend Through a "Dialectic"

Is it an "admixture" that makes up sublime feeling, strictly speaking? "Strictly speaking" here means to speak in the terms of the critique. "Admixture" is not a term of the critique. It designates the juxtaposition or the coexistence before the "greatness" of two feelings in one and the same "state" of thought, and it both presents and conceives. If such were in fact the case, the feeling resulting from this "subjective" coexistence would have no finality, and could lay no claim to the quality of an aesthetic judgment that is finally affirmative, that is to say, a pleasure ("finally" in both senses of the word: as result, and as granted to an end not conceived but subjectively perceived). (Instead, one might perhaps compare this "admixture" with the anguish aroused in the psyche by the approach of the "real" of desire, in excess of all "imaginary" demand. But this parallel could not readily be articulated, for neither the field nor the approach of the field is, for Freud or Lacan, of the same order of the fields of the transcendental critique.)

Sublime feeling is aesthetic because, like taste, it is subjectively final without the concept of an end. Thus one must find a finality, if not an end, in the very differend that reason has with the imagination. What arouses sublime feeling, or is at least the occasion for it, seems "to contravene the ends [*zweckwidrig*] of our power of judgment" and "to be ill-adapted [*unangemessen*] to our faculty of presentation" and an "outrage [*gewälttätig*] on the imagination" (91; *88*), but this outrage is judged all the more sublime and the state of thought consequently all the more final.

One is tempted to conceive of the finalization of this extreme discordance as a dialectical operation. Dialectical in a non-Kantian, more Hegelian sense, but well known in the paradoxes of logic under the name given to it by the first Sophist, the argument called the *antistrephon*, or retortion. Using a response made by Gorgias to his student Evathle as a model, I will summarize the dialectical figure in the following way: it is precisely in affirming that the series of your judgments is finite that you deny it, for in so doing you add a new judgment to this series. It is precisely, says reason to the imagination, in showing that you cannot "comprehend" more magnitudes in a single intuition than you are doing that you show you can, for in order to show the limit, you must also show beyond the limit. Such that the pleasure in infinitude, which is mine, is already latent in the unhappiness you feel in your finitude. The process consists in displacing the examination of judgment from its (negative) quality to its (assertive) modality: you say that . . . is not, but you affirm it. The *modus* of a proposition is in effect independent from its content, the *dictum*.

Kant's text occasionally lends itself to this "dialectical" reading:

> When a magnitude begins to tax the utmost stretch of our faculty of comprehension in a single intuition, and still numerical magnitudes . . . call upon the imagination for aesthetic comprehension in a greater unity, the mind then gets a feeling of being aesthetically con-

fined within bounds. Nevertheless, with a view to the extension of imagination necessary for adequacy with what is unbounded in our faculty of reason, namely, the Idea of the absolute, the attendant displeasure, and, in this [*mithin*], the want of finality in our faculty of imagination, is still represented as final for Ideas of reason and their animation. (109, t.m.; *105*)

"In this" does translate *mithin* a little excessively. However, the crux of the argument is the same: the relation between the imagination and reason is not final, and thus unpleasant, or it is at least neutral, making it final and thus pleasant.

The following lines that conclude the same passage are even more explicit on this point: "But in this very way [*eben dadurch*; in the want of finality of the imagination for reason] the aesthetic judgment itself is subjectively final for reason as a source of Ideas . . . and the object is received as sublime with a pleasure that is only possible through the mediation of a displeasure [*nur vermittelst einer Unlust*]" (ibid., t.m.). The *dadurch*—thanks to this, in this, by means of this—and the "through the mediation" (*vermittelst*) suggest the dialectical reading I have evoked. Even the beginnings of the "suppression" (of the *Aufhebung* [or the *relève*: tr.]) by the negative, which would be expected in such a reading, are not missing: the subjective finality of sublime feeling that results from the want of finality of the imagination for reason is finality (I repeat: of this feeling "itself" as a whole and as result) for reason, for the source of the Ideas. This suppression can be understood "dialectically": the absolute auto-affirmation of thinking as reason overcomes (preserves and suppresses) its negativity as imagination.

This "taking up," this *Erheben*, of reason (the sublime is *erhaben*), which is at the same time the "relieving of," the *Aufheben* of the imagination (the German, like the Latin *tollere*, evokes the action both of removing and of elevating), seems thus to be a legitimate meaning of the procedure described by the texts cited. As in the dialectical operation, each "moment" of thought—presentation, concept—has its absolute "for itself." But in relation to the other, the absolute of imagination is not of equal power. The absolute of reason is the impossible of imagination; the absolute of the imagination would only be a moment relative to the absolute of reason. The latter would therefore be, in itself, the only absolute. And because what is in question here is felt by the thought thinking the absolute, the displeasure that it feels in thinking the impossible absolute (impossible for the imagination) is effaced (yet preserved) before and in the pleasure that it feels in thinking the possible absolute (possible for reason).

However, this reading is not the correct one. It is not critical but speculative. By this I mean that it makes the two powers in conflict "homogeneous" in order to transform them into moments of a finalized process. The dialectic seems heedlessly to relativize the absolute of imagination in relation to the absolute of reason, the "first measure" of one compared to the "infinite as whole" of the other. This "heedlessness" consists in admitting of a third instance between imagination and reason that authorizes the transition from one to the other. As if the question that directs all of the third *Critique*, that of "transition" precisely, were already resolved, and as if the Analytic of the Sublime did not refute the promise of an agreement of thought with itself and with the nature that constitutes the feeling of the beautiful. For the "casualties" of the so-called dialectic of the sublime are considerable: what is lost without being taken up in the sublime is all of nature as the "writing" of forms, and everything by which thought is attached, finalized with regard to this writing—its very power of forms.

The third instance to which both powers—imagination and reason—are supposed to have recourse in the hypothesis of a dialectical reading is "becoming" itself, as in the *Science of Logic*, or "the life of the spirit," as in the *Phenomenology of the Spirit*. This instance is certainly only *mentio*, the act of the *mens* (of the spirit), and the contradiction of this act by the *mens*, the construction of a presence and its deconstruction, thus pure "taking up," which insists but is not an instance. As it is, this power, which is always in excess of its acts, has no trouble striding across the "abysses" that paralyze critical thought and no trouble relativizing the "absolutes" it believes to have localized. Here lies all of the work of this power.

It is not graspable except as this undecidable, affirmative work of the negative. Which here would be the work of reason. Consequently one would have to say that the imagination is reason arrested in one of its formations, in one of its acts, and that as a reason temporarily limited, it will not fail to pass these limits and to settle further on, in another so-called instance or faculty that is less limited, for example, understanding, the "enlarging" of which will in turn lead to the autopositioning of the spirit by itself as the only true absolute in the form of reason.

A dialectical reading of this kind has no access to a sublime that is subjectively felt by thought as differend. One has only to refer to what concerns the sublime in the Hegelian (and Romantic) aesthetic in general. It is clear that for critical thought such a reading expresses the transcendental illusion of which reason is always the victim, or it expresses a failing in the "domiciliation" of the acts of thought. An examination of this shortcoming was made in the Appendix to the first *Critique* devoted to reflection, on the subject of Leibniz's intellectualism (KRV, 276–96; *309–33*; see Chapter 1, pp. 26–32). Whether it is in regard to "becoming" or to the "life of the spirit," this refutation holds for the speculative dialectic.

Dynamical Synthesis of the Cause and the Conditioned

The texts that allow one to identify the dynamical synthesis and to distinguish it from a "dialectical" synthesis have already been cited (see Chapter 3, pp. 77–81 and 89–96 in particular). They are essentially the exposition of the axioms of intuition and the remark inserted between the solution of the transcendental mathematical Ideas and the solution of the transcendental dynamical Ideas (respectively, KRV A and B, 197–201; *217–20*, and KRV, 461–64; *519–22*). I will only recall the crux of the argument to illustrate its consequences for the dynamical synthesis in sublime feeling. To introduce the general critical "solution" (*Entscheidung*) of the Antithetic (KRV, 443–49; *496–504*), Kant dismantles the reasoning that supports both theses and antitheses. The reasoning is the same whatever the stakes of each antinomy may be. For in all cases it is a question of thinking the world as a totality of phenomena: is this totality limited or unlimited in spatiotemporal extension (according to quantity), in intensive complexity (according to quality), in causality (according to relation), in the necessity to exist (according to modality)?

What supports the arguments is the following reasoning: "If the conditioned is given, the entire series of all its conditions is likewise given; objects of the senses are given as conditioned; therefore, etc." (KRV, 443; *496*). Upon which the critique reasons as follows: it is true that the objects of the senses are given to us as phenomena, for they are necessarily filtered through the forms of sensibility, the schemas of the imagination, and the principles of understanding. What "gives" them to us, the thing or the being from which these phenomena reach our apprehension, we know nothing about. By definition, it is not a phenomenon, but an object of thought, a noumenon, a thing-in-itself.

But the major premise of this reasoning is incorrect in the way it is formulated. From the premise that every phenomenon is given as conditioned (as an object of the mathematical syntheses involved in forms, schemas, and principles), it does not follow that the "entire series" of all its conditions is given. The entire series might be given, Kant continues, if the givens were things-in-themselves. For then their conditions, which are homogeneous to them, would also be things-in-themselves, and one could say that the series of the conditions would in turn be given (as thing-in-itself). But the given is not the thing as it is in itself. It is what is apprehended of the thing, in the broad sense, and more precisely what is grasped by intuition in an "apprehension" and by imagination in a "comprehension." Moreover, these acts of synthesis, which are minimal in providing a given, are limited, if only in "magnitude," by a "measure" that the faculty of presentation cannot exceed (here we see how the "mathematical" analysis of the sublime naturally relays the critical argument of the Antithetic). The synthesis of the "entire series" of phenomena exceeds this limit. Thus there is no intuitive apprehension or imaginative comprehension of it. Consequently, the "entire series" is not "given." The "regression" in the series of conditions can indeed continue *ad infinitum*. It is none other than the "progression" in composition, the *Zusammensetzung*, of the elements, expounded in Chapter 4 on the sublime examined mathematically. Intuition and imagination can follow understanding *ad infinitum* without encountering any obstacles. But what they cannot do is "give" the whole of the series, that is, in the problematic of the antithetic, "give" the world in its totality. The polemic regarding the infinitude or the finitude of the world is thus empty, and both parties are nonsuited.

However, as we know, the dismissal of the double complaint is only legitimate insofar as one is debating a limit phenomenon on both sides, which is a pure absurdity, for any phenomenon is given only in the syntheses that associate it with other phenomena, in a contingent but homogeneous way. Such is not the case for cause and for the necessity of existence. The synthesis of cause with effect is necessary *a priori*—one cannot be thought without the other—but it also unites two heterogeneous elements. Effect is given as a phenomenon. If one looks for the cause, understanding can only provide other phenomena as conditions of the effect, thus answering the question "mathematically": How does the phenomenon appear? But to provide its cause (or the necessity of its being) is to answer the question why?

Kant explains this difference through the aspect of temporality, which is of great consequence for sublime feeling. The relation of a cause and an effect is not that of a before and an after. For the before is always, by mathematical synthesis, the after of a more before. "Between" cause and effect there is, from the temporal point of view, an event that does not belong to the succession. The effect is said to result from the cause. If the cause does not act, the phenomenon can still be given, but it is not the effect of the cause. We would say that it remains to be explained. The moments that form the temporal context of a moment are given to regression (or to progression) in succession. But the "action" of the cause that "produces" the effect is only a principle of the unintelligibility of the phenomenon. This principle is not a phenomenon in the series; it gives the reason for which the phenomenon appears in it. It is an Idea. The notion of causality, which is the Idea of a cause's action that produces an effect, is not at all satisfied if understanding provides it with a series, even a very large series, of the conditions of the phenomenon. There are many conditions for a body to fall or to ignite; they do not give the reason for the fall or the fire. In this, causality is not a synthesis, the certainty of which can be "intuitive"; its certainty is "discursive" (KRV, 197; *216*).

One easily speaks of a phenomenon as the "cause" of a phenomenon. But even so, one has to distinguish this "causality," which is sensible, from the intelligible causality that is at issue here. "Whatever in an object of the sense is not itself phenomenon [*apparance*: tr.], I entitle *intelligible*. If, therefore, that which in the sensible world must be regarded as phenomenon has in itself a faculty which is not an object of sensible intuition, but through which it can be the cause of phenomena, the *causality* of this being can be regarded from two points of view. Regarded as the causality of the thing-in-itself, it is *intelligible* in its *action*; regarded as the causality of a phenomenon in the world of sense, it is *sensible* in its *effects*" (KRV, 467; *527*).

I put forward the "event" that is the putting into action of the intelligible causality and that does not belong to phenomenal time. Kant's text does not mention this term. But it marks the independence of the causal "agent" in relation to the time of succession. "Now this acting subject [*dieses handelnde Subjekt*, the source of the action that causes the effect] would not, in its intelligible character, stand under any conditions of time [*unter keinen Zeitbedingungen stehen*]; time is only a condition of phenomena not of things-in-themselves. In it [in this "subject"] no action would *begin* or *cease* [*würde keine Handlung* entstehen, *oder* vergehen] and it would not, therefore, be subordinated [*unterworfen*] to the law of the determination of all that is alterable in time [*alles Veränderlichen*], namely, that everything that happens must have its cause in the *phenomena* that precede it" (KRV, 468, t.m.; *528*).

The verbal mode remains conditional in order to mark the problematic nature of what is implied. For, in truth, we do not know anything about this "agent" or about this "subject." This "agent" or "subject" is the object of an Idea. But it is precisely because of this status that one can negatively characterize its mode of action in relation to succession. The action of the cause cannot be caused by what has already taken place, for the "already" belongs to the time of succession, and in this case the cause would lose its character of intelligible cause. But as soon as it produces its effect, this effect is "real"; it is a phenomenon, it is "given" in the necessary *a priori* conditions for phenomena to be given. The intelligible cause may be said to be first, but its authority does not belong to succession.

Several properties of the agent of causal action are thus determined negatively: the agent is an entity that is only intelligible (not "presentable"); it does not contribute to the knowledge of phenomena according to understanding; it is unconditioned; it is not situated in succession. The before and the after that support the imagination and understanding in their progression or regression *ad infinitum* are unknown to it. This agent exercises or actualizes its power, that is, it produces a phenomenon as being its effect, according to "a rule and order [*Regel und Ordnung*] altogether different from the order of nature" (KRV, 474; *536*). Thus "all that *has happened* [*alles was . . .* geschehen ist] in the course of nature, and in accordance with its empirical grounds, must inevitably have happened [*unausbleiblich geschehen mußte*], *ought* perhaps *not to have happened* [sollte *vielleicht . . .* nicht geschehen sein]" (ibid., t.m.). Here we see the difference between *sollen* and *müssen*. What had to happen, according to the necessity of the laws of understanding (*müssen*), perhaps did not have to happen according to the "free" causality of the agent (*sollen*). What must happen perhaps must not.

The critical meditation on the time of causal action thus leads to a split in the sense of the word "duty." As necessity (*müssen*), "duty" designates the predictability of successions in nature under the rule of understanding. As obligation (*sollen*), "duty" signifies that it is "time" for the agent to exert its action ("time," which in classical Greek or the Greek of the Septuagint or the Greek of Paul of Tarsus is called *kairos*). The agent decides what this "time" is. The decision is not motivated; it is not conditioned, because the causality of the agent is not. The phenomenon does not itself result from this "due" (*sollen*) action, but must "also" be the effect of this action, and no longer simply the conditioned of the conditions that envelop it. The phenomenon remains conditioned according to the rule and order of nature; it becomes the effect of an unconditioned cause according to the altogether different rule and order of reason (unknown to us).

This cause belongs to reason because it is the object of an Idea, of a concept of reason. But insofar as it is considered the acting cause of production, not of the phenomenon but of the nature of its effect, this reason is itself considered to be acting. In the same way that there is no effect without cause, there is no cause without effect. This is what the *Sollen* says: this action must be "effected." One begins with the speculative examination of the properties of intelligible causality, and these properties are negative. But because they are speculatively negative, they form the *a priori* conditions of a causality freed from all condition, that is, the conditions of freedom. Without this free causality, there could never be moral judgment. All *sollen* would be reducible to a *müssen*. What is inscribed in the *Sollen* is that the agent is only agent if it acts. While it is first the object of an Idea of speculative reason, free causality reveals itself to be practical reason in action. One must not ask reason "to explain" (*erklären*) the origin of the actions that result from this causality. One must recognize in reason itself, whose Idea this causality is, "the cause capable of *producing* [erzeugen] them" (KRV, 474; 536).

This example of dynamical synthesis had to be examined closely because it is much more than an example. It underlies a large part of the critical system. This synthesis makes the union of nature and freedom possible for thought despite their absolute heterogeneity. The same phenomenon explainable through the series of conditions of which it is an element can also be grasped as the effect of a free causality. This "grasping" is not the apprehension of a given or its subsumption under a concept of understanding.

-rs "writing" of Chikrschaft

Rather, it is like listening to a "sign." This is the name Kant gives a phenomenon in which the effect of free causality is also "perceived": the "sensible sign" of the thing, the "transcendental cause of its empirical character" (*das sinnliche Zeichen der transzendentalen Ursache;* KRV, 472, t.m.; *533*). Through such signs one can discern that causality by freedom is active in the natural history, that is the history of man for as long as men themselves "hear" the "presence" of freedom in phenomena (second "Conflict of the Faculties"). A "reading" of or a listening to these signs has nothing to do with a determination by concept. This "reading" requires a "manner" much more than a method (182; *174*). But the "reading" applies to the same objects. In the dynamical synthesis, a phenomenon enclosed within an immanent necessity occasionally serves as a sign of a transcendental obligation.

Necessity of the Synthesis of Sensations in Sublime Feeling

Considered dynamically, sublime judgment must present the case of a similar synthesis. This synthesis must necessarily unite two heterogeneous elements. One can foresee that a given presented in intuition will be "grasped" in intuition as the sign of an Idea of reason. But because it is a question here of an aesthetic reflective judgment, the synthesis must concern not the object, the phenomenal given taken as a sign of a noumenal causality, but the state of thought, i.e., sensation. Thus sensation must be double, or split into two heterogeneous yet indissociable sensations. We are of course referring to terror, which has to do with the presentable, and to exaltation, which refers to the unpresentable.

Let us first try to understand why the unity of these two sensations or of the two faces of sublime feeling is necessary. The imagination tries with "the greatest effort" (*die größte Bestrebung:* 106; *103*) to present a "comprehension," the absolute for which reason has an Idea. If the thought that imagines (always in Kant's sense: that presents here and now) opposed the thought that conceives of the absolute with a pure and simple refusal, there would be no sublime feeling. The same would be true if reason demanded nothing, that is, if thought were not available, "liable," did not have the necessary *Empfänglichkeit* (115; *III*) to the Ideas of reason for them to "arise" on the occasion of this almost impossible presentation. The latter must make a "sign" of transcendence. The "Savoyard peasant" who sees Saussure exalted by the immensity of mountain glaciers judges him to be simply a fool (115; *III*). This is because the peasant is not "cultured," "tutored" in matters of Ideas of reason (115–16; *III*).

In reality these two cases of insensibility to the sublime are one and the same. The imagination can refuse to present the "almost too great" just as the "almost too great" may not signal to thought the "presence" of an Idea of reason. The imagination contents itself, one might say, with "surveying" the given magnitudes by progressive composition. The imagination will do this under the sole direction of understanding; it can rest assured that understanding will not ask it to grasp "in a glance" all the units that compose these magnitudes. Thought will thus remain confined in the recurrent mathematical synthesis of a series that can be infinite.

If the synthesis of sensations is necessary in sublime feeling, it is because the imagination does violence to itself in order to present a magnitude, which is a sign of the subjective absolute of magnitude (magnitude itself). Moreover, the imagination does violence to itself because reason has the strength to demand this of it. Such is the situation (as we have seen on pp. 131–37) with regard to the Idea of an absolute "agent" and not merely of an "absolute whole." For the first Idea immediately requires its realization. By "immediately" one must understand not "right now," for the absolute agent does not belong to succession, but, rather, "without mediation." The synthesis of sensations in sublime feeling only becomes necessary with the transformation of the absolute of magnitude into the absolute of causality. The absolute ceases to be merely the object of a speculative Idea; the absolute is the subject acting absolutely, and this is why it requires the presentation of the "almost too great" as a sign of itself in aesthetic feeling.

This explains why the Analytic of the Sublime as it is considered dynamically opens on the theme of force and no longer of magnitude, at the risk of creating the confusion we have discussed above. Nature has might (force), this might inspires "fear" (*Furcht*) in thought, but the latter discovers that it too has might, enough "dominion" (*Gewalt*) to resist that of nature (109–10; *105–6*). It is not a question, as we have already said, of a real or empirical fear, which cannot give rise to sublime feeling any more than thought "captivated by inclination and appetite can [play the part of a judge] of the beautiful" (110; *106*). What matters in the formulation of sublime feeling is the sensation that there is cause to be fearful, a terror that corresponds to "this is frightening," that is, to a reflective judgment in the tautegorical sense.

This specification leads to a first remark pursuant to the way in which absolute causality makes a "sign" in sublime feeling. The "acting subject" demands the presentation of sublime feeling under the sign of an "almost too great" or, we can now add, of an "almost too strong." But the acting subject does not require its "being effected," that is, the inscription in the order of phenomena of an action that is an effect or a sign of its absolute causality. In other words, the Idea of freedom leads not to moral action but to aesthetic feeling. The Idea of freedom is not present to thought as an incentive to make exist what is not, but, rather, what should be (*sollen*); the Idea of freedom is present to thought as fear and exaltation because what is (the phenomenon) is almost nothing next to what freedom could and should cause to be. Thus moral law, which is simply the obligation freely to carry out free causality, is felt not in the form or according to the "state" of thought, which is its subjective signal, I mean—respect. The latter (as we have said in Chapter 1, pp. 36–43) is an empty sentimental temper that shows only that thought is ready to "carry out" the absolute causality, to fulfill the duty (*sollen*) of realizing it. This respectful temper is immediately determined by first causality when thinking thinks it; it is first causality itself as felt, but felt as an incentive to act. In sublime feeling, first causality does not become an incentive for the thought that wants, for volition, or, as Kant says, for the faculty of desire. Sublime feeling is aesthetic and, as such, only interests, among the powers of thought, the power of feeling pleasure or displeasure, and not the power of knowing or the power of desiring (and acting). This difference is considerable. In the sublime, absolute causality is "present" only insofar as it pleases or displeases. In fact absolute causality is present as it pleases and displeases at the same time. If such were not the case, the "Analytic of the Sublime" would be another chapter in the *Critique of Practical Reason*. But the separation of the two powers of thought, of desire and of feeling pleasure or displeasure, which the table of faculties clearly displays at the end of the Introduction to the third *Critique* (*39*; *36*), prevents this confusion and safeguards the irreducible specificity of the aesthetic, even the sublime aesthetic. The table also reminds us that the final end is not finality: the concept of first causality or freedom is given by reason as the end to will; finality (paradoxical in the case of the sublime), which is expressed in aesthetic feeling, is subjectively "judged" (tautegorically, as sensation) by a power of judgment that operates without the mediation of a concept.

A second remark must be made on the subject of the "replacement" of the "absolute whole" with the "absolute cause," which occurs with the transition from a mathematical examination of aesthetic judgment upon the sublime, to its dynamical examination. The Idea of the infinite as a whole, absolutely, cannot give rise to a necessary synthesis of the heterogeneous, that is, to a dynamical synthesis complete with presentation. As the object of an Idea, this absolute infinite is obviously not presentable, and in this sense there is indeed heterogeneity of this object of thought with any object presentable in intuition. But the synthesis of one with the other is not necessary, for it is not written in the Idea of the actual infinite magnitude that it *must* be presented, only that it cannot be. This is why the imagination, responsible for this presentation, does not succeed in fulfilling it. But what remains unexplained, with only the Idea of the absolute whole, is why reason demands a presentation of the absolute. Reason maintains the object it conceives as absolute whole outside of the series of phenomena estimable by understanding in magnitude and outside of what the imagination can compose in its wake, for the Idea of the infinite as totality is altogether different from the concept of an infinite series of apprehensions and progressive predications. Indeed the Idea is the "maximization" of the concept or its passage to the limit, but it jumps the limit, and this suffices to render its object unpresentable and thus to make any attempt at presentation in a "comprehension" fail. But, once again, this "intelligible" status of the infinite does not explain why the imagination is called upon to give the infinite a presentation nonetheless.

Only the Idea of absolute causality can legitimate the *double bind* in which the imagination is caught and kept prisoner in sublime feeling: to present the unpresentable. For only the Idea of absolute causality contains within it, as its very content, the obligation of its realization. We have shown how this "being effected" is not moral action. However, the *duty* to "effect" is precisely what, in the order of aesthetic feeling, is translated as the necessity for the imagination to present an object that cannot be presented. Because the imagination cannot succeed, its failure will at least have the sense of a testimony to the "presence" of this causality. Lacking the power to present it—there being no possible presentation—the imagination will present that there is an unpresentable object, absolute causality. Thus the distress of the imagination becomes the sign of the intelligible in the sensible. But, once again, the intelligible must demand this sign, and only the free "agency of the subject" has this essential property. Only with this agent, thanks to this "acting subject" that demands its "incarnation," is the synthesis—of what is heterogeneous in the feeling provided by natural magnitudes and forces (which are very large in the order of phenomena, signs of an absolute magnitude, in extension or in potential in the order of the noumena)—also a necessary synthesis. The synthesis thus is properly dynamical.

Heterogeneity of the Sensations of Time in the Sublime Synthesis

It is useful to clarify the heterogeneous character of the two elements unified in the sublime feeling by an examination of the aspect of temporality. A passage from paragraph 27, devoted to the exposition of the quality of sublime delight, invites the reader to do so. I neglected doing so until now because the consequences of this examination are significant only in relation to the dynamical synthesis. The passage in question begins with the following: *Messung eines Raums (als Auffassung)* (measurement of space [as apprehension]: 107; *104*). The text insists on the "contra-final" (*zweckwidrig*) character of the "effort" (*Bestrebung*) that is required of the imagination in sublime judgment for its normal functioning (ibid.). Kant meticulously points to what the reversal of the "mode of representation" (*die Vorstellungsart*: 108; *104*), which conforms to the finality of the imagination, consists in. We know the localization of the reversal: it is in the transition from apprehension to comprehension (see Chapter 4, pp. 102–9). The apprehension of a magnitude, even a very great magnitude, always remains possible part by part; it is relayed by the "composition" of the parts apprehended one after the other. It allows for the "description" (*Beschreibung*) of this magnitude thanks to the "objective movement" (*objektive Bewegung*, that is, movement of successive syntheses of the properties of the object), and this movement is a "progression" (*ein Progressus*: 108; *104*). Thus the imagination works in a way that is conformable to its finality, that is, in a way suitable to providing a presentation of the object.

However, when the imagination must comprehend the manifold in a unity that is no longer one "of thought" (thus no longer one of composition), but "of intuition," when the imagination must provide a comprehension "at one glance" (*in einem Augenblick*) of what has been apprehended in successively apprehended parts, *des Sukzessiv-Aufgefaßten* (ibid.), then the imagination works "regressively": there is *Regressus*. Furthermore, this regression strikes a blow at what is the most essential to the imagination, "the time condition in the progression" (*die Zeitbedingung im Progressus*: ibid.), in its own progression. What time condition? The very one that is discussed in the Preliminary Remark to the Deduction of the categories, to which we have previously referred: what intuition has apprehended in a unity at first grasp, the imagination comprehends in a unity at second grasp by exercising its faculty of

Comprehension as such (which not just exp, which requires appr) is temporal-time?

"reproduction" (KRV A, 132–33; *145–46*). Thus we noted that the imagination could follow understanding in its progression *ad infinitum* toward very great units of magnitudes (see Chapter 4, pp. 102–9). But what one remarks here is more serious than an obstacle to the *Zusammenfassung* of important magnitudes. It is the destruction of the temporality proper to all presentation, of which the syntheses examined in the first *Critique* constitute the *a priori* conditions. More specifically, the simultaneous grasp of the successive destroys the *Zeitfolge*, the "time series" (KRV A, 132; *145*), needed by objective description, especially if the magnitude to be described is great. But more serious still, this time series is not only indispensable to the presentation of an object in intuition, it is "a condition of the internal sense" (*eine Bedingung des inneren Sinnes*: ibid.).

The transcendental aesthetic of the first *Critique* showed that time has no reality in itself but is a formal condition of the intuition of givens in general. The form that is proper to this condition is succession: "Time has only one dimension; different times are not simultaneous but successive" (KRV, 75; *74*). Space, on the contrary, is the *a priori* condition for givens to be intuited "outside and alongside one another" (KRV A and B, 68; *67*). But time alone is the "formal *a priori* condition of all appearances whatsoever" (KRV, 77; *77*). For givens, outer and inner alike, are subject to its form, succession, whereas inner givens are not subject to the spatial form of juxtaposition (which, temporally speaking, signifies coexistence). From this it follows that time, as the succession imposed on "givens" for them to be given, "is nothing but the form of inner sense, that is, of the intuition of ourselves and of our inner state" (ibid., 77; *76–77*).

Thus the grasp in "one glance" of what is successive, which reason demands of the imagination in the judgment upon the sublime, and which must render intuitable the "coexistence" (*Zugleichsein*) of what can only be given successively, does "violence" not only to the *a priori* condition of the intuition of any given or succession, but to the eminent and unique condition that such a grasp imposes on the "intuition of ourselves and of our state." If the imagination were able to satisfy reason, time as the form of inner sense would be altered, at least for the duration of the *Zugleich* (but then how would this be determined?). This would mean that there would no longer be an inner sense to organize our representations in a time series. The "subject" would be deprived of the means of constituting its subjectivity. For, under the name of the "I think," the "subject" is nothing other than the consciousness of the originary synthetic unity to which all representations are imputed. Without this imputation, called apperception, representations would not be those of a subject. Moreover, this imputation would be impossible if the representations were not themselves already given in the form of a succession. I remind the reader, all too briefly, of this analysis in the second edition of the first *Critique* under the title "Transcendental Deduction of the Pure Concepts of Understanding" (KRV B, 152–75; *140–91*), only to show how the "regression" of the imagination in sublime feeling strikes a blow at the very foundation of the "subject." Taste promised him a beautiful life; the sublime threatens to make him disappear. We will return to this (see Chapter 7, pp. 179–81).

The regression is thus "contra-final" to the temporal synthesis, which is itself constitutive of the synthesis of apperception, that is, it is constitutive for the "I think." But the analysis of the Transcendental Aesthetic of the first *Critique* only considers thought in its power to know. One could say (see Chapter 1, pp. 15–26) that in the exercise of its other powers—that of feeling pleasure and displeasure, of particular interest to us here—the "I think" is not necessarily required. One could say that thought is not the "I think," and that the subjective is not the subject. Furthermore, one could say that the time of aesthetic feeling is not necessarily the same as the time of cognition. Kant does not seem to doubt this. For however disastrous it may be for inner sense, the "regression" demanded of the imagination is nonetheless declared to be "subjectively" felt and felt as *zweckwidrig*, as contravening the finality of the faculty of presentation (108; *104*). Although this feeling cannot be related to the unity of an "I think," as can a moment in a series of inner representations, it is nonetheless felt, in the tautegorical sense of reflection. It was never said that thought as reflection, as pure faculty of judging, presupposes an "I think." On the contrary, it is said that "the subjective condition of all judgments is the judging faculty itself" (143; *137*). Moreover, because this "power of judgment" (*das Vermögen zu urteilen*: ibid.) truly exceeds what the "I think" and its temporal synthesis can do by succession, it can find a finality in the threat, a finality with regard to the destination or vocation exceeding its sole cognitive vocation "for the whole province of the mind" (*für die ganze Bestimmung des Gemüts*) when succession is threatened with disappearance (108; *104*).

Given the above, let us now return to the question of the heterogeneity of the sensations felt together in sublime feeling. At the very moment (I dare say) when the thought that imagines seems threatened with annihilation by its "regression," that is, by working against the current of the succession it usually needs, the (rational) thought of reason also feels serial time to be annihilated in the Idea of the infinite as absolute whole and, further still, as we have shown, in the Idea of absolute causality. The power to engender an "effect" without being determined to do it by a condition does not involve the temporality wherein phenomena are perceived and explained according to their linkage. It escapes the elementary syntheses of intuition, imagination, and understanding, that is, respectively, form, schema, and the axiom of time as magnitude added to itself.

Sublime feeling is remarkable in this respect, in the double weakening of the principle of succession: a weakening in a strict sense due to the "regression" of the imagination, a weakening (in a loose sense), an extemporalization due to the "presence" of the Idea of reason. One might think that it was the same single departure from inner sense. In reality it is a question of two very similar but heterogeneous feelings. For the imagination, this "departure" is made regressively, in the fear of losing the minimal power that thinking has of synthesizing givens (its own included) by succession. For reason, on the other hand, the departure is made (and always already made) in a leap, in the exaltation of recovering the maximal power that thinking has of beginning a series of givens without being bound to it (KRV, *475–79*; *536–41*). The first "no time" threatens the faculty of knowledge, the second "no time" establishes the faculty of pure desire.

Thus it is very difficult to classify Kantism among philosophies of the subject, as is sometimes done.

§6 A Few Signs of
Heterogeneity

Resistance

The most difficult and subtle trait to decipher in sublime feeling is the extreme dissonance between the powers of thought, which is simultaneously felt as the sublime feeling's supreme consonance with itself. Later we will examine the way in which the text of the Analytic (and even of the analytics of the beautiful and the sublime) "deduces" this consonance on the basis of a supersensible principle. First we will try to measure the sublime paradox by examining the terms, certain terms that are linked to it. "Resistance," "negative presentation," "enthusiasm," and "simplicity" are the recurring terms in the General Remark with which "Exposition of Aesthetic Reflective Judgments" concludes (117–30; *113–25*).

The critical concept of "resistance" (*Widerstand*: 118; *114*) characterizes precisely the relation of sublime feeling to "the interest of sense" (*das Interesse der Sinne*: ibid.). This latter notion refers to the discussion about the specific nature of aesthetic delight in the "First Moment" of the "Analytic of the Beautiful" under the category of quality. The quality of taste is to please. This pleasure is distinct from the pleasure provided by the delight of an inclination, different also from the pleasure that a good action can produce, i.e., the "delight" of moral law. The criterion of this double difference is unique: interest. "All interest presupposes a want, or calls one forth; and, being a ground determining approval, de-

147

prives the judgment on the object of its freedom" (49; *47*). "Presupposes . . . or calls . . . forth" a need. "Inclination" (*Neigung*: ibid.) is a delight determined by the need of the senses. Animals feel it in the same way that men do. The law of reason, which is proper to humans, determines an interest for the objects in which it is judged capable of realizing itself. Thus interest is placed in a different relation to determination, depending on whether it belongs to the senses or to reason. The interest of the senses presupposes need; inclination is the delight of this interest. The interest of practical reason, or what determines practical reason to exercise the power of its absolute causality (KPV, 124; *138*), "produces an interest . . . and this we call moral interest" (KPV, 83; *94*), an interest that consists in obedience to the law. But in both cases, delight is linked to a determination, whether empirical or transcendental (and even transcendent).

On the contrary, "favor" (*Gunst*: 49; *47*), which is the aesthetic delight owing to the beautiful, is not determined by any interest for the object that occasions it, and it calls forth none. This delight is thus the only "free" (ibid.) delight, free from all determination. The beautiful is what simply pleases, *was bloß gefällt* (ibid.). Surprising simplicity: the pleasure of the beautiful comes, occurs to thought without the latter feeling any need for it. Nothing motivates it. We are reminded in the "General Remark" closing the exposition of aesthetic judgments that the beautiful "is what pleases in the mere estimate [*in der bloßen Beurteilung*] formed of it (consequently not by intervention of any feeling of sense in accordance with a concept of the understanding)" (118; *114*). *Also nicht vermittelst,* "without the intervention" of a sensation that would be subsumed under a concept. The mediation that is lacking is clearly designated; it is that of the schema. The *Empfindung des Sinnes,* the "feeling of sense," is sensation insofar as it relates to the object, that is, the sensation examined in the first *Critique* and not the sensation as thinking feels it reflexively. The estimate of taste is free of any cognitive condition, either of sensibility or of understanding (i.e., of sensorial sensibility).

In summary, the beautiful pleases in the absence of any sensible interest. As for the sublime, it also "pleases immediately" (*unvermittelbar gefällt*) but it pleases "by its opposition [resistance] to the interest of sense" (*durch seinen Widerstand gegen das Interesse der Sinne*: 118; *114*). "*Unvermittelbar*" (without mediation) but "*durch*" (through, by means of) a resistance. We find this trait of resistance (the *wider*) "against" (the *gegen*) marked once again a few lines later: the beautiful "prepares us to love [*lieben*] something, even nature, apart from any interest," the sublime "to esteem something highly [*hochzuschätzen*] even in opposition to our (sensible) interest" (119; *114*). The "in opposition to," the *wider*, is an essential figure of sublime feeling, as is the "through," the *durch*. Both signal a resistance. The sublime is not unaware of the sensible interest; it opposes it. This intrinsic opposition is expressed in the affectual (I ask the reader to permit me the use of this word) differend that constitutes the sublime feeling: of fear and exaltation. A differend, which, in turn, is the subjective state of thought at the mercy of the differend of its powers to present and to conceive.

The term "resistance" (*Widerstand*), linked to that of "differend" (*Widerstreit*: 107; *103*), deserves further elaboration. Not all resistance presupposes and expresses a differend. In a political order, for example, the opposition of one party to another may only be motivated by a dispute about the legitimacy or the authority of the government. On the other hand, one cannot conceive of a differend that would not distinguish itself by at least one of the parties being in conflict with the other, perhaps even by their reciprocal opposition. Conciliation, indeed to be hoped for, does not truly erase the differend; it displaces it, and its sign, resistance itself, will reappear elsewhere. (The model of these displacements is given by the resistance of the unconscious in psychoanalysis.)

Here the resistance, which marks the sublime feeling, bears testimony to what the dynamical synthesis is, of which the sublime feeling is the result. This synthesis involves the incommensurability of one power of thought with another. If, however, we accept along with Kant that their dissonance and not its resolution attests to a finality, a supreme consonance of thought with itself, then we have to conclude that it is essential for thought to feel reflexively its heterogeneity when it brings itself to its own limits (something it cannot avoid doing). It can do one thing and its opposite, present an object in a finite way and conceive of an object as actually infinite. It can feel this double power, as a pleasure taken in form and as exaltation owing to the Idea. In the sublime thought can feel the nullity of this pleasure in the eyes of this exaltation. When this happens thought feels itself in the truth of its split. This split suspends it above or apart from two ways of understanding this split, both of which are denegation: ordinary empiricism that draws from the split a lesson of wisdom in deception, and speculative idealism that uses the split as the pretext to authorize a delirium in the absolute. Thus the sublime feeling, as has already been suggested (see Chapter 2, pp. 50–56), is the subjective state critical thought must feel in its being carried to its limits (therefore beyond them) and its resistance to this impetus, or, conversely, what it must feel in its passion to determine and in its resistance to this passion. One might consider this a philosophical neurosis. Rather, it is a faithfulness par excellence to the philosophical feeling, "brooding melancholy," as Kant suggested in his *Observations on the Feeling of the Beautiful and the Sublime*. The absolute is never there, never given in a presentation, but it is always "present" as a call to think beyond the "there." Ungraspable, but unforgettable. Never restored, never abandoned.

Negative Presentation

This mode of "presence" of the absolute is the grounds for the "negative presentation" invoked in the final Remark (127–32; *122–27*). The vocabulary is one of energy (see Chapter 2, pp. 60–67). Although the senses are opposed in sublime feeling and "nothing . . . meets the eye of sense" (127; *122*), the feeling provided by the unpresentable "presence" of the absolute is not lost, *verloren* (ibid.); it is not reduced to a "cold and lifeless approbation," without "any moving force," without "emotion" (ibid.). The reverse is true, *gerade umgekehrt* (ibid.). There follows an argument that may surprise the reader because it seems to annul the contradictory economy of sublime feeling. If there is no fear of a decrease in tension—due to an eclipsing of what can be presented by the imagination with regard to the absolute Idea—it is because the imagination, believed to have been blocked at the limits of its "first measure," has a "feeling of being unbounded" (*fühlt sich . . . unbegrenzt*: ibid.), thanks to the elimination, the "thrusting aside" (*Wegschaffung*: ibid.) of its own barriers. The imagination can even lose control, become "unbridled" (*zügellos*: 128; *123*) and can drag thought into the "delirium" (*Wahnsinn*: ibid.) of enthusiasm.

This is a temporary and remissible delirium, unlike *Schwärmerei*. In mania the imagination claims "positively to present" the absolute. Although the imagination gets carried away in *Wahnsinn*, presentation extends beyond its fundamental measure but remains negative. The obligation to which the imagination is subjected by reason does not only leave the imagination terrified, but gives it the courage to force its barriers and attempt a "presentation of the infinite" (127; *122*). This attempt can never end in "anything more than a negative presentation" (ibid.). What is this negative presentation? It is neither the absence of presentation nor the presentation of nothingness. It is negative in the eyes of the sensible but at the same time is still a "mode of presentation" (*eine Darstellungsart*: ibid.). This mode is withdrawn, in retreat (*abgezogene*), and the presentation it furnishes consists in an *Absonderung*, a putting apart and to the side, an "abs-traction" (ibid.). The mode escapes, removes itself (*abgezogene*) from the "first measure" of the imagination. What is presented according to this mode is separated from what is normally presented according to this measure; it is isolated, *ab-*, in a special status, *sonder*. Here the imagination has a way of presenting that "ex-ceeds" its norm, or, rather, "se-cedes" from it.

The play of the faculties in sublime judgment is thus far more complex than one could have imagined. Their differend cannot consist in the simple incommensurability of their respective causes (in the juridical sense). The differend of the finite and the infinite can only be felt fully in thought if the finite thought (that of form) removes itself from its finality in order to try to put itself at the measure of the other party. There is no differend without this gesture. Moreover, because this gesture cannot succeed, there will remain in the order of presentation only a trace, the trace of a retreat, the sign of a "presence" that will never be a presentation. "Negative presentation" is the sign of the presence of the absolute, and it is or can only make a sign of being absent from the forms of the presentable. Thus the absolute remains unpresentable; no given is subsumable under its concept. But the imagination can signal its "presence," an almost insane mirage, in the emptiness it discovers beyond its capacity to "comprehend." This gesture must only be understood reflexively. Only through its sensation can the thought that imagines be aware of this "presence" without presentation.

The differend does not signify that the two parties do not understand each other. It requires that each know the idiom of the other (form, Idea), although each cannot satisfy the demand of the other by means of its own idiom. This is why the various sublime feelings, whatever their particularities may be, are all of a "strenuous" (*wackerer*: 125; *120*) courageous type. Far from closing itself off in the "own right" of its proper finality and renouncing the trial, each party, or one at least, accepts to undergo and to suffer the wrong that the claim of the other forces upon it and tries to show with the means it has at its disposal the inanity of the claim. "Negative presentation" is, in this sense, merely the demonstration of the inanity of the demand that the absolute be presented. In excluding itself from its own limits of presentation, the imagination suggests the presence of what it cannot present. It unbinds itself, unleashes itself, but it does this by removing itself from its finality and thus annihilating itself according to this finality. It follows that the said "presence" is not an object of the imagination; it is only felt subjectively by thought, as this gesture of retraction.

Two brief observations to conclude this point. First, we understand how useless it is to imagine that one has refuted the notion of a differend by showing that the latter presupposes the communication of opposing causes. It is necessary to their differend for the parties to "understand" each other. But neither party succeeds in making the demand of the other legitimate for itself. Furthermore, the shock of the thought of the absolute for the thinking of forms expresses and sanctions a major shift in the stakes of art and literature. This shift does not have the characteristics of a "revolution." Historically, it is a slow, uncertain movement, always threatened by repression, through which the faculty of presentation seeks to remove itself from the *technē* of beautiful forms. One can trace its avatars in the West, back to the High Middle Ages, via the dispute between the Victorines and the Bernardines, via the baroque motif that overtakes and opposes a renewed classicism, the Quarrel of the Ancients and the Moderns, via the appropriation of Longinus's treatise and the discussion of the figure of the sublime in the eighteenth century, in which Kant's Analytic is an important element. This shift in the finality of art and literature was pursued in Romanticism and the avant-garde and is still being debated. Its stakes can be formulated simply: is it possible, and how would it be possible, to testify to the absolute by means of artistic and literary presentations, which are always dependent on forms? Whatever the case may be, the beautiful ceases to be their "object," or else the meaning of the word is indeed subverted.

Enthusiasm

Another important motif of the General Remark is that of enthusiasm. "I must dwell a while on the latter point," Kant writes (124; *119*). Enthusiasm is important. The "intellectual" delight in sublime feeling proceeds, as his analysis of the dynamical point of view shows, from the relation of thought to the absolute of free causality that founds moral law. This delight is "negative" "from the aesthetic side," "opposed to the interest" of sensibility (123; *118–19*). Thus it requires "sacrifices" (*Aufopferungen*: 123; *118*), deprivation or "spoliation" (*Beraubung*: 120, 123; *116, 118*). We will examine this question further a little later (see Chapter 7, pp. 187–90). Kant dwells on this question in order to dissipate a common error by which one confuses enthusiasm with the respect due the law or what matters to it, in particular God (113–14; *109–10*). Enthusiasm is, rather, "the Idea of the Good to which affection is added [*mit Affekt*]" (124, t.m.; *119*). The presence of this affection is enough to deprive enthusiasm of any ethical value: "On this account it cannot merit any delight on the part of reason" (124; *119–20*), that is, serve to carry out free causality by obedience to the law. "Every affection is blind either as to the choice of its end, or, supposing this had been furnished by reason, in the way it is effected" (124, t.m.; *119*). The law of practical reason must only be effected by reason. The law of practical reason cannot be effected by what it prescribes, for it does not prescribe anything that is determined or could be determinate as object for the will. It effects, by making itself directly the incentive of the will. Such is respect, the only pure moral feeling (KPV, 74–110; *84–123*). This purity transcendentally requires a "holiness" of will (KPV, 84; *96*), freed from any interest other than the interest of the law for its realization. This is not the case with enthusiasm. By provoking the extreme tension that is subjectively experienced as terror before the loss of presentation and as "ardor" (*Schwung*: 127; *122*) in the face of what exceeds presentation, that is, absolute causality, enthusiasm relates thought to the law with an affectual "strength" (*mutig*: 125; *120*).

In showing how enthusiasm contravenes moral feeling, Kant is led to denounce another kind of confusion. First of all, one must not think that the affectual "content," so to speak, determines the sublimity of a feeling. Any emotion, any subjective "state" of thought can pass over into the sublime: anger, desperation (ibid.), sadness (130; *124*), admiration (125; *120*), and even "freedom from affection" (*die Affektlosigkeit*) or apathy, a state of disaffection (124; *120*), can become sublime. The sublime can be distinguished not by these affectual qualities or nuances but, rather, by the quantity of energy that is expended on the occasion of the object said to be sublime. "Faint-hearted" (*verzagte*), exhausted despair is not sublime; only "the rage of forlorn hope," "indignant" (*entrüstete*), the energy of desperation is sublime (125; *120*). This energy gives the particular affectual quality its sublime value, makes it "noble" (ibid.). Impassiveness is noble, as is the *Affektlosigkeit* that results within a person from the unshakable resolution to follow "unswerving principles"; a manner of writing, a way of carrying oneself, a garment, a building that conveys this extreme firmness are noble as they strenuously "uphold" principles. These states and these noble works provoke "admiration," which is an "astonishment" that persists after the surprise of novelty (ibid.). The quantity of energy is inscribed in the quantity of time, as the words "strenuously" and "enduring" indicate (ibid.). Given this characterization by tension alone, we see how far the sublime is from the absolutely neutral feeling of respect.

Another remark must be added to this one. Affectual tension is necessary to the sublime, but it is not sufficient. There are "impetuous movements of the mind" (*stürmische Gemütsbewegungen*: 126; *121*) in religious edification, for example, or in the social breadth of certain "ideas" that have nothing of the sublime in them, for thought does not feel itself imperiously called by the absolute Idea. The "presence" of the latter must be felt as being stronger than all possible presentation. The "supersensible" (ibid.) must signal itself as the supreme end of thought, through the sign of the intrinsically contradictory "state" of thought. Tumult is only sublime if it proceeds from resistance, and from the endurance of the resistance that the supersensible Idea opposes to the resistance of the presentable. The impetuousness of political masses or sports crowds is not enthusiasm. "For" (*sonst*) in the absence of the obstinate call of impetuous emotion, the rapture that thought feels before the exploit of the competitive or political performance, or religious eloquence, "belong[s] only to *motion*," to the movement of gymnastics "which we welcome in the interests of good health" (126; *121*). The play of affections does in effect stir one. Following which, one takes pleasure in an "agreeable lassitude," which is the restoration of one's vital forces, the same effect that the "Eastern voluptuaries" obtain in massage, but in this case a massage without masseur (ibid.). The *Denkungsart*, the "way of thinking" (ibid.) that involves the struggle of thinking with itself, is missing from this.

Will we conclude from this argument that sublime emotion is contrary to the hygiene of thought? On the subject of the well-being of the body, Kant, in the third "Conflict of the Faculties," observes that the body's well-being is never determinable in experience and that one has only an Idea of it. As for thought, its true well-being is to be ill with the absolute. Thought is in a "good state" only when this "state" signals to thought its vocation, which is to think the absolute, but with the resistance that the "fundamental measure" of all presentation opposes to the actuality of the absolute. The feeling of its destination and its deception can lead to a "delirium." But this delirium is good because it is remissible first of all, and above all because it makes the absolute "almost intuitable" (*gleichsam anschaulich*: 106; *102*) for a moment.

Simplicity

One last term deserves examination, which the General Remark seems to introduce in passing: this is "simplicity" (*die Einfalt*: 128; *123*). The German word evokes not only what is not complex but also what is not subtle: candor, and even foolishness. The word is inserted here without any apparent reason, following the passage devoted to the distinction between delirium and mania. Simplicity, we read, "is, as it were [*gleichsam*], the style adopted by nature in the sublime" (ibid.). It is an "artless finality" (*kunstlose Zweckmäßigkeit*) and as such, that is, as nature without art, it is also the style "of morality."

This brusque observation echoes the dispute that swept intellectual Europe and occupied it at the time, whether the sublime style is the "grand style" in the sense of ancient rhetoric or, on the contrary, the absence of all style. What is at stake in this controversy is, once again, the conflict between an aesthetic of "presence" and the pagan poetics of good form. The treatise of Longinus was hesitant. Boileau, its translator, orients himself more clearly in the direction of the thesis of simplicity as he multiplies his observations on Longinus. Fénelon opts without hesitation for bareness. The phrase of predication is all the more sublime in that it is stripped of ornament, of embellishment, of artifice, as if it came straight from the mouth of the predicator, from the divine voice.

In Kant this is the "artless finality" of sublime style: without artifice.

But let us remember that this candid "style" belongs to morality.
Thus there would be an aesthetic of morality, or at least touching
on morality. In context, it could only be the aesthetic of the sublime: "the intellectual and intrinsically final (moral) Good, estimated aesthetically, instead of being represented as beautiful, must,
rather, be represented as sublime" (123; *119*). That is, it must be
represented as affecting thought in a way that is double, in fear
and in exaltation. We will see that this is not the last word the critique has to say about the aesthetic of morality (see Chapter 9, pp.
234–39). Thus the thesis of simplicity declares that this very complex duality of sensations, which requires nothing less than a dynamical synthesis to be correctly determined, is simplicity itself.
This duality is simple owing to its occasion, the magnitude or the
power that can arouse this complex feeling. The spontaneity of
this complex feeling is simple, just as virtue is simple. None of
this needs embellishment, or even a particular intention; it is without design and without art (*unabsichtlich und ohne Kunst*: 125; *120*).
It is what we call natural. Morality itself is like something natural
in thought, "a second (supersensible) nature." Thinking knows its
"laws," without having an "intuition" of the "supersensible faculty"
within it to legitimate them (128; *123*).

This simplicity announces neither the end of art nor the beginning of ethics. As style, it belongs to the aesthetic. It is the sign
made by the absolute in the forms of nature and in human mores,
in *Sittlichkeit*. The absolute sign in all simplicity. In art, the formulation of the absolute under this sign gives rise to various
"schools," suprematism, abstraction, minimalism, etc., in which
the absolute can signal itself simply in presentation. Morality, on
the other hand, considered in itself, has no style at all. Style is a
manner of presentation destined to affect thought. But moral law
affects thought without affecting it and without manner; moral
law occupies thought directly without any presentation by its
"presence" alone, which is respect. Respect is the absolute in "negative presentation" in the sense that presentation is intrinsically

absent in respect. Respect is such a strange feeling that no object, even an immoderate or formless one, can provoke it, so strange that it escapes the values of pleasure and displeasure. But for this very reason it is the absolute model of the simple feeling that sublime art (vainly) attempts to arouse. This art would have to be "foolish," the way nature is in its magnitude or its "rude" force.

§7 Aesthetics and Ethics in the Beautiful and the Sublime

Delight

Usage, interest, benefit, sacrifice: the text of the *Critiques* works its themes, the true, the Good, the beautiful, with the help of operators (the ones we have just mentioned, but there are others—for example, incitement, incentive) borrowed from the world of economics. Even *Vermögen* makes one think of a potential financier or industrialist. This is because there is an economy of the faculties. We caught a glimpse of it when we discussed animation (see Chapter 2, pp. 60–67). It always intervenes on two occasions: when the cooperation of the faculties must be elaborated and when it is a matter of understanding how "the facultary" in general, which is only a power, comes to be actualized in empirical reality. It intervenes when it is a matter of knowing how the capital of the thinking powers is invested, "realized" in acts.

By pointing to interest in sublime feeling, we touch on a nerve center of the "organism" or flow chart of the faculties. The analysis of the beautiful allows one to hope for the advent of a subject as unity of the faculties, and for a legitimation of the agreement of real objects with the authentic destination of this subject, in the Idea of nature. A meteor dropped into the work devoted to this twofold project, the Analytic of the Sublime, a "mere appendage" (93; *90*; see Chapter 2, pp. 50–56), seems to put an end to these hopes. Yet what is of interest in sublime feeling is precisely what detonates this disappointment.

The feeling of the beautiful is a reflective judgment, singular with claims to the universal: immediate, disinterested. It only involves a faculty of the soul, that of pleasure and displeasure. It takes place on the occasion of a form. On this point its fate as disinterested pleasure is played out. For if it proceeded from the merest attachment to the matter of the given, to a color, to a tone, it would regress to an "agreeableness," to the kind of pleasure that results from a gratified "inclination." The object would have exerted on the mind a "charm" through its existence here and now (65–68; *62–66*).

Charm is a case of interest—the empirical, "pathological" case. The will's maxim, what we would call the finality of desire, is dictated by the "enjoyment" (*Genießen*: 45; *43*) of the object. Thinking feels an interest in the existence of the object (43–46; *41–43*). Thinking feels an interest for an empirical object, an interest in serfdom, and a pleasure in dependence.

One might think it sufficient to discriminate between pure taste and impure taste to emancipate aesthetic pleasure from the enjoyment of the object. One might think it sufficient to distinguish *Reflexionsgeschmack* (the taste of reflection) from *Sinnengeschmack* (the taste of the senses: 54; *52*). Reflection in general, especially in this exemplary "turn" of the immediate judgment in the beautiful, i.e., feeling, excludes all interest defined by a submission of the will to a determined object. Reflection in general consists in judging without the determination of a criterion, without categorical rules of judgment, and thus without being able to anticipate the kind of object or the unique object that could provide pleasure.

However, in distinguishing between tastes according to the faculties of knowledge (determinant judgment belongs to understanding, reflective judgment to the faculty of judgment), one overlooks another distinction made by the "mental faculties" (39; *36*) according to whether they are pure or empirically applied. Kant opposes three kinds of delight (in the broad sense), three kinds of relations to the feeling of pleasure and displeasure. An object can "gratify" (*vergnügen*), it can simply "please" (*gefallen*), it can be "esteemed, approved" (*geschätzt, gebilligt werden*: 49; 47). The object is then called agreeable, beautiful, or good, respectively. The incentive that corresponds to this object for thought is, respectively, inclination, favor, or respect. Favor alone, thus accorded the beautiful, is a "disinterested and *free* delight," writes Kant, "the only free liking" (49; 47). The taste of the senses presupposes inclination, and wants gratification in the strict sense; the taste of the senses is interested in the agreeable. The taste of reflection presupposes favor. "Pleasure" (*Gefallen*) is its lot. And the beautiful is the "object" that is allotted. The German word *Gefallen* is indicative of how the beautiful befalls it, falls from the sky, is not expected. One is neither ready nor prepared for it. To speak of this ingenuousness of delight (in general), French has the expression: "a happiness" (*un bonheur*) which is not happiness see Chapter 2, pp. 60–67). Disinterest is the condition for "happinesses" (*avoir des bonheurs*). But not a guarantee. "Genius" is the "happy relation" between the powers of knowledge (*besteht . . . in dem glücklichen Verhältnisse*: 179; *172*); it cannot be taught and cannot be learned. Genius is to the creation of forms what taste is to their estimation.

Two further remarks on the subject of this distinction. When aesthetic judgment is applied empirically, it may be that "what has already pleased of itself and without regard to any interest whatsoever" thereafter arouses an interest for its existence, for the existence of this something (155; *147–48*). Thus, for example, the inclination to live in society can take over from pure aesthetic pleasure: sociability finds it can realize itself through taste, for taste involves the demand to be communicable to all (155; *148–49*). Nevertheless, one must separate this latter demand, which is inscribed *a priori* in the transcendental analysis of aesthetic feeling, from all empirical inclination to communicate this feeling. In short, one must recognize that the promise of a universal communication of taste, which is analytically attached to taste, is not due to any interest for a determinable community (156; *149*). Pure "favor" cannot be an inclination, or else the beautiful would be agreeable and there would be no aesthetic pleasure.

This argument emerges from the distinction between the transcendental and the empirical. But it also calls forth, and this is the second observation, the differences between the "mental faculties." Delight in the strict sense gratifies an inclination. It involves an economy, which is one of desire. Delight implies that there was a lack and a time awaiting its suppression, satiation, the "enough," the *genug* that can be heard in *Vergnügung*. However, taste did not wait for anything in order to take place. If it obeys a finality, even a transcendental analysis could not produce the determined concept of its end, of the object that would satisfy it. Taste is not determined. This does not mean it is infinite. But the delight in which taste consists is independent of any leaning. There is no desire for the beautiful. It is either one or the other, desire or beauty. That is to say: it is either the faculty of desire or the faculty of pleasure and displeasure. Moreover, it is no easy task for us Westerners, haunted as we are by the passion of the will, to think that this liking or this grace, this *Gunst*, is not sought after. A pleasure "first" takes place, which does not come to satisfy anything and which cannot disappoint anything. Its occurrence is not relative to anything. It is an incentive, a "favor," that nothing prompts.

I return to the three delights. The third, "esteemed" and "approved," has for its incentive respect and for its object the Good. The relations of the aesthetic and the ethical are already in play in the pleasure of esteem as compared with the happiness of taste. With this localization, the point of intersection of the sublime with transcendental sentimentality can already be determined. The object, the Good, is made equivalent to that of an empirical need, at least with regard to the constraint it imposes. Favor alone provides a "free liking." Respect, as we have seen, is itself a free affection. But the law and its prescription, be it only a form of the actions to accomplish, impose on the will interest for certain objects. As we are in the practical realm, under the law "of action," these objects are actions or, rather, because the law is a formal one, maxims of action. And prescription makes them of great interest. "For where moral law dictates, there is, objectively, no room left for free choice as to what one has to do" (50; *47*). There is a return of the constraint imposed by the object, even if subjectively and empirically the "good maxims," that is, good objects, remain to be determined according to the case.

There is constraint because there is a return of the faculty of desire. "Esteem," in this regard, is subject to the same fate as "satiation" (*Vergnügung*), which is the fate proper to the faculty of desire: to attain what "is good" (46; *43–44*). In what it is reasonable to judge good, one does indeed distinguish the *wozu gut* and the *an sich gut,* the "good for" and the "good in itself," but both presuppose the "concept of an end." One must still put aside what is useful (the "good for"), the agreeable in which reason has no part (KPV, 59–65; *68–74*). At the two extremes of delight, the agreeable and the good—passing through the useful—however different they may be with regard to reason, have a common trait that distinguishes them from aesthetic pleasure: interest, "an interest in their object" (48; *46*). Even pure moral Good does not differ from the others except in the quality of the interest that it arouses: pure moral Good calls forth "the highest interest" (ibid.). Moreover, this resemblance resides in the will, which sets aesthetic pleasure apart from the rest. For where there is will, there is interest: "To will something and to take delight in its existence, i.e., to take an interest in it, are identical" (ibid.).

The Beautiful, Symbol of the Good

The disjunction between the aesthetic and the ethical seems final. This disjunction responds to the heterogeneity of the two "mental faculties" that are in play, the feeling of pleasure and displeasure and the faculty of desire, respectively. Yet in the third *Critique* the object is to bridge the power of knowledge and the power of will, and the feeling in question, the aesthetic feeling, is to serve as the central pillar upon which to build a double-arched bridge between these powers. It would seem here that the first arch had failed to materialize, the one that was supposed to open the way from will to feeling. What prevents one from building it is interest. At the same time all hope of unifying thought in a "subject," of unifying its manifold powers, disappears. There will always be a differend between "to taste" and "to desire." And thus not one but two heteronomous subjects, the one that is constantly born to itself (see pp. 181–87 below) without being interested in doing so, without wanting it, in the pure pleasure of the beautiful, and the one that is always held to act in the interest of the realization of the law.

This divorce cannot be concluded without much debate. The critical judge multiplies the conciliation procedures, in particular in paragraphs 42 and 59, which have been read as if they discussed Kant's "thesis" on the problem. The feeling of the beautiful, it seems, conceals an interest in the end, an "intellectual interest" (§42, 157; *149*), to be understood non-empirically. The feeling of the beautiful conceals an interest precisely in realizing what moral law prescribes, an "intellectual" interest because it is attached to the "object" that practical reason prescribes to the will for it to realize the Good (158–61; *151–53*). Moreover, in paragraph 59 this thesis is reaffirmed in greater detail, and it seems possible to rebuild the missing arch of the bridge by means of a particular construction of great service in critical strategy. The construction allows one to span the "abysses" created by the heteronomy of the faculties. It is called hypotyposis, *subjectio ad aspectum*, a submission to sight, i.e., the operation that consists in putting in view something that (analogically) corresponds to an invisible object (§59, 221–25; *211–15*). Which is the case of the object of an Idea of reason, unpresentable in intuition, but of which one can present an intuitive analogue, which is then a "symbol." Beauty can thus be "the symbol of the morally good" (223; *213*).

The way being thus opened, more than one thinker, hastily concluding the Good from the beautiful, has rushed forward and succeeded in crossing the bridge (despite the many warnings of Kant) in order to reimplant the metaphysical bridgehead on critical soil, in order to reaffirm the archaic argument, archaic for Western thought, according to which the outcome, having moved from the beautiful to the Good, is the Good and that in *feeling* the Good, one will *do* good. Furthermore, in making the beautiful felt, one will make others do good. In shaping the given according to the beautiful, with taste, one preaches the individual *ethos* or the community *politikon*. The way toward an "aesthetic education," which was lost for a moment, is reopened without taking any account of the explicit reservation Kant incessantly opposes to a conclusive use of analogy. As when he writes, for example: "In the case of two dissimilar things we may admittedly form some *conception* of one of them by an *analogy* which it bears to the other, and to do so even on the point on which they are dissimilar; but from that in which they are dissimilar we cannot draw any *inference* from one to the other on the strength of the analogy" ([Part II] 136–37; *337–38*). One can in short say that "*as* the beautiful, *so* the good," but not "*if* the beautiful, *then* the good" (or the reverse). An aesthetic ethics and politics are in advance unauthorized, according to this reservation. They are exactly what Kant calls a transcendental "illusion" or "appearance."

I would add conversely that one should not confuse the aspiration, the call by which thought is affected, the debt that it accepts to contract when it engages in the realization of the beautiful work—in what we would call writing, in a literary and artistic sense, maintained at least under the demand of the beautiful—one should not confuse this obedience with listening to the moral law, with the feeling of the duty to act according to the principle of universalization that it involves as prescriptive reason or as sole rational dictate (see Chapter 5, pp. 123–27). To make the work directly a testament to the law, one occults the aesthetic difference; one obscures a territory, that of beautiful forms, and what is at stake in them, the pure pleasure that they provide, both of which need to be protected from any interference. In this sense "writing," making the beautiful out of words, is not a manner, not even a hopeless one, of settling with the law. Even as a "negative presentation" (see Chapter 6, pp. 150–53), a "sublime" writing would not be equivalent to an action. In other words, the "antinomy of reason . . . for *the feeling of pleasure and displeasure*" should not be confused with the "antinomy of reason . . . *for the faculty of desire*" (214; *204*). The "aesthetic use of judgment" is not the "practical employment of self-legislative reason" (ibid.).

The principle of the heterogeneity of the faculties prevents one from confusing the beautiful with the good. It dispels the illusion that subordinates the feeling of pleasure and displeasure to the faculty of knowledge. It also dispels the illusion "that the judgment of taste is in fact a disguised judgment of reason on the perfection discovered in a thing" (ibid.), that is, the difference between the two judgments being reduced to the "distinction" between them (70; *68*): taste is a "confused . . . concept" (*verworrener Begriff*) of an object, the perfection of which is "clearly defined" (*deutlicher Begriff*: ibid.) in principle. This is a Leibnizian thesis against which the whole of the third *Critique* argues according to a general strategy that autonomizes space-time in relation to understanding and autonomizes reflection in relation to determination, a strategy already begun in the first *Critique* (see Chapter 1, pp. 32–35).

The initial confusion of the good and the beautiful that the critique dispels should also discourage all "philosophy of the will" beginning with the "will to power," which reduces ethics and politics to "values" and thus authorizes itself to treat them as equal to "forms." "Affirmation" in Nietzsche is to be understood as formation, as artistic creation. The good and secondarily the true are supported only by their "beauty." This is an extreme expression of the obsession to shape, no more authorized, following the critique, than that of a preestablished harmony. This always forces the unity of being.

Let us return to our bridge. The analogical construction is far from being the basis of a true bridge. We have just evoked some of the perils that a thought too quickly engaged along this fragile passage is sure to encounter. Kant tries to consolidate the passage because the unification for which he aims, that of the system, has a great need for it (see Chapter 1, pp. 1–8). I will examine the strategy of this consolidation. We will be better able to gauge its scope when we situate sublime feeling in relation to ethics.

The Analogy of the Beautiful with the Good as It Is Logically Argued

There are two sets of arguments, of two different sorts. The first set of arguments calls attention to the transcendental properties common to aesthetic and moral judgment, to the similar aspects of the two that permit such an analogy to be made. I will call these arguments *logical* because they limit themselves to comparing the two judgments according to what transcendental logic alone permits. The other set of arguments, on the contrary, appeals to the regulative Idea of a nature finalized according to the model of art. The arguments use the "guiding thread" that the teleological critique draws from the concrete texture of the existences that make up the world. We will call them *teleological* with the reservation required by the use of this term in Kant's work, and in the third *Critique* in particular. They follow, or at least accompany, the elaboration of the Idea of nature in the latter *Critique*, whereas the first kind of argument is foreign to it and one might say prior to it.

The distinction between these two kinds of argument is made in paragraph III of the Introduction to our *Critique*. The faculty of judging, it is written, must make a transition, an *Übergang*, between the realm of nature and the realm of freedom "just as [*eben-sowohl als*] in its logical employment [*im logischen Gebrauch*] it makes possible the transition from understanding to reason" (17; *15*). The first transition requires a teleological principle, the second the simple, logical extension of the concept beyond experience. Nonetheless, it is a matter of unifying the true and the good, and not, as we have here, the beautiful and the good, that is, the faculty of judging with practical reason.

Logically, the beautiful and the good have a family resemblance. They please immediately, without or before any interest, according to a free relation of the faculties to which they respectively belong; they are judged according to a mode of necessity, as universally communicable (224–25; *214–15*). These similarities, a little forced, require correction, according to Kant. These corrections are such that the difference between the good and the beautiful is as marked as before. The concept of the law is what inspires moral feeling without mediation; it is an inconceivable form of the imagination, at least for a moment, which is the occasion for taste. (One is indeed "forced" *before* knowing what it is one is forced to, although the law that forces is conceivable.) The will is free in morality, in that it is subordinate to a prescription of rational form (the "typic" of legality: KPV, 70–74; *79–84*); whereas in taste the imagination is free. The imagination produces new forms way "beyond" what is "conformable to the concept" that limits the schema (179; *171*), to such an extent that it creates "as it were, a second nature out of the material supplied to it by actual nature" (176; *168*). This freedom incites or excites the understanding to compete in conception with the creativity of the imagination. From this results a "play" between the faculties that is itself "free," a "furtherance," a *Beförderung* (143; *137*). The claim of singular taste to a universal communication is not supported by the authority of any concept, whereas the universalization of the maxim is analytically required in the very definition of the concept of the law. The beautiful concedes nothing to interest, which I distinguish here as the final term in the comparison: "it pleases *apart from all interest*," whereas the "morally good is . . . necessarily bound up with an interest" (224; *214*).

The opposition is not, however, as radical as I have made it out to be, even in the logical argument. The good is bound to an interest, but this interest does not precede moral judgment, but results from it (ibid.). This specification is repeated: practical judgment is not "founded" on any interest, "*though here it produces one*" (159; *152*). This reversal of the position of interest is essential to the critique of morality. The law does not *result* from the interest of the will in the good, it dictates it. This is the "paradox of method": "*The concept of good and evil is not defined prior to the moral law, to which, it would seem, the former would have to serve as foundation; rather, the concept of good and evil must be defined after and by means of the law*" (KPV, 65; *74*). If in morality the will aimed for the good as its object "before" the good was prescribed to it, the will would be subordinated to this good object, just as it is to an empirical, desirable, agreeable, or useful object. There would then be no transcendental difference between *pathos* and pure *ethos*. Only a difference of object. In both cases, one would have an imperative on condition, which is the condition of the object, thus "interested," hypothetical. If you want this (the good or chocolate), do that.

To escape this ruinous consequence, that is, "heteronomy" (KPV, 67; *76*), which is ruinous for ethical difference and leads to skepticism or cynicism (some like the good, others like chocolate), the order of determination must be reversed. The law "immediately" grasps the will by obligation, without regard to any object. Thus it only prescribes prescription itself to the will. The law's *dictum* (its content) is reduced to the commandment, without object. According to its *modus* (the modality of the prescription), it must necessarily prescribe the prescription. The law is posed as being unable not to be posed. Consequently it must be the law for every moral "subject," for all the you's. It is universally imposed.

The same can be said for the judgment of taste. All must judge what I judge beautiful to be beautiful. "The judgment of taste exacts agreement from everyone; and a person who describes something as beautiful insists that everyone *ought* [solle] to give the object in question his approval and follow suit in describing it as beautiful" (82; *79*). Kant underlines the analogy: "The feeling in the judgment of taste comes to be exacted [*zugemutet*] from everyone as a sort of duty [*gleichsam als Pflicht*]" (154; *147*). The analogy goes so far as to assimilate an important property of aesthetic interest to one of moral interest: the interest, which the thought that judges the beautiful has in its object, is "immediate" (*unmittelbares Interesse*), "just the same" (*gleichmäßiges... sowie*) as the interest it takes in its object when it judges the good (161; *153*).

The analogy must, however, stop here. The "interests" in play in aesthetic judgment and in moral judgment are similarly immediate, although aesthetic judgment is "free" and moral judgment is "founded on objective laws" (160; *153*). One could say that moral law does not prescribe *what* is good, but, on the contrary, leaves judgment free (responsible) to decide on the object that deserves to be esteemed good. This is why the interest moral law has in this object is immediate, not determined by a prior concept of the good. But this same immediate interest results from the "presence," in the thought that wants or desires, of the Idea of absolute causality. This "presence" is respect. It is what determines, not the object of morality, but the will to realize morality. Thus in ethics interest is "founded," merely founded, on a concept of reason, that of freedom, which the law transcribes by prescribing *that* this freedom be made real. This Idea is absolutely universal, because its object, first causality, is an absolute. The law can thus specify not *what* must be done for it to be realized but that, whatever one does, it must be done "in such a way that" any will will also want to do it in order to realize freedom. The prescription to universalize the maxim— according to which the will decides on an object that it judges good (an action to accomplish)—is inherent in the law because the law is moral, that is to say, because it is absolute causality as it is exercised on and in the thought that desires.

If the good is interesting, it is because freedom must be realized, and this is what the law says. But the beautiful is only "interesting" insofar as reflective thought has no interest in it. "No interest, whether of sense or reason, extorts approval" (49; *47*). Taste's demand to be communicable to all would not be a *Sollen* identical to that of moral duty except if this universalization were "of itself" (*an sich*) to "carry with it an interest for us" (*schon ein Interesse für uns bei sich führen müsse*: 154; *147*). However, only the universalization of the moral maxim has in and of itself the power to carry an interest for thought. We have just seen how and why. It is because it proceeds from an Idea, from the Idea of reason that contains the demand for its realization by the will. Its power or, rather, the necessity is such that "we are not entitled to draw [it] as a conclusion [*schließen*] from the character [*aus der Beschaffenheit*] of a merely reflective judgment [*bloß reflektierenden*]" (ibid.). We are not entitled to draw it as a conclusion from a power of thought that is not supported by a universal concept of judging the beautiful—and certainly not by the concept of absolute causality that carries the dictate to realize its object. We are not entitled to draw it as a conclusion from a power of thought that thinks completely otherwise and does not have at its disposal the force to oblige "everyone" (*jedermann*), either in or of itself, or for us.

If there is a cousinship between the two judgments, it must be "à la mode de Bretagne," constructed upon an improbable analogy.

One would need for "it to go over" into the Good from the beautiful. But according to strict transcendental logic "it goes over" rather badly. There is no interest at all, but, rather, sentimental immediacy, in taste. In ethics there is interest, which is undoubtedly secondary but secondary because, precisely, it is deduced from the concept of the law; in ethics there is interest that is "mediatized"—an implicit interest. Interest is what results in ethics. Disinterest is what initiates in aesthetics.

The Nerve of the Teleological Argument

Does the argument that I have called *teleological* better attest to the kinship of the beautiful with the good? The reasoning as follows:

1. The mind has no interest in the law. But the law commands it to do good, and interests it in "acts" that are capable of actualizing the good. (This demand to actualize is exercised, furthermore, over all of the faculties, which, of themselves, are but "optional" possibilities.)

2. The mind has no interest in the beautiful. But the beautiful occurs, and this gives pure reflective (disinterested) judgment the opportunity to be exercised, to be realized, as the sensation of pure pleasure. What furnishes this opportunity seems to be art, which produces the beautiful. But on the condition that art itself solicit no interest, and thus that it obey no interest.

3. Moreover, the model for disinterested actualization of the beautiful is furnished by "nature." It expects no gain, that we know of, from the landscapes, the harmonies it offers to the mind. It has no concept of the end it aims at producing the beautiful. Art is pure only if it produces works the way "nature" does, itself the paradigm of pure art.

4. "Nature" as artist and/or work of art in providing occasions for pure aesthetic pleasure (of taste) for the mind thus attests that a disinterested judgment or activity that is merely possible can be actualized. Thus it shows itself favorable to the demand to actual-

ize the possible in general, the "facultary" or the optional. In particular to the demand to actualize the faculty of acting in a disinterested way, i.e., rational will.

5. Thus practical reason discovers an interest in the disinterested pleasure aroused by "natural" beauty (157–61; *149–52*; and KPV, 124–26; *138–40*).

Such is the thrust of the "teleological" argument by which critical thought supports the affinity of the beautiful with the good. One might be tempted to give it a dialectically logical turn: an (ethical) interest for (aesthetic) disinterest. But this dialectic would not be critical. The critique is held to explaining the condition of the so-called dialectic, and this condition is not "conceptual" in the Hegelian sense; it is the regulative Idea of a nature finalized (as an art can be) upon the actualization of the mental powers. Far from authorizing a logic of negation that would in its own way homogenize the "yes" and the "no," that is, interest and disinterest here, in a movement of "supercession" (see Chapter 5, pp. 127–31), this Idea must on the contrary, according to the critique, establish its legitimacy (be "deduced" in the Kantian sense: KRV, 120; *126*). The deduction reveals the exercise of a third faculty, that of reflective judgment, which, to be in play in knowledge and morality, disposes of its own *Boden*, its own territory of legislation (15; *13*), art and nature, where it is "purely" exercised in a way that is "appropriate to it." This does indeed complicate the matter of unification, which is consequently in suspension because of the "indemonstrable" Idea (210–12; *201–2*) of a natural teleology of art— and which is required to include a supplementary faculty in the synthesis of the first two. Thus it is critically that one must examine the play of interest and disinterest that allows one in principle to bring together or pair (to "bridge") aesthetic favor and ethical respect. An examination that is all the more "useful," for it reveals the exact point at which sublime feeling scrambles the play by breaking the fragile alliance between the two "delights." The consequences that the localization of this fracture may have both on the Idea of "nature" and on the general project of constituting the mind as a subjective unity are easy to establish. Only the first set of consequences will be treated here. We will only point to the second set concerning the subject.

"Facultary" Interest and Primacy of the Practical

One must begin again with the faculty's demand to actualize. This demand extends to all the powers, all the faculties of the mind. They are only possibilities. How do they become mental acts? How is it that on a certain occasion (at the "right moment"), understanding or, rather, taste or perhaps the will is exercised? How is the divide between *posse* and *esse* crossed? It is crossed precisely by "interest."

In the second *Critique*, Kant seeks to establish the primacy of pure practical reason over pure speculative reason (KPV, 124–26; *138–40*). This primacy, he explains, cannot be intrinsic. One cannot say that the practical usage of reason affords further insight than its theoretical usage. Further in itself. One feels like saying: a "better" ontological grasp.

Formulated critically, this primacy is not metaphysical, or even transcendental. They are the conditions according to which a power of thought *can*. It would be absurd to claim that some conditions are more "radical" than others. On the other hand, when it is a matter of effecting *any* one of these powers, it is permitted, and it is even inevitable, to ask why on a particular occasion the "exercise" of a given faculty takes place and why a particular power, rather than another, finds "employment." The term "employment," frequently repeated along with "interest" and "incentive" throughout the *Critiques*, should be examined. The employment of a faculty is like the transformation of its transcendental "value" into mental acts such as production and consumption. The faculty is what the rules of the game permit, and its use is the shot one takes, to speak like Wittgenstein. This transformation, this realization which is similar to that of the transformation of currency into goods, is dictated by an interest. Interest is the "principle that contains the condition under which alone its [each of the "mental powers"] exercise is advanced" (KPV, 124; *138*). Interest does not therefore consist in the "mere agreement [of reason] with itself" according to each of its faculties (that the status of its "*a priori* conditions" fixes), but "only [in] its extension [*Erweiterung*]" (ibid.). The interest in the employment of a faculty is an interest with regard to the faculty itself: in employing it, thought carries out its potential, "realizes" its credit, as much as possible. Thus it "extends, enlarges" the scope of the faculty by manifesting its power *in actu*. The faculty is like a bank of possible judgments; it is in its best interest that an entrepreneur dig into the resources of the bank to make use of them.

But the entrepreneur needs an "incentive." In experience this incentive is the flip side of facultary interest. The entrepreneur needs a kind of incitement to invest in the facultary power. The interest of the bank to "realize" must be matched by an interest of reality to invest in a facultary power, an interest of empirical thought to register the mark of one of its powers in experience. This interest is not *a priori*; it must be calculated. It must be calculated because empirical thought, when it actualizes one of its powers, always takes a risk, the risk of a loss. An interest "can never be attributed to a being which lacks reason; it indicates an incentive of the will so far as it is presented by reason" (KPV, 82; *93*). A reasonable calculation must be made because the actualization of a power of thought is not without risk for empirical thought. The risk of bankruptcy, of a dead loss, a deficit. The debit balance threatens the actualization of a rational potential, because obstacles oppose the actualization. "All three concepts—of incentive, interest, and maxim [which would be the strategy of the entrepreneur in the metaphor]—can, however, be applied only to finite beings. For without exception they presuppose a limitation of the nature of being . . . that being must be impelled [*angetrieben*] in some manner to action [this is the incitement to invest], since an internal obstacle stands against it" (KPV, 82; *93*). When thought is interested *by* the actualization of one of its faculties, it is interested *in* it: the actualization becomes thought's rational incentive and thought has to sacrifice any other interest that is not reasonable, that is rationally impure. This is why rational interest must be negotiated. The entrepreneur is not a saint.

In the passage I am discussing, Kant analyzes the incentive and the interest of, for, and in rational morality; he analyzes the incentive that incites one to do good and the interest that this incitement (the maxim) can have for thought. The obstacle is easy to discern: what has to be set apart in and by the actualization of practical reason, in and by the "employment" of moral law, is the pleasure taken by the empirical ego in itself, its preference for itself, its conceit. "The representation of moral law deprives self-love [*der Selbstliebe*] of its influence and self-conceit [*dem Eigendünkel*] of its delusion [*den Wahn*]" (KPV, 78, t.m.; *89*). Kant does not have the words to explain what thinking must "sacrifice" to realize moral law. However, one would be wrong in emphasizing the calculation of the sacrifices to be made in view of actualizing the good prescribed by the law. One would be confusing respect with enthusiasm, ethics with sublime aesthetics. This is the whole question.

Practical reason is interested in its actualization not merely as a faculty, like all the other faculties beginning with understanding. It is interested in its actualization because it is practical, that is, it carries in its intrinsic condition of possibility, in the imperative form of the law, the obligation to be realized. "Act": this is what practical reason prescribes to practical thought (to empirical will) and this means nothing other than—actualize me. But in order to obtain this effect, there must be an incentive in the will capable of overcoming the internal obstacles, i.e., the preestablished incentives, that is, the will's attachment to the empirical ego.

The interest of practical reason can only be understood if practical reason creates in the ego an "interest" relieved of its choice object, the ego itself. But "to relieve" not only implies changing the object of interest and reorienting the interest in the ego to the law, it also implies transforming the nature of the interest. For what rational law requires is *its* interest and not the interest of the ego. Moreover, this interest induces, from the empirical point of view, a paradoxical incentive, a "disinterest." It does not offer the ego a new object of cathexis, in whose appropriation it might have something to gain. The law itself cannot be this object. It does not offer the ego any "content" that would allow for the ego's own interest to overdetermine (including by "sublimation" in the Freudian sense) the interest of the law. It must not permit the least ambiguity in the obedience it requires. In listening to the law, the ego cannot hope for any advantage in happiness, in pride, and the like. It must fall in with the law without any (empirical) subjective interest. Thus it must produce in itself a disinterested incentive without "pathos," without calculation. Such is the interest *of* the practical rational faculty: it must actualize itself without arousing an empirical interest *for* it (KPV, 78–79; *88–89*).

Incentive and interest are less clearly circumscribed with regard to the theoretical power of reason in the first *Critique* and I will leave them aside here (KRV, 422–30; *470–80*). What is certain is that they are different from the incentive and interest that cause practical reason to be "exercised." This is why there is a problem as to the *Verbindung* (KPV, 124; *138*) of interests, their connection to one another. The problem is not dramatic according to Kant in the sense of one interest having to "give precedence" to the other. It might be if theoretical interest and practical interest "contradict[ed]" each other (ibid.), which is not necessarily the case. The question is only one of hierarchy or "primacy": Which is the "highest" interest, to extend knowledge or to extend morality?

We know the answer: without undermining the inner functioning and interest of knowledge, the primacy of interest belongs to practical reason. But the argument backing this primacy deserves some attention. The hegemony of the practical is not due, or not solely, as we are in the habit of saying, to ethics being what alone gives to thought a necessary access—by obligation, that is, by intimation of moral law—to the supersensible, i.e., freedom (the absolute of causality). Knowledge does not lead to the supersensible (the absolute of the world) except by a "maximization" of its concepts (KRV, 449–54; *504–10*), which is inevitable but without cognitive use: the "precept to advance toward completeness by an ascent to ever-higher conditions" (*Vorschrift, sich . . . der Vollständigkeit derselben zu nähern*: KRV, 307, t.m.; *346*) is also what turns the concepts into Ideas that cannot be determined by intuition, "indemonstrable" (210; *201*). No, hegemony is first a tautol-

ogy. "Nor could we reverse the order [of the subordination of speculative reason to practical reason] and expect practical reason to
submit to speculative reason, because every interest is ultimately
practical" (KPV, 126; *140*).

Every interest is practical. On the one hand, transcendental interest attests to a sort of "need" to actualize the faculty, a pressure
on the possible to be realized, which is pure *prattein*. We might
say: a kind of facultary "will to be" (which would require further
examination). And on the other hand, on the side of the empirical,
this facultary "will" cannot be effected unless it can make itself
heard by a thought immersed in the world of empirical interests,
conditions, and charms. This thought must "pay attention"
(*Achtung*, respect), have regard for the facultary "pressure" (whatever it may be), be "mobilized" by this pressure. Such is precisely
the condition of actualizing the facultary power, considered from
the point of view of a reasonable, practical, and finite being: the
being must be moved by this power.

Thus even the interest of speculative reason is "only conditional"
(KPV, 126; *140*). This does not mean that science passes into the
service of morality. But what actualizes knowledge, what prompts
scientific research (according to its own rules, of course, and not
according to moral law), what extends its realm, this very thing is
dependent on a transcendental interest right at first, on a "will to
effect" the potential of understanding; it is dependent on a will to
"use," on an impatience to perform cognitive feats, in order to establish in the world a knowledge about it. In the empirical, the
realization of knowledge requires the other "interest" that corresponds or responds to a speculative interest of reason, an "incentive," the "subjective determining ground of a will" (KPV, 74; *84*),
which is not immediately omniscient (benevolent when it is a matter of actualizing the Good), and whose theoretical (or practical)
rational spontaneity is hindered and must be "incited." The will of
a being that has constitutively to do with ignorance (or with
meanness). (And perhaps, as it involves the interest of the reflective
faculty, with ugliness, with what is disgusting, with the insipid?)

In morality, the obstacles to be overcome are the likings that in-

hibit the exercise of good will. Empirical will is always already invested in and fixated on "charms." It is preoccupied. The purely
reasonable, practical incentive can only arise accompanied by
"pain" (KPV, 75; *85*), by mourning objects that are captivating, by
losing fixed cathexes. This mourning must affect the "object" that
is an obstacle to the good incentive, the obstacle to respect par excellence: "the self" (*das Selbst*: KPV, 77; *87*), which nevertheless,
according to Freud, stays on, and supports itself with the loss of
captivating objects. This dark side of respect is the "humiliation" of
"pretensions," of the empirical ego's "conceit," of the overestima-
tion of the self by the self (ibid.). Narcissism must be thrown off,
overcome. The ego feels bound only by duty, affected by respect
for the law, and prepared to realize it, insofar as it feels itself unbound and its "pathological" dependence broken. Dis-occupied.
It never completely accomplishes this. This mourning remains a
melancholy. Dark side, finitude. The will is not holy, and the ill is
radical. However, this is but the obverse of respect, and not its
condition.

Seen in its more favorable light, respect is "an incentive" (KPV,
82; *93*). It is the empirical listening to pure practical reason. It is
the law itself listened to. It is interesting because "from the concept
of an incentive there comes that of an *interest*" (ibid.). This is an
interest independent of empirical interests, "the mere interest in
obedience to the law" (ibid.). This interest is without interest, in
that it does not result from a calculation of enjoyment. "Thus respect for the law is not the incentive to morality [*nicht Triebfeder
zur Sittlichkeit*]; it is morality itself, regarded subjectively as an incentive" (*die Sittlichkeit selbst, subjektiv als Triebfeder betrachtet*:
KPV, 78; *89*). Just like listening to the order to do good, it is the
whole condition of ethics. This is what the German *Achtung* says.
Thus the law makes itself an incentive, in its more favorable light.
As regard.

Achtung is closer to *regard*, a regard for something that is not
there, that is not an object and does not give rise to passionate in-
trigue or to a passion for knowledge or to a passion to desire and
love. It is barely a feeling, which would necessarily be "pathologi-

cal"; it is a "singular" (*sonderbar*) feeling, "of such a peculiar kind" (*so eigentümlicher Art*: ibid.). The law clears a space for its "presence" in the dense texture of the conditioned. Being unconditional, "categorical," it acquires simplicity and levity. The space it clears does not consist in anything. One recognizes the "sign" of the law because regard always stems from duty, whatever the circumstance—even "a humble plain" one (KPV, 79; *90*). Regard is an incentive at rest, a sentimental state *a priori*, an a-pathetic pathos. "The negative effect on feeling . . . is itself feeling" (KPV, 75; *85*). We must recall that apathy, *apatheia*, *Affektlosigkeit*, is to be counted among the sublime feelings, with the advantage over enthusiasm that it has "the delight of pure reason on its side" (125; *120*), which enthusiasm does not, for it contains too much *pathos*. There is a great range of disinterested feelings, a range that goes from pure aesthetic favor to pure ethical regard. And the intermediary "tones" are all sublime.

The Family Story of the Sublime

There are not one but many sublime feelings, as we have seen (see Chapter 6, pp. 153–56): there is an entire family, or, rather, an entire generation. Let me embellish for a moment the story of this *genos*. On the family tree of the "mental faculties" the female parent is a "sensation" (39; *36*), a state of the faculty of pleasure and displeasure, the same as the male parent. But the father is content and the mother is miserable. The sublime child will be sentimentally impaired, contradictory: pain and delight. This is because in the genealogy of the faculties said to be "of knowledge" (in the broad sense, as the powers of thought relate to objects), the parents come from two different families. She is "judgment" and he is "reason." She is an artist and he a moralist. She "reflects" and he "determines." The (paternal) moral law determines itself and determines thought to act. Reason wants good children, requires that just moral maxims be engendered. But the mother, the free, reflective imagination, knows only how to deploy forms without prior rules and without a known or knowable end.

In her relationship with understanding, "before" encountering reason, it so happened that this freedom of "forms" was able to unite with the power to regulate and that from this encounter an exemplary "happiness" was born (see pp. 159–63 above). But in any case no children. Beauty is not the fruit of a contract; rather, it is the flower of love, and, like anything not conceived out of interest, it passes.

The sublime is the child of an unhappy encounter, that of the Idea with form. Unhappy because this Idea is unable to make concessions. The law (the father) is so authoritarian, so unconditional, and the regard the law requires so exclusive that he, the father, will do nothing to obtain consent, even through a delicious rivalry with the imagination. He requires the imagination's "retraction" (see Chapter 6, pp. 147–53). He pushes forms aside, or, rather, forms part before his presence, tear themselves apart, extend themselves to inordinate proportions. He fertilizes the virgin who has devoted herself to forms, without regard for her favor. He demands regard only for himself, for the law and its realization. He has no need for a beautiful nature. He desperately needs an imagination that is violated, exceeded, exhausted. She will die in giving birth to the sublime. She will think she is dying (see Chapter 4, pp. 102–9).

Thus the sublime inherits an air of respect from reason, its father. However, the *Erhabene* is not *Erhebung* (KPV, 83; *94*), is not the pure elation, *Erhabenheit* which the law inspires (ibid., *90*; *102*). Violence and courage (125; *120*) are necessary to the sublime; it tears at itself, undoes itself. Whereas respect simply arises and addresses. Violence must be done to the imagination because it is through its pain, through the mediation of its violation, that the joy of seeing or of almost seeing the law is obtained. The sublime "renders almost intuitable [*gleichsam anschaulich*] the supremacy of our cognitive faculties on the rational side over the greatest faculty of sensibility" (106, t.m.; *102*). Moreover, this "pleasure . . . is only possible through the mediation of a displeasure" (109, t.m.; *105*).

The mourning involved in the respect for the law is the dark side of respect, but not its means. The self cries out because its will is not holy. Yet it is not necessary for the self to cry out. It is a fact of finitude. Respect cannot be measured in sacrifices. The law does not wish anyone any pain; it does not wish anything. The sublime, on the contrary, requires one to suffer. It must cause displeasure. It is "contra-final" (*zweckwidrig*), "ill-adapted." This just makes it more sublime "on that account" (*dennoch nur um desto erhabener zu sein geurteilt wird*: 91, t.m.; *88*). It needs "presentation," which is the function of the imagination, its mother, and "conceit"—the native illness of servile will—in order to manifest their nullity before the greatness of the law.

Teleology in the Beautiful and the Sublime

The reader will perhaps smile at this puerile scenario. Yet it is a "manner" (*Manier*) of exposition (182; *174*) permitted in matters of aesthetics. Let us return to the *modus logicus*, which here is *teleologicus*. Kant is well aware that the cousinship between the good and the sublime is closer than that between the beautiful and the sublime. "Intellectual . . . (moral) good, estimated aesthetically, instead of being represented as beautiful, must rather be represented as sublime [*nicht sowohl schon als vielmehr erhaben vorgestellt*]" (123; *119*). This is the thesis. The effect of this kinship on the status of nature in the sublime aesthetic can be seen as follows: "The concept of the sublime in nature is far less important and rich in consequences [*bei weitem nicht so wichtig und an Folgerungen reichhaltig*] than that of its beauty. It gives on the whole no indication of anything final in nature itself, but only in the possible *employment* of our intuitions of it in inducing a feeling in our own selves of a finality quite independent of nature [*um eine von der Natur ganz unabhängige Zweckmäßigkeit in uns selbst fühlbar zu machen*]": (92–93, t.m.; *89–90*).

The word "employment" (*Gebrauch*) is emphasized in the text. In order to understand its scope, one must return to the teleological argument and to the parallel in the paradox of interests that appears in it between aesthetic favor and ethical regard. I have said that the interest of practical reason is to have itself listened to without interest. This is the respect for the law. The interest of the faculty of reflective judgment is to offer the mind occasions to judge without interest, without pathological inclination, without cognitive incentive, without even the intention of doing good: such is favor for the beautiful. The *employment* of the two faculties, which are heterogeneous in the *a priori* conditions of their respective functioning, requires the same kind of paradoxical *incentive*: a disinterested interest. Favor is less suspect the more beauty—of which it is the occasion—belongs to nature; the law is interested in nature as what spontaneously arouses a disinterested delight (see pp. 171–73 above).

What the teleological argument adds to the strictly analogical, logical argument of the affinity of the beautiful with the good is a gesture. The mind gestures when it enjoys a landscape. Let us call natural beauties *landscapes*, whatever they may be, and stripped, as Kant requires, of their material charms (64–68; *61–66*). They "speak" to us or through them nature "speaks to us figuratively" (*figürlich zu uns spricht*: 160, t.m.; *153*), as a coded writing, a "cipher" (*Chiffreschrift*: ibid.). The code of this writing remains unknown. It is impossible to decode the landscapes, to "give [their] exponents" (*exponieren*: 212; *202*) conceptually. They are accessible only by feeling, by taste. This *only* in itself suggests a retreat, a sidelong look, at the "in our own selves" (*in uns selbst*: 93; *90*). The mind feels a quasi finality, a quasi intentionality, and a quasi regularity in the mute messages, that is, the landscapes. However, "as we never meet with such an end outside ourselves, we naturally look for it in ourselves, and, in fact, in that which constitutes the ultimate end of our existence—the moral side of our being" (160, t.m.; *153*).

This gesturing back is surreptitious. In the sublime we spoke of "subreption" (*Subreption*: 106; *102*) and of a "substitution of a respect for the object in place of one for the idea of humanity in our own self—the subject" (ibid.). It is this projection, this objectification that the Analytic of the Sublime critiques; there are no sublime objects but only sublime feelings (103–5; *100–101*; see also Chapter 2, pp. 67–73). There is already an implicit subreption in taste, but one that works backward, from the objective toward the subjective. The landscape alludes to the destination of thought. The favor with which it is welcomed induces a timid, suspended "gesture," a gesture of respect. But the allusion to the law goes no further than this oblique glance. One has to elaborate the conditions of "objective" teleology in order to legitimate this gesture (161; *153*). Natural finality is only made up of a network of "guiding thread[s]" (*Leitfäden:* [part II] 36, 40; *250, 253*). The gesture of aesthetic subreption takes hold of one of these threads.

But the sublime cuts the thread, interrupts the allusion, aggravates the subreption. "It gives on the whole no indication of anything final in nature itself, but only in the possible employment of our intuitions of it" (93; *90*). It is ignorant of nature, for nature must remain *unerklärlich* (not able to be elucidated, explained, or proclaimed: [part II] 48; *260*) for the *Aufklärer*. This protects the enigma of the sublime against metaphysical delirium (Leibniz, Hegel). The sublime cares nothing about the move toward ethics that the aesthetic of nature enables and that the law seems to require for its realization.

In the sublime, nature does not give thought a sign, an indirect sign of its destination. Rather, thought makes "use" of nature. The object "wanting in form or figure" (*formlos oder ungestalt*), "formless and in conflict with ends" (*formlos und unzweckmäßig*), is "put to a subjectively final *use* [gebraucht], but is not estimated as subjectively final *on its own account* and because of its form. (It is, as it were, a *species finalis accepta, non data.*)" (134; *128–29*). Indeed, we see a reversal of the relation to the object, but above all a reversal of interests, and thus a putting into question of interesting disinterests. Natural anti-finality, or, to be brief, anti-nature, can be said to have a possible use. We have seen what "anti-nature," a term that is not Kantian, might mean in the economy of thought considered in its subjective nature. The word designates "rude nature" (see Chapter 3, pp. 77–81) insofar as the latter inclines thought to neglect its beautiful forms: it may be "that the object, when we perceive it, has nothing for our reflection that [would] be purposive for a[ny] determination of its form" (FI, 439). This does not refer to the "monstrous" (100; *97*), as we have read (see Chapter 4, pp. 102–9). Form simply ceases to be relevant in matters of aesthetic perception. The sublime does not receive the object according to its form, according to its subjective, inner finality. Form does not cause the soul to ring with "happiness."

What "use" does thought make of nature or of anti-nature in the sublime? The First Introduction says a "contingent use" (FI, 439). "A *purposiveness of nature* concerning the subject" ceases to induce "in" thought its own proper "natural" finality, felt as an agreement of its manifold powers. On the contrary, the "purposiveness lying *a priori* in the subject," "an *a priori* principle (though this principle is only subjective)," makes "a possible purposive *use*... of certain sensible intuitions." This use is contingent because it does not require that one "presuppose a special technic of nature" (FI, 439). Natural art, of which taste was the repercussion, the "inner" harmonic in thought, is silent.

On the contrary, thought imposes its own finality on what remains of nature when natural form is no longer "given" (*data*) as a work of art, but only "received," "taken" (*accepta*), diverted. Moreover, (ethical) destination, the sublime of which is too strenuous a feeling, is not suggested to thought by the work of nature, the "landscape," even indirectly, as with taste; rather, thought arbitrarily actualizes its destination in a "contingent" way with regard to the object, and in an autonomous way with regard to itself, by grasping the occasion furnished not by the landscape but by the quasi amorphousness of a "rude" magnitude (100; *97*).

The part played by the imagination (or sensibility) in sublime judgment must consequently be reduced, "retracted"; the content of forms is weak in sublime presentation (see Chapter 6, pp. 150–53). This is why, for Kant, the sublime is said to be an "intellectual feeling" (*Geistesgefühl*), as opposed to taste. Its true force consists in a destination proper to thought, which is indifferent to the finality of forms. What arouses and sustains sublime feeling is not only "a finality on the part of objects in their relation to the reflective judgment in the subject" but "also, conversely, a finality on the part of the subject, answering to the concept of freedom, in respect of the form, or even formlessness, of objects" (33, t.m.; *29*). Here we have a reversal if not a conflict of the finalities. Through the beautiful the "subject" is made to listen to nature, as well as to its own "subject" nature. In the sublime, nature is put in drastic contrast to this other thought required by the law, a thought that is only "subject" because it is absolutely subject to obligation. For the *Geistesgefühl* is not a stranger to "respect for moral Ideas" (202; *193*). And, as it should be, the "delight" that affects this thought is not a pleasure, a *Vergnügen*, but a *Selbstschätzung*, a self-esteem (49, 202; *47, 193*; see Chapter 9, pp. 226–31).

In pursuing the reversal of finalities, one might wonder whether the very "spiritual" feeling, which expects and learns nothing of its object, but instead *serves* as its occasion—a given more "captured" than "given": "rude" nature, forms at the limit of the presentable—still deserves to be called aesthetic. "Yet" it must be, Kant writes, "because it too expresses a subjective purposiveness that does not rest on a concept of the object" (FI, 440). Like taste, the sublime is a reflective judgment "without concepts of the object, but [a reflective judgment] merely in regard to subjective purposiveness" (ibid.). Thus the sublime can be classified as aesthetic because *aisthēsis*, sensation, here means not "the representation of a thing (through sense as a receptivity pertaining to the faculty of knowledge)," but "a modification of the feeling of pleasure or displeasure," a representation that refers "solely [*lediglich*] to the subject and is not available for any cognition, not even for that by which the subject *cognizes* itself" (45, t.m.; *42–43*). What judges (itself) *by* the state of thought, by its internal "sensation," is aesthetic. This sensation is not information about the object, whether it be internal or external (see Chapter 1, pp. 8–15). What is informative, on the contrary, is the sensation furnished by the senses. It is even an indispensable component in judgments of knowledge. The sensation refers to logic (71; *68*; and KRV, 66–67; *64–65*). As for the "spiritual feeling," it belongs to the aesthetic despite its indifference to sensible forms, for, like taste, it is a non-cognitive judgment that thinking makes that concerns not an object, but the occasion of an object. The sensation concerns the occasion of an object according only to the subjective state in which thinking finds itself on this occasion.

The occasion of this judging sensation simply does not have the same status when it feels the beautiful and when it feels the sublime, and thought is not in the same state. This alterity depends on the occasion and affects the order of respective interests that are in play. The object said to be sublime is no longer the occasion given to a form to transform itself immediately into a "happiness" of the soul by a transitiveness of the finalities, in the way the natural "code" converts itself to an affectual disposition. It is through its absence of form, or, rather, considered "without" its forms, beyond or outside them, that the object—in spite of itself, so to speak—furnishes practical reason the opportunity to reinforce its hold on thought and to extend its power according to its facultary interest. And of course, thought, thus constrained by the law, turns to the law or exposes itself to the law without being pushed by an interest, thus by the singular incentive of ethics, that is, regard, *Achtung* (see Chapter 9, pp. 226–31). But can the same be said for the dark side of the sublime—a dark side darker than that of respect, because here it is constitutive of the feeling and not merely its verso? And will it be said that sublime indifference to form is still the sign of a "disinterest"?

In terms of the transcendental interest that leads the faculties to actualize themselves, the debacle of forms, or the "retreat" of the imagination (see Chapter 6, pp. 150–53) that the sublime implies, results in a reshuffling of the interfacultary hierarchies. Understanding (or thought in its cognitive usage) must relinquish its power, whereas in taste, as we recall (see Chapter 2, pp. 60–67), forms, in defying, in exciting the understanding, appeal to its actualization as a power. The perspectives of knowledge that the beautiful leaves accessible, albeit aporetically (206–9; *197–200*), are at once barred by the sublime. Reason, on the other hand, the faculty of pure Ideas, and first that of absolute causality, seems to have a great interest in the disorganization of the given and the defeat of the understanding and the imagination. In the space thus created by "negative presentation," reason can in effect render al-

most "intuitable" (106; *102*) to thought the Idea of its true destination, which is to be moral.

The Sublime Sacrifice

Were we to raise the question of the interest or disinterest felt by
empirical thought affected by sublime emotion, and were we to
put aside the "disinterested interest" that it feels when it discovers
the moral law within itself, we would see that the indifference it
shows the object's forms involves, more than a disinterest or interest, a simple *uninterest*. The forms of the imagination seem irrele-
vant to the arousal of "spiritual feeling."

However, a closer examination reveals that this "thrusting aside"
(*Absonderung*: 127; *122*) of forms is not without interest for
thought in the discovery of its true destination. Their irrelevance is
a means toward this discovery, and the pain that the impossibility
of presentation gives to thought, is a "mediation" authorizing exalted pleasure to discover the true (ethical) destination of thought,
thus evoking respect. This is because the "forgetting" of forms—
however "contra-final" it may appear to taste and to the finality of
nature—is nevertheless finalized, or finalizable, upon the Idea of
this ultimate destination. The "displeasure" that insists on showing
just how "contra-final" reason is to the imagination "is still represented as final" (109; *105*). There is something like a logic of the
"worst possible" or at least an aesthetic of the worst that "plays" not
the ugly but the amorphous. The more an anti-landscape exceeds
all putting into form, the more the power of pure (practical) reason finds itself "extended" or actualized, the more its greatness is
revealed. It counts on favor's misery to bring out the elevation of
its law. We have already seen this (see Chapter 5, pp. 123–27). Unlike what takes place in respect, which only arouses displeasure
secondarily, in an extrinsic way, the sublime "mediatizes" ("dynamically" speaking) the light with the dark. A clear space is drawn
upon a dark contrast.

This biased perhaps perverse interest, this profit derived from
the quasi "insignificance [of nature] before the Ideas of reason"

(105; *101*; see Chapter 4, pp. 102–9), is what motivates or accompanies the "use"—the "contingent" use—that thought *makes* of nature (of anti-nature) in the sublime. Let us reread this passage: "The concept of the sublime . . . gives on the whole no indication of anything final in nature itself, but only in the possible *employment* of our intuitions of it in inducing a feeling [*fühlbar*] in our own selves of a finality quite independent of nature" (93; *90*). On the side of actual thought this "in order to induce a feeling" betrays a powerful interest. The collapse of forms is interesting, as is the subordination of the imagination to a finality that is incompatible with its own finality, that is, the free production of forms. "The imagination by its own act depriv[es] itself of its freedom by receiving a final determination in accordance with a law other than that of its empirical employment" (120; *116*). What profit can be expected from the *Beraubung*, the "spoliation," to which it consents (ibid.)? The profit one would expect from a sacrifice. Who is the beneficiary? Nature is sacrificed on the altar of the law. "In this way [the imagination] gains an extension [*Erweiterung*] and a might greater than that which it sacrifices [*aufopfert*]. But the ground of this is concealed from it, and in its place it *feels* the sacrifice or deprivation, as well as its cause, to which it is subjected" (ibid., t.m.).

The "contingent use" of nature thus proceeds from a sacrificial economy of the facultary powers. The kind of regard the sublime has for the law is acquired and signaled by using natural forms in a way that was not their intended use for thought, by misusing them. This constitutes a conversion (or perversion) in destination, which perhaps still connotes the institution of the sacred. The latter requires the destruction or consumption of the given, of the present "wealth," the *Stoff* of free natural form (180; *171–72*; see Chapter 2, pp. 60–67), in order to obtain in return the counter-gift of the unpresented. "It is only through sacrifices that this might [of moral law] makes itself known to us aesthetically" (123; *118*). Aesthetically. When one lights the beautiful on fire, the sign of the good arises from its cinders. Any sacrifice involves this sacrilege. A pardon can only be obtained by abandoning, by banishing a first gift, which must itself be infinitely precious. The nature sacrificed is sacred. Sublime interest evokes such a sacrilege. One is tempted to say: an ontological sacrilege. In any case, here, a facultary sacrilege. The law of practical reason, the law of the law, weighs with all its weight on the law of productive imagination. It uses it. It subordinates it as far as its *a priori* conditions of possibility, its own autonomy, which is also its heterogeneity with respect to the conditions of morality. However, the servitude of the imagination is "voluntary," violently interested. The faculty of free forms "depriv[es] itself of its freedom" (120; *116*), and it does this in order to induce "a feeling" for a law that is not its own (93; *90*). By sacrificing itself, the imagination sacrifices nature, which is aesthetically sacred, in order to exalt holy law.

As in any sacrificial rite, there is in the sacrifice of the imagination a calculation of interest, a reckoning of feeling. Give up favor, and you will find regard. It seems easy to back this calculation up with the calculation supporting a "dialectic" (for example, the "master-slave": renounce pleasure and one will have recognition and spirit). This would be the case if Kant let himself be Hegel (see Chapter 5, pp. 127–31). If he thought the law were negotiable at the expense of the beautiful in the gift-for-a-gift logic that dictates dialectical logic and guarantees its profit, its final *Resultat*, even if always deferred.

On the contrary, this economy of the bad, of plus through minus, this interested frenzy in denaturation that Kant calls enthusiasm (but it has siblings) is denounced as a blindness owing to the "choice" of its end or "in the way it is effected" (124; *119*). As an "affection of a strenuous type," a violence of feeling, the sublime "cannot merit any delight on the part of reason" (124; *119–20*; see Chapter 6, pp. 153–56). This "use" thus remains useless, without ethical result. The law will not allow itself to yield to the consumption of forms. For, quite simply, the law requires regard alone, a pure, disinterested obedience. It will have nothing to do with demonstrations of heroism. Respect cannot be obtained by means of mortification. It is an immediate and *a priori* reverence. That this veneration should have for its *effect*, as I have said, the humiliation of self-love, is one thing. But it is another altogether for the sacrifice of the ego, or that of the imagination's forms, to be the *condition* of respect. Respect takes place without condition; it is, let me repeat, "morality itself, regarded ... as an incentive" in empirical will (KPV, 78; *89*). Respect cannot be acquired, even if one were to offer the price of all of nature. Like the law, respect cannot be the object of a trade, even one that is expiatory.

This is especially true of a transcendental trade. By this I mean: especially when the trade implies that one power of thought "gives way" to another—for example, the faculty of presenting forms to the one of being obligated by the law. This is especially true when one faculty concedes not only primacy in extension, but gives way *on* the very conditions of possibility, *on* its autonomy—in this case, on the freedom of presentation and its disinterestedness. This surrender overwhelms not only the specific functioning of the imagination. This surrender also disorganizes the very principle of practical reason, which is precisely the unconditioned of the law and the regard owed to it. Thus the general economy of the faculties is affected by this crisis.

The second *Critique* uses the word *Frevel* (KPV, 126; *140*) to refer to this radical concession, to this subordination of one faculty to another, which also entails the disorganization of the other (in this case, the constant threat of the subordination of practical reason to speculative reason, and the overturning of an order). It signifies an outrage to piety, a sacrilege. There is *frevelhaft* in the sublime. In other words, respect, in its pure ideal, that is, the fair face of the law, cannot enter into account, be counted in an economy of sacrifice. It involves an an-economy, which would be of the order of holiness. Its dark face and the loss that ensues result from empirical will being not holy, but finite. Furthermore, sacrifice cannot use this finitude to buy holiness. (Practical) reason could not be "satisfied" with such folly, which masks a "frivolous" wager.

§ 8 The Communication of Taste

Demand for a Universal Communication

Taste and sublime feeling must be described by the critique as feelings devoid of all interest, in order to be distinguished from inclinations presupposing needs, or from a moral feeling that produces a need for the good (48–50; *46–48*). This condition of possibility of aesthetic feeling was established in the name of its quality. But we have seen that another aspect also distinguishes taste, and also the sublime, from the other feelings, and this aspect is no less important—far from it. Taste is a sensation that immediately demands to be communicated. It demands this immediately. This exigency or expectation is inscribed in the sensation, without any extrinsic mediation. One could say that taste immediately demands to be communicated immediately. This does not mean in the same instant, but, rather, without the mediation of any argument, as if by a direct transitiveness. Immediacy of a demand to be communicated without mediation. We have seen (see Chapter 3, pp. 81–89) how the critical analysis of this double immediation is made doubly, both in the name of quality and in the name of modality. Moreover, the importance of quality and modality is such that they alone are responsible for the legitimation of taste as a judgment necessary *a priori*; they are responsible for its critical "deduction": "The solution [*Auflösung*] of these logical peculiarities," i.e., universality and necessity, "will itself suffice for a deduction of this strange faculty [*dieses sonderbaren Vermögens*]" (136; *130–31*).

According to the category of quantity, the demand to be communicated in the judgment upon the beautiful calls directly for a universality that is itself immediate. According to modality, the demand to be communicated spontaneously requires its necessity to be accepted without discussion. (To simplify matters, and following Kant's own example, I am using the designations of the categories of pure understanding instead of the "headings" of reflection, which would be identity/difference and determination/determinable, respectively, and which, in principle, are the only appropriate designations for the subjective judgments of pure aesthetic feelings. The first "heading" suggests by comparison that all that is beautiful gives pleasure, and the second suggests that the beautiful is unable not to give pleasure.)

We have also seen (see Chapter 2, pp. 60–67) how the analysis of the demand for universality and the demand for necessity come together in the notion of a possible communication of taste. "Possible communication" is one word, *Mitteilbarkeit,* communicability. This notion is the topic of paragraph 39: "Von der Mitteilbarkeit einer Empfindung" (Whether a sensation is communicable: 148, t.m.; *142*). Thus the quantitative analysis of the claim to universality, to *Allgemeinheit*, leads the critique to the Idea of an *allgemeine Stimme*, a "universal voice" (56; *54*). What does this voice say? It says there is "a possibility" (*Möglichkeit*) of an aesthetic judgment—this very sensation—being considered "valid for everyone" (*als für jedermann gültig*) "at the same time" (*zugleich*: ibid.). The judgment of taste does not "postulate" an *Einstimmung*, "the agreement" (the *chorus*) of everyone; it only "imputes [*es sinnt . . . an*] this agreement to everyone" (ibid.).

The judgment of taste imputes the agreement "as an instance of the rule" (*als ein Fall der Regel*: ibid.). Every "agreement," every pure pleasure felt before the same form, is an instance and, as such, remains a singular judgment. By calling it an instance, one nonetheless refers it to a general rule of aesthetic judgment, of which it would be the particular instance. This rule is not given, for sensation judges without the mediation of a determinate concept. Understanding is at work in taste only as the power, *Vermögen*, of concepts, but it does not determine the object through a concept of beauty by means of a rule of attribution. If there is a rule, the sensation or the pleasure of the beautiful "waits [*erwartet*] for confirmation [*Bestätigung*]" (ibid.), for approval through homology. It looks for confirmation "not from concepts" (*nicht von Begriffen*), but "from the concurrence of others" (*von anderer Beitritt*: ibid.), from their "access" to the same sensation. The rule of taste that is "imputed" in singular pleasure would thus be induced on the basis of equally singular pleasures felt by "others," on the basis of their proliferation, which would be so many instances confirming the rule.

This is a common reading and one the text seems to authorize. Thus: "To say: this flower is beautiful, is tantamount [*ebensoviel*] to repeating its own proper claim [*ihren eigenen Anspruch*] to the delight of everyone" (136, t.m.; *131*). One must remember that in the *Anthropology from a Pragmatic Point of View* (§44) the faculty of "finding [*auszufinden*] the particular [*das Besondere*] for the general (the rule) [*zum Allgemein (der Regel)*]" is called *Urteilskraft*, judgment. Conversely, "the faculty of discovering [*ausdenken*] the general for the particular" is spirit, *der Witz* (*ingenium*). Indeed the *Anthropology* is only an anthropology and should not be involved in the affairs of a critique. Nevertheless, one can draw from this distinction the following question, When the sensation of taste is said to "look for" the concurrence of others, is it in the way the *Witz* prepares to think the general on the basis of particular instances or is it in the way the *Urteilskraft* inquires after instances that may fall under a rule it already has? Evidently what taste "waits for" or "promises itself" (57; *54*) is neither. It cannot be a matter of applying a rule of taste already determined to the "instances" of aesthetic judgments, because the latter judge without rules. Nor can one find this rule on the basis of the judgments of others, however numerous they may be in their consensus, for two reasons. The first is automatic: empirical induction is not legitimation in the eyes of the critique. The synthesis implied in the *vs. Arendt?*

judgment of taste must be transcendentally "deduced" as the *a priori* condition of this judgment; the unanimity observed in fact (if it exists) is not a valid legitimation. The other reason applies to aesthetic judgment proper: once again, aesthetic judgment is not aware of a conceptual rule. It does not presuppose it, nor is the rule its aim as it may be for reflection in its cognitive usage. It is tautegorical, but not heuristic.

Thus the "universal voice" should not be confused with the agreement that everyone can in effect give to the singular sensation of pure pleasure inspired by a form. Nevertheless, the "universal capacity for being communicated incident to the mental state in the given representation [*die allgemeine Mitteilungsfähigkeit des Gemütszustandes in der gegebenen Vorstellung*] . . . must be fundamental [*zum Grunde liegen muß*]" in a judgment of taste (57; *55*). The character of communicability is indeed distinctive. But the legitimacy of this strange demand still remains to be deduced. This is what is done explicitly by the deduction in paragraph 30 and in subsequent paragraphs (133–34; *128–29*). But the materials for the deduction are already to be found in the Analytic of the Beautiful.

Let us first examine what relates to quantity. We have already observed that a slippage occurs, by which the universal claim made by a judgment upon the beautiful is treated as a claim toward universal communication, the latter understood in turn—at least apparently—as the communication of this judgment to "everyone" (see Chapter 3, pp. 81–89). It is difficult to see why the logical universality of a judgment would be guaranteed or even signaled by the unanimity of the individuals judging. The fact that this judgment is reflective and not determinant does not make matters any easier. The reflexive "heading" of unity replaces the determinant category "universality," but this does not make it any clearer why it must have the agreement of others to be valid.

I will briefly recall what appears to be the structure of the reasoning behind this "slippage." First of all, as we have just indicated, universality must be thought of as a reflexive "heading," because the judgment upon the beautiful is a reflective judgment. Second, this "heading," unity, indicates that the whole of the form judged to be beautiful "applies" to the totality of the state of thought called pure pleasure: this is the reflective analogue to universality in determination. Third of all, this "application," or attribution, is neither an application nor an attribution, because the beautiful is not an objective predicate, and pleasure is not a concept, the possible "subject" of a judgment. One must not fall victim to the predicative form that we give to our taste by "subreption" when we say, for example, "This form is beautiful." Formulated correctly, taste says: "Given this form, thought feels a pure pleasure (that is immotivated and whole)."

However, this formulation conceals something equivocal: what is "the thought" that feels this pleasure? Is it the instantaneous thought that "apprehends" and "reproduces," that "comprehends" the said form, the thought "contained in a single moment," the "absolute unity" (KRV A, 131; *143*) where the manifold is first synthesized and then actually reproduced in order to present itself as form (ibid., 132–33; *145–46*)—as a free form in taste, but nonetheless always presentable within the limits of the "first measure" of the imagination (98; *95*; see also Chapter 1, pp. 8–15, and Chapter 4, pp. 98–102). Or are we speaking of "thought" in general, of all thought as it thinks this form, thought thus seen as a permanent object, identical to itself through the successive and/or coexistent proliferation of thoughts that take hold of it? Is "thought" thought as an immediate whole, as occurrence, or else thought in totality, all thought, as capacity? The definite article is equivocal (in French, but also in German). It designates the universal: man [*l'homme*: tr.] is mortal (all men are); or the singular: the man is blond (the man of whom I speak). The same is true of "the thought" in our formulation.

For there to be taste, singular thought in its actual occurrence must be affected as a whole by a pure pleasure on the occasion of the presentation of the form judged to be beautiful. This is its definition with regard to quality. But this quality maintains the quantity of the judgment in its singularity, in a unique and exclusive universality. This indeed suffices to distinguish it from the "delight" afforded by the "agreeable" (49; *46–47*) or the positive "esteem" given to the "good" (ibid.), but it is not enough to confer upon it any universality proper. Whence it follows from the slippage we have signaled that "communicability" would cease to be a transcendental aspect of taste.

How serious would this be? Does "disinterest" not suffice in authenticating pleasure as pure aesthetic? In authenticating it, certainly, for its quality is enough to distinguish it, though not to legitimate it. Without this universality of communication, even as a simple demand, the aesthetic cannot be founded. To found the judgment of taste means, in critical terms, to deduce its possibility *a priori*, and not simply to describe its distinctive characteristics. For the critical project, these serve only to establish the necessary *a priori* conditions for these characteristics to be what they are. As necessary *a priori*, these conditions are universal, that is, true for any singular aesthetic judgment. Thus one must be able to demonstrate that this judgment, in its empirical and contingent singularity, presupposes certain conditions without which it could not in fact present itself, as it presents itself, as singular and contingent. These conditions said to be transcendental are universal and necessary for all judgments of this nature. Thus it is neither the singularity nor the contingency of aesthetic judgment that leads the critique to these conditions. No more than does its quality of "disinterest," which is perfectly compatible with its singularity and its contingency. It is only this—often forgotten—aspect, the demand to be communicated universally and necessarily. This is why a possible communication of the mental state is "fundamental" to the judgment of taste (57; *55*), with pleasure as "its consequent" (*zur Folge*: ibid.). Aesthetic pleasure has its "determining ground" (*Grund*: 58; *55*) in judgment, and, finally, the "universality of the subjective conditions of estimating objects forms the sole foundation [*allein . . . gründet*] of this universal subjective validity of the delight that we connect with representation of the object" (59; *56*).

One could oppose the above text to that of paragraph 1 where, on the contrary, it seems that "the feeling of pleasure and displeasure . . . forms the basis [*gründet*] of a quite separate faculty of discriminating and estimating" (42; *40*). The order of foundation

seems reversed in favor of pleasure, thus of the singular, to the
detriment of the faculty of judging and its *a priori* conditions. But
this is because the object of this last passage is quite different. The
paragraph aims at distinguishing a faculty "that contributes nothing to knowledge" of the object (42; *40*) from "one's cognitive faculties, be the mode of representation clear or confused" (ibid.).
(The "confused" mode refers once again to Leibniz's intellectualism.) What "forms the basis" of the feeling is the capacity of
thought to relate a thought (a representation) not to the object
thought, but to thinking itself according to its "state," a strictly
"subjective" and even tautegorical capacity to think. What the text
does, in short, is to translate from the "mental faculty" (*Vermögen
des Gemüts*) of the feeling of pleasure and displeasure to the "cognitive faculty" (*Erkenntnisvermögen*) of pure judgment without re-
sorting to understanding (39; *36*). "To form the basis" here means
to institute this correspondence.

Let us return to "communicability." This demand is much more
than a remarkable aspect of taste. It serves as the basis for its universal validity. The hypothesis of an aesthetic sense, common to all
thought, the *sensus communis* (83–85; *80–82*), will be formed on
the basis on this demand. With this demand and through the hypothesis of a *sensus communis*, the critique will discover the principle of a supersensible substrate that finalizes all thought (207–8;
198). This demand is what will permit the antinomy of the critique of taste to be debated: the antinomy states that there can be
no "dispute" and "decision," *disputieren* and *entscheiden*, about
taste, but that there can always be "contention" (*streiten*) about it
(205–6, t.m.; *196–97*); this of course has to do with the status of its
universality and necessity. Thus it must be understood that in our
formulation—"given this form, thought feels a pure pleasure"—
the term "thought" signifies both the whole of a given thought
that actually occurs, and all thought thinking the same form. It
signifies singular thought and the universal condition of thought,
at the same time. This paradoxical coexistence is precisely what is
marked analytically by the double immediacy mentioned earlier: as
singular, thought is immediately affected by pleasure on the occa-

sion of a given form; as universal, it immediately calls for the communication of its affection.

Demand for a Necessary Communication

As it examines the judgment of taste through the category of
modality (or the corresponding reflexive "heading" determina-
tion/determinable: KRV, 280–81; *314–15*), the critique explores the
question of possible communication. And it offers a solution. This
"Fourth Moment" of the "Analytic of the Beautiful" first determines the modality of the judgment of taste by elimination. The
logical category of modality commands the synthesis that unites
the terms involved in a judgment when the latter poses the synthesis in terms of "possibility," "existence," or "necessity" (KRV, 113;
118). In the case of an aesthetic reflective judgment, the three values of modality would be as follows: it can happen that a form
provides pleasure for thought; or it is a fact that it gives thought
pleasure; or it is impossible for it not to give pleasure. The first
judgment would be "problematic" (KRV, 107; *110*); the second,
which posits the form as "actually" (*wirklich*: 81; *78*) giving pleasure, would be "assertoric." In the third, a form declared beautiful
is thus judged to provide pleasure, and the synthesis of form and
delight is posed as necessary, making the judgment "apodictic."

This would indeed be the case if the judgment in question were
a determinant judgment and attributed a property to the concept
of the object that belonged to it necessarily. But such is not the
case in a judgment of taste, for the beautiful is not an objective
predicate but the name of a subjective state of thought projected
onto an object. It is nonetheless true that the union of the object's
form with the state of thought is necessary. In calling the form
beautiful, we mean that all thought should be in the state where
our thought finds itself in the presence of this form. But it
"should" merely. We may evoke or invoke this necessity without
being able to give "its exponents" (*exponieren*: 212; *202*). To give its
exponents is to reduce "a representation of the imagination to concepts [*auf Begriffe bringen*]" (ibid.). However, the judgment made

by our feeling regarding a form operates without a concept. If it expresses a necessary link between sensation and the occasion of sensation, it does so only insofar as "we tolerate no one else being of a different opinion" (*verstatten wir keinem, anderer Meinung zu sein*: 84; *81*). This puts the critique back on the path of "communicability."

This mental experience, so to speak, or this "imaginary variation" by which we try to feel what others should feel on the same occasion, endows our judgment with a special necessity, one that is not logical but what Kant calls "exemplary" (*exemplarisch*: 81; *78*): "a necessity of the assent of all to a judgment" (*eine Notwendigkeit der Beistimmung aller zu einem Urteil*: ibid.). The shift is plain to see: the judgment is not necessary, but the agreement of all thought on the subject of this judgment is. A legitimate shift, for the thought that judges the judgment is the same thought which, as (logical) "subject" of this judgment, is supposed to judge the form to which the judgment refers. From this simple evocation, thus, the judgment of taste presents itself as "exemplifying [*ein Beispiel*] a universal rule incapable of formulation" (ibid.). As with the claim to universality previously, the demand for necessity evokes the phantom of a conceptual rule. But this rule cannot be formulated (by understanding, whose function it is); therefore the demand for necessity remains unfounded conceptually. Lacking this rule, the critique must find some reflexive "principle" (82–83; *79–80*) authorizing sensation to claim its communication as necessary. This principle must determine "by means of feeling only and not through concepts" what pleases and yet has "universal validity" (ibid.). The necessity called for by the judgment of taste will be exemplary only if it is legitimated by this principle.

In what does this principle consist? It can be called *Gemeinsinn*, "common sense" (ibid.). It is not "good sense," which is the ordinary faculty of reasoning attributed to every thinking being, but a disposition to "feel," which would be communicable to all (150–51; *144–45*). Its function would be (the entire description is in the conditional, as this principle remains problematic at this stage of the deduction) to authorize the universal exemplarity of the necessity felt singularly in taste: "I put forward my judgment of taste as an example [*Beispiel*] of the judgment of common sense, and attribute to it on that account *exemplary* [exemplarische] validity" (84, t.m.; *81*). This principle of common sense would thus fulfill the function of the missing rule.

Given this, can it be said that one is justified in presupposing this principle? The argument authorizing this presupposition, outlined in the Introduction (31–33; *28–29*), is given in paragraph 21. It can be elaborated in the following way:

1. Cognitions and judgments must (*müssen*: 83; *80*) be universally communicated, "together with their attendant conviction [*Überzeugung*]" (ibid.). Why must they be? Because without this universal communication, there would only be individual opinions, incapable of showing the agreement (*Übereinstimmung*) of these cognitions and judgments with their object. Moreover, the skepticism that would result from this incapacity is untenable, as the first *Critique* shows.

2. The possibility of universal communication, required of knowledge, must also be required of the "mental state" (*Gemütszustand*: ibid.) accompanying knowledge. For all thought occupied with knowing an object is at the same time affected by its act of knowing and thus finds itself in a certain "state": for example "conviction," which is a delight due to knowledge. By reversing the order, one could even say that this subjective "condition," this *Stimmung*, i.e., the state in which thought finds itself when it knows, is also a "subjective condition of . . . knowing" (*die subjektive Bedingung des Erkennens*: ibid., t.m.), a condition, this time, in the sense of a condition of possibility. If there were not a disposition of thought about which it was immediately informed and was favorable to its act of knowing, the latter would not exist for thought and thought would not know. The subjective here, that is, the reflective, overrides the objective or the determinant. (This could only surprise a hasty reader of the *Critique*s and of the Appendix to the first *Critique* in particular, which is devoted to the "concepts" of reflection.) Of course subjective sensation is the "effect" (*die Wirkung*) of facilitating the play between understanding

and the imagination, the faculties of objective knowledge (60; 57); but conversely "knowledge, as effect" (*das Erkenntnis als Wirkung*: 83; 80) could not arise without the *Stimmung*, the "disposition" of thought that allows for the agreement of the two faculties. This reversal is of great importance: the rank of a condition of knowledge, a *Bedingung*, is conferred upon the *Stimmung*. Moreover, as this condition must be universal for the condition connected to cognition and determinant judgment to be communicable, as it is in effect, the *Stimmung* must itself be universally communicable.

3. There is a disposition of thought particularly "suited," particularly "due" (I am trying to convey the *welche sich . . . gebührt* [ibid.]), to the representation of an object from which cognition will result. It corresponds to a "proportion" (*eine Proportion*: ibid.) of the two powers—imagination and understanding—the one in relation to the other. The disposition of thought, estimated according to pleasure and displeasure (the mental faculty), can thus be translated in terms of the faculties of knowledge. An object is given by sensibility, and the imagination sets to work arranging, *Zusammensetzung* (83; 80), the given manifold in a schema; the imagination puts the understanding to work so that it "recognizes" the object through concepts. We recognize the "ratio" required of the faculties of knowledge for the knowledge of the object to be effective. This ratio was described in the first *Critique*.

4. Is this ratio felt by thought to be "good," to be a pleasure? One cannot be certain. Many ratios are possible. The ratio of the faculties at work in obtaining a cognition generally depends upon the object to be known (*auf Erkenntnis* [*gegebener Gegenstände überhaupt*]). In critical terms "cognition . . . generally" includes knowledge that determines an object of experience in the strict sense, but it also includes the representation of a practical action to be accomplished, or the representation of a free form to be presented for pure pleasure, or the representation of a "transcendent" object, the Idea of which reason has and upon which it speculates, or finally the representation of an object of which pure understanding tries to determine the "notion," without considering experience, etc. It is clear that in each of these cases, the proportion

of imagination and understanding "invested" in the act of thinking is not the same.

5. "However [given the above], there must be (*gleichwohl aber muß es*: ibid.) one ratio among all those possible that is "best adapted" (*die zuträglichste*: ibid.) to the relation between the two powers (of presentation and concepts): a kind of optimal ratio. Optimal for what, adapted for what? For the "mental powers" (*Gemütskräfte*: ibid.) in view of knowledge in general.

6. This ratio can be recognized, for it is felt immediately by thought. Thus one returns from the analysis of the powers of knowing to the examination of the reflective disposition of thought as the power of feeling pleasure and displeasure. And neither the "good" proportion nor the "happy" disposition, which is its sign (both the cause and the effect), is determinable "through concepts." They are only determinable "through feeling." Here we recognize the absolutely tautegorical property of reflective thought: its "state" is the sign of itself. Paragraph 9 shows that it cannot be determined conceptually. If it could be, thought would be informed and made "conscious" of its pleasure in an "intellectual" way, as in the cognition of an object by means of an "objective schematism" (59; 57–58). But this is impossible. For thought has no knowledge in the strict sense (by schema and concept) of its subjective states; it has a sensation of them, and the sensation is its state.

7. In conclusion, the knowledge of an object must be communicable and the subjective disposition suited to it must be communicable. The proper disposition (pleasure) must also be communicable. Thus it is permitted to presuppose a "common sense," that is, a common aptitude for feeling the good proportion of the faculties of knowledge. Moreover, this is not only permitted but is as necessary as the "communicability" of knowledge.

Hesitation About the Demand

Despite its rigor, this demonstration does not fully satisfy the critique. It leaves open the question of the transcendental status

that should be given to a *sensus communis*. "Psychological observations" (84; *81*) are certainly not what can determine this status. It is
transcendental, but where should it be "housed"? The question is a
reflective one. This consideration is for the "transcendental topic"; it requires this additional determination.

The question is addressed in paragraph 22 in the form of an alternative. However, in order to grasp the stakes of the alternative,
one must clearly circumscribe its object. Its object is not the *sensus
communis* itself. It is the "ideal norm" (*die ideale Norm*: 84; *81*), "a
mere ideal" that the pleasure in the beautiful seems to involve as
soon as it claims a universalization of its singular judgment. If I demand that you find beautiful what I find beautiful, is it not because my taste obeys a norm? "Imputes," "waits for," "promises itself" assent: all of these terms give themselves a "duty," a *Sollen*. As
we have already read, "a person who describes something as beautiful insists that everyone *ought* to give the object in question his
approval and follow suit in describing it as beautiful" (82; *79*; see
Chapter 7, pp. 161–71). But we also saw that the *Sollen* cannot
claim the status of a moral duty: "The *ought* in aesthetic judgments, therefore, despite an accordance with all the requisite data
for passing judgment, is still only pronounced conditionally" (82;
79). The aesthetic "ought" obliges only on condition that the judgment involving it be the instance of a principle of obligation that is
universally valid, because this judgment—which is subjective, singular, and without concept—has no authority to obligate. And
supposing further that this principle could be demonstrated, one
would always need to be "assured" (*immer sicher*) that "the case"
(*der Fall*), that is, a given judgment of taste in its singular occurrence, was indeed subsumed "under that ground" (ibid.), and did
not oblige for other motives than this pure principle. Aesthetic
obligation would then have a validity similar to that of an "objective principle" (*gleich einem objektive*: 85; *81*). But the condition is
repeated: provided one were assured that the subsumption of the
singular judgment of taste under the principle was "correct" (ibid.).

The term "subsumption," which is used twice to designate the
condition of validity of aesthetic obligation, leads one to think of

the principle—to which this obligation refers—as a rule of understanding. Just as a judgment of experience acquires its cognitive
validity and the right to universalization from the synthesis it performs upon the givens being subsumed under a rule of understanding, so it stands for a judgment upon the beautiful. Its validity is subject to a similar condition, that of the subsumption of its
synthesis under a principle. One could "rightly convert . . . into a
rule for everyone" (*für jedermann mit Recht zur Regel machen*: 84;
81) a singular judgment, an "instance" of taste, if it satisfied this
condition of subsumption.

However, this interpretation of the principle as a cognitive rule
must be abandoned for three reasons: the first is that the judgment of taste is subjective, even if it requires universality and necessity, and cannot fall under a rule of understanding. The second
is that in a judgment of taste the imagination does not work according to schemas. And finally such a rule is not binding, strictly
speaking. It requires that the instance be subsumed to it for it to be
known, that is, determined by a concept. However, a *sensus communis* is felt as an "ideal norm" that everyone in turn "should" observe when judging the form judged to be beautiful. What obli-
gates, what is felt by thought as a *Sollen*, as a "you must," is called
not a rule but a norm. Moral law is a norm. It prescribes impera-
tively and without condition. Moreover, unlike a rule of understanding, the law does not determine *what it is* one must do, the
instance, but *that* something must be done, given the instance, for
the law to be realized. When the principle of universalization,
which legitimates the singular aesthetic judgment to demand its
communication, works as an "ideal norm," it acts more like a
moral law. And its norm, like that of moral law, would have to remain "indeterminate" (*unbestimmte*: 85; *82*).

In summary, by requiring communication, taste would exem-
plify a norm. This norm would remain indeterminate (aesthetic
judgment must remain free); it would be founded on an unconditional and universal principle.

But before accepting the deduction of the said principle, one
must still confront the difficulty of localizing the facultary realm.

In other words: when thinking judges a form to be beautiful, does it *require* all thought to feel the form to be beautiful, or does it *oblige* all thought to feel this form to be beautiful? Our text invokes the necessity of aesthetic judgment. But the necessity, *stricto sensu*, is the impossibility of an opposing judgment. Is this the case with taste? Not at all. To each his own, as they say. When one judges a body to be weighty, the opposite judgment is excluded. Form is not beautiful in the same way that a body is weighty. Thus the necessity is not "apodictic." It is exemplary (81; *78*), but how does one house an "exemplary necessity" in a transcendental topic? *Exemplarisch* is not of the same *topos* as *Beispiel. Sollen*, obligation, is not *müssen*, necessity.

Yet the critique seems to have some difficulty in separating them in its description of aesthetic obligation. The following passage is evidence of this: "The 'ought' [*das Sollen*], i.e., the objective necessity [*die objektive Notwendigkeit*] of the coincidence of the feeling of all [*Zusammenfließen*] with the particular feeling of each, only betoken[s] the possibility of arriving at some sort of unanimity [*einträchtig*] in these matters, and the judgment of taste only adduce[s] an example [*ein Beispiel*] of the application of this principle" (85, t.m.; *82*). The exemplary is a simple example of application, and the *Sollen* is an objective necessity: here we return to the cognitive hypothesis. It thus becomes urgent to localize the principle authorizing communicability. If this principle is required like a rule, it belongs to the realm of understanding, which is impossible. If the principle is obligatory like a norm, it depends on practical reason, which is equally impossible (see Chapter 7, pp. 159–73). This alternative is displaced by another, more subtle one described in paragraph 22. The solution to the latter is deferred and given only in paragraphs 57 and 59.

Localization of the Principle Behind the Demand

Where must one house the principle upon which the demand for communicability, inherent in a judgment of taste, is based? To which faculty does it belong? To which power of thought? In paragraph 22, the question is formulated in a new way: "Is taste . . . a natural and original faculty [*ein ursprüngliches und naturliches . . . Vermögen*], or is it only the Idea of one that is artificial and to be acquired by us?" (*oder nur die Idee von einem noch zu erwerbenden und künstlichen Vermögen?*: 85, t.m.; *82*). Three oppositions are to be understood: either taste is a power already given, or it only requires the Idea of a power; either thought is originally endowed with this power, or it must take hold of it; either this power belongs to the nature of thought, or it is the fruit of its art.

The question might be surprising on the whole. Had it not already been established that the capacity for thought to be and feel good on the occasion of the perception of a form was spontaneous, constitutive? Had the "subjective" not been precisely conceived as this affectivity or immediate affectuality of thought in its objects? Could it be that thought has to deploy its artful resources, that it has to deploy an art—to become an artist, even deceitful, *künstliche*—in order to be capable of feeling the beautiful?

This is in effect surprising. Furthermore, it is not taste as pure, disinterested sensation that is put into question in this way, but its demand to be universally and necessarily communicated. The beginning of the passage leaves no room for doubt: the question is to know whether "a common sense [does] in fact exist [*ob es in der Tat . . . gebe*] as a constitutive principle of the possibility of experience, or [whether it is] formed for us as a regulative principle by a still higher [*noch höheres*] principle of reason, that for higher ends first [*allererst*] seeks to beget in us [*in uns hervorzubringen*] a common sense" (85, t.m.; *82*). The first hypothesis is clearly that of a principle working as a rule of understanding for a knowledge of experience. One must remember that this hypothesis was authorized by the deduction procedure of a *sensus communis*, supported entirely by a reference to the subjective condition of all knowledge *stricto sensu*. According to the second hypothesis, on the other hand, that of a "higher principle of reason," the critique must acknowledge that a *sensus communis* is not itself the principle behind an aesthetic norm. *Sensus communis* is subordinated to this other principle; it is regulated, *regulativ*, by it and this other principle "beget[s]" (*hervorbringen*) in us a common sense. The said "common sense" is reclassified as a trace, a sign which, in the order of the aesthetic, recalls an Idea that regulates thought from afar as thought takes pleasure in the beautiful and demands its communication. Thus we understand how, according to this hypothesis, aesthetic thought (the feeling of the beautiful, taste) belongs to another power, that this higher power is not yet at thought's disposal, and that thought will need plenty of art to attain it. For even in its demand for communication, taste is only (*allererst*) a premise and has no ultimate finality.

This is the enigma, which begins to sound a little intellectualist: taste would merely be the still confused actualization of a purely rational power of thought—to come—which is not limited to making experience "possible." This is the correct hypothesis nonetheless, as we will see. However, the communicability demanded by taste cannot be supported solely by demonstrating its involvement in all acts of theoretical knowledge. For a very simple reason: this demand acts not as a rule of understanding, but as a norm of reason. Norm implies a finality, whereas rule does not.

Solution to the Antinomy of Taste

Let us look now at paragraphs 57 and 59 where the hypothesis we have just outlined is argued. These paragraphs belong to the "Dialectic of Aesthetic Judgment." They follow the "Solution of the Antinomy of Taste" (206–15; *197–205*). I will remind the reader of the latter's content.

Above all else, one must keep in mind that the antinomy is not the antinomy of taste itself but that of the "critique of taste" (204; *195*). On the subject of taste, the critique should and must support two apparently contradictory propositions: taste is a singular, subjective judgment that does not make use of any concept; taste is a judgment that lays claim to universality and necessity, which are categories of the understanding, i.e., the faculty of concepts. The thesis of the antinomy (which proceeds by refutation, as in the Antithetic of the first *Critique*) follows from the first proposition: if one judged the beautiful according to a concept, one could make a decision about what was beautiful "by means of proofs." However, such is not the case (206; *197*). The antithesis follows from the second hypothesis: if one were to judge the beautiful without any concept, one could make no claim as "to the necessary agreement of others with this judgment" (ibid., t.m.), and discussion would be impossible. Again, this is not the case.

In order to resolve this—its—aporia, the critique begins by distinguishing between two kinds of argumentative interlocutions. "To dispute" (*disputieren*) is an exchange of arguments that obeys the rules of conceptual logic and objective knowledge with a view to reaching an agreement of the interlocutors upon the object of the *disputatio*. It involves the giving of proofs: during the course of the dispute phenomena are put forward to prove that a given empirical concept does in fact have its object present in experience (211; *201*). And if the concepts in question are used by the judgments *a priori*, then one puts forward the schemas themselves (222–23; *212*). They ascertain that the object of the judgments is presentable *a priori* in experience. In both cases—the simply empirical judgment or the *a priori* judgment—the *disputatio* has recourse to a *Darstellen*, to presentation (210; *201*), to a "direct" *Darstellung* (223; *212*), and has the power to convince. The imagination, the faculty of presentation, and the understanding that furnishes the concepts thus cooperate in giving proof of the argument's truth and allow one to come to a "decision" (*entscheiden*: 205; *196*) about the argument and its opposition.

We have already seen that when the object of the dispute is taste, a decision cannot be reached between judgments on the subject of the beautiful. Lacking concepts, devoid of rules, indifferent to knowable experience, judgments of taste are incapable of furnishing logical arguments and proofs of their aesthetic validity through presentation. If, however, they provide matter for interlocution, for "discussion," the latter cannot be a *disputatio*; it is *ein Streiten*, a subject of "contention" (205, t.m.; *196*), one might say, a battle. One fights. Each party tries to supply arguments for its judgment on the beautiful in order to reach an agreement with the other. But the "hope" (*die Hoffnung*: ibid.) of reaching this agreement will be forever disappointed. A consensus will never be established on the basis of communicable reasons and proofs that would enable one to declare the dispute resolved. Thus, unable to be resolved, the debate about the beautiful lives on. And the debate lives on not, or not only, because it cannot be stopped. After all, the adversaries could, as in the first two antinomies of the first *Critique*, be dismissed (see Chapter 1, pp. 36–43), and the debate would come to a halt for lack of debaters. No, the debate lives on because a "higher" finality, of which neither of the interlocutors is aware, "inhabits," so to speak, the object of the debate and haunts the debate itself. Here I evoke the enigmatic instance, which, from above and beyond, ceaselessly calls for the communication of aesthetic feeling and consequently for the discussion of this feeling.

The interminable debate guides the critical solution of the antinomy. For the debate is, in itself, the sign of the way in which to proceed in unifying what is heterogeneous, and of unifying it in a necessary way. The solution can only be sought on the side of a dynamical synthesis (see Chapter 3, pp. 60–67). The text recalls what is essential in this matter: the principle of this synthesis is "the possibility of two apparently conflicting propositions [*dem Scheine nach*] not being in fact [*in der Tat*] contradictory, but rather being capable of consisting together [*nebeneinander*]" (208, t.m.; *199*). The unfolding of this solution, its *Gang*, is similar to the procedure involved in the resolution of the last two antinomies of pure theoretical reason (ibid.).

One should and one must give reason to the thesis stating that there are no concepts in taste that allow it to be disputed, and also to the antithesis that says there must be concepts to at least push one to debate it, for debate is an argument. For there is indeed no determinable concept at work in the judgment of taste. However, this judgment nevertheless obeys, in a regulative way, an "undetermined" and "indeterminable" concept (206; *197*). There is no concept here that is "provable" (*erweislich*: ibid.) on the basis of an intuition, as the dispute demands. But there is nevertheless a concept, or else we could never understand the demand for communication in taste that motivates the debate and the hope of coming to an agreement. This demand and this hope are the seal, the sign with which the power of concepts marks pure reflection, i.e., the feeling of the beautiful. Because of this seal, aesthetic judgment is removed from the limited particularity of a *Privaturteil* (207; *198*), of a judgment devoid of all communication, incommunicable like a judgment of the senses. Aesthetic judgment judges without rules, but not without a regulative Idea. The call to communicate proceeds from this regulation.

An indeterminable concept, the object of which remains unpresentable, is called an Idea (KRV, 308–26; *347–68*). Thinking in the strict sense knows nothing about the object of this Idea. In the demand to be communicated, which is constitutive of the pleasure provided by the beautiful, the critique discovers the sign of an Idea. This Idea makes taste possible according to its very distinctive delight, which is this demand itself. In estimating the beautiful, thought knows nothing of this Idea; it is affected by it, it hears its voice, a voice evoking the concert of voices, a voice promising, looking toward, and prescribing the "universal voice" (56; *54*). Such is the indetermination of the concept (of reason) "underly[ing]" the conditions of aesthetic judgment.

Limit-Ideas

This concept of reason is called *das Übersinnlich*, the "supersensible" (56; *54*). It refers to what lies above the sensible, without any further determination than its localization in relation to the sensible. The voice that calls for the communication of sensation is not the voice of sensation. The sensation related to the state of thought is traversed by "another sensation" that thinking feels as a *call* lodged in its pleasure. For the supersensible affects thought simply by making a "sign" to it of a regulative norm, and this is what transforms the singular feeling into an "example" to be followed necessarily and universally.

It is not difficult to localize this voice in the transcendental topic. The dynamical resolution of the antinomy suggests it is an Idea of reason, for taste gives rise to argumentation, and reason cannot supply any proofs in the form of presentations—only a concept without corresponding intuition. Like any Idea, this Idea is "indemonstrable" (*indemonstrabel*: 210; *201*). *Demonstrieren* is "*ostendere, exhibere*," to present the object of a concept in intuition (211; *201–2*). For example, the Idea at the foundation of morality, the "concept of transcendental freedom" (211; *202*), is indemonstrable, as the *Critique of Practical Reason* makes clear. The Idea of the supersensible is not only a "transcendental rational concept" (*ein transzendentale Vernunftbegriff*: 207; *197*), it is a "transcendent concept" (*ein transzendenter Begriff*: 210; *200*), according to the distinction made by the first *Critique* in the "Concluding Note on the Whole Antinomy of Pure Reason" (KRV, 483–84; *546–47*). What is conceived in the transcendent concept exceeds all sensible intuition and escapes all means of proof.

So long as an Idea regulates the legitimate use of a faculty in its realm or territory, it is transcendental. It is transcendent when it makes for itself "objects for which experience supplies no material" (KRV, 483; *547*), either in the realm or the territory. It is not determinable by the means that govern judgment in this field; "it is a mere thought entity" (*ein bloßes Gedankending*: ibid., 484; *547*). The "thought entity" was defined in the table of Nothing as an "empty concept without object, *ens rationis*" (ibid., 295–96; *332–33*). It is the "blank" concept for an object for which intuition has nothing to show. But in itself or as an object of thought, this empty concept is no less certain; its transcendence is certain. The concept of the supersensible is transcendent, but certain. Its certainty is "immediate"; it cannot be obtained by giving proofs, which are impossible (210–11; *201–2*). It is transcendental in that it is required by critical reflection in the judgment of taste when reflection looks to legitimate the demand for the communication of taste. It is transcendent in that its object remains unknown. In other words, this demand to be communicated is not equivalent to the presentation of the object of the supersensible. The demand is but the "presence" or the sign of this object that is absolutely absent, insensible, in the strictest sense of the word "knowledge."

One might say, and Kant himself writes, that these properties are also those of the Idea of freedom: the Idea of freedom is transcendental, for it makes morality possible and governs the realm of practical reason; it is transcendent because its "presence" is signaled only by the feeling of respect, which also implies the obligation to be universally communicated. This is not to say that both Ideas, the one governing the aesthetic and the one governing the ethical, are the same. They are not identical but are in a relation of "analogy" (222; *212*). More precisely, the beautiful is to the good what an indirect presentation is to an unpresentable concept (ibid.). This "hypotyposis" is called "symbolic" (ibid.). We have already examined the fourfold reason for this analogy, expounded in paragraph 59 (see Chapter 7, pp. 166–71).

In fact, although the text encourages such a reading—for the critique of aesthetic judgment ends with the analogy of the beautiful and the good—the transcendent concept of the supersensible uncovered by the examination of this judgment *is not* the object of the comparison of the beautiful with the good. What is compared to the Idea of practical reason, transcendental freedom, is the Idea proper to the faculty of aesthetic judgment, the aesthetic Idea. This latter expression, introduced in "technical" terms in the First Remark of paragraph 57, is repeated, as we have already seen (see Chapter 2, pp. 60–67) from the analysis of genius (175–82; *167–74*). The expression designates a mode of presentation of forms by the imagination in which no determined concept could be adequate to the presentation, nor could it be rendered by any intelligible language (175–76; *167–68*). One is tempted to say that if in fact there is an Idea of the faculty of aesthetic judgment analogous to that of practical reason, it is transcendental freedom once again—but the transcendental freedom of the imagination and not of the will. Thus the Idea of aesthetic judgment is the "counterpart" to the Idea of reason (176; *168*): presentation without adequate concept, concept without adequate presentation.

In the Dialectic this symmetry motivates the opposition of the "inexponible" (*inexponibel*) and the "indemonstrable" (*indemonstrabel*: 210; *201*). To give exponents is to put a representation of the imagination into concepts; thus the aesthetic Idea, which does not permit this, is inexponible. The Idea of reason is indemonstrable because the opposite is true: the concept does not find adequate intuition. This opposition is enough to prevent any confusion, and even any continuity, between the ethical and the aesthetic. Their relation must be maintained by the critique in the form of an analogy. The aesthetic inexponibility can be no more than a symbol of indemonstrability. Although taste is linked to a good proportion of the faculties of knowledge (but only seen as the subjective condition of the possibility of experience, the *sensus communis*), there is in both the aesthetic and the ethical a kind of excess in the play of one faculty with the other: too much imaginative presentation, too much rational obligation.

The final analogy, discussed in paragraph 59, thus establishes a parallel between the Idea of the beautiful and the Idea of the good, a "demonstration" and an "exposition" (one must be wary of these words). The analogy is not at all about the indeterminate concept of the supersensible. The supersensible is of even higher rank. For what the supersensible must establish is the agreement or the affinity of the faculties themselves with each other, despite the extreme differences between Ideas (we have touched on those concerning the ethical and the aesthetic) encountered by these faculties at the very limit of their power when they seek to discover the supreme condition of the specific conditions of possibility of their respective territories or realms. The faculty of desire culminates in the Idea of a transcendental freedom for the ethical realm, and the faculty of presentation culminates in the Idea of a transcendental freedom for the territory of the aesthetic. But they are not alone. Understanding also cannot avoid maximizing its concepts (that condition the possibility of a knowledge of experience) to the Ideas of "absolute completeness" (*absolute Vollständigkeit*) that form the table of cosmological concepts: "composition" (*Zusammensetzung*), "division," "origination" (*Entstehung*), and the "dependence of existence" (KRV, 390, t.m.; *444*). The antinomies resulting from these concepts, when they are maximized to the absolute, show once again that understanding, otherwise master of rules in the territory of the knowledge of nature, contradicts itself when it attempts to know these limit-Ideas. They belong to theoretical reason in its transcendental freedom to conceive.

When each of the faculties of knowledge (in the broad sense) reaches its point of breathlessness, its hubris, it is seized by its intrinsic weakness. The antinomy is the logical (transcendental) mark of the contradiction, i.e., the limit. Because there are "three faculties of cognition," there are three antinomies: "*for the cognitive faculty* an antinomy of reason in respect of the theoretical employment of understanding carried to the point of the unconditioned"; "*for the feeling of pleasure and displeasure* an antinomy of reason in respect of the aesthetic employment of judgment"—and here one might add: to the point of the universality necessary to taste; "*for the faculty of desire* an antinomy in respect of the practical employment of self-legislative reason," or to the point of the autonomy of desire in the law (214, t.m.; *204*).

The "to the point of the unconditioned," which is indicative of the limit from which the antinomy arises, and which I will allow myself to specify for the two following antinomies, indicates that it is indeed a question of the unthinkable horizon that each power of thought approaches in its passion to legitimate itself. It is a question of horizons because the unconditioned of the conditions of thought in each of its capacities is always deferred, and its search has no end. In the name of "reason" one is entitled to hear the interminable heuristic act of critical reflection itself. With the means reflection has at its disposal in each of the realms or territories mentioned, reflection cannot determine the absolutes upon which these means depend. The unconditioned of knowledge cannot be known. The absolute law of the faculty of desire cannot be desired. The supersensible principle that founds the demand for the universal communication of taste is not the object of an aesthetic pleasure. However, the horizon is "present" everywhere. What we are calling "presence" in contradistinction to presentation is the effect of this transcendence, its sign, on theoretical, practical, and aesthetic thought. If "reason" is truly reflection when it arrives at these border regions, at these borders, one can see the advantage

the reflective faculty of judgment has in aesthetic judgment when
it approaches the absolute.

The Supersensible Substrate

The Idea of the supersensible was discussed under the name of
the "intelligible" in the first *Critique* (KRV, 467–69.; *527–29*) in the
resolution of the third cosmological antinomy with the dynamical
synthesis of condition and cause (see Chapter 5, pp. 131–37). This
same Idea appears under the name of the "supersensible" in the
Critique of Practical Reason (KPV, 56–59; *65–67*): it is the "theoretically empty" concept, but one that conditions the very possibility
of morality, of an "empirically unconditioned causality" (ibid., 58;
66). The Idea of the supersensible is not, however, one of the limit-
Ideas of a realm or territory, or, rather, it is all of these Ideas. Let us
say that these Ideas, listed as we have read in the exposition of the
three antinomies (214; *204*), are in effect horizons specified according to the faculty, but that the supersensible is the horizon of
these horizons, the notion the critique needs to unify them. The
supersensible guarantees that these profoundly heterogeneous capacities of thinking—theoretical, practical, and aesthetic—nonetheless share an affinity with each other. This affinity is revealed by
way of the similarity of their respective inconsistencies. Each faculty is seized with the impossibility of thinking its limit with the
means it has at its disposal, but that it must try to think this limit
is the sign of the supersensible. This sign is transitive in relation to
the heterogeneity of the faculties.

But this sign does not put an end to their heterogeneity. On the
contrary, the supersensible must signal itself (*sich zeigen*: 215, t.m.;
205) in each of the three facultary orders. It is the "substrate" that
makes one nature out of the totality of phenomena (*Substrat der
Natur*: ibid.). But it is also the principle of affinity of this nature
with our power of knowing envisaged subjectively as the pleasure
of taste (*Prinzip der subjecktiven Zweckmäßigkeit der Natur für
unser Erkenntnisvermögen*: ibid.). The supersensible is also the principle according to which transcendental freedom poses its ends

and the principle that accords these ends with morality, "*Prinzip der Zwecke der Freiheit und Prinzip der Überinstimmung derselben mit jener in Sittlichen*" (ibid.). These three different functions are assured by the Idea of the supersensible. In the final analysis they are not only what accords each faculty with the exercise of its power; they are brought together by the common sign of their incompetence to think this exercise to its conclusion, to exercise their power in thinking this power itself.

Thus the supersensible—the unique name for this "boundedness" or this "unboundedness"—is what makes all manners of thinking "compossible" insofar as they all think excessively. One must think excessively, until one reaches a discordance, in order to hear the voice of concordance.

Moreover this voice is the one that can be heard in the presupposition of a *sensus communis* for the aesthetic faculty. The true deduction of the demand for communication is thus the following: (1) The feeling, altogether singular, of the beautiful immediately involves the demand to be universally and necessarily communicated. (2) In order to found this contradictory demand, a *sensus communis* must be presupposed. (3) This presupposition, itself paradoxical, is only permitted if in turn a principle can assure thought of its consistency with regard to all of its "objects" (including itself) when this consistency appears impossible. This principle of harmonious accord must serve as nature in all acts of thought, all judgments, however heterogeneous they may be. This "natural" principle is called "the supersensible substrate of all the subject's faculties" (212; *203*), of all the faculties of the "subject," that is, of thought. It is "that which forms the point of reference for the harmonious accord [*zusammenstimmend*] of all our faculties of cognition—the production of which accord is the ultimate end set by the intelligible basis of our nature" (ibid., t.m.).

The antinomy of taste (indisputable/disputable) is finally resolved by having recourse to this indeterminable "nature." This "nature" also works when thinking is blocked as it reaches its limits. With this substrate the dead ends can be commuted to passageways. The dynamical synthesis provides the general model for this mutation. Aesthetic feeling, as I have said, has the advantage in that it gives virtually direct access to the Idea of this substrate. We have seen (see Chapter 7, pp. 171–73) that there is an "aesthetic and unconditioned finality in . . . art" (212; *203*) unconditioned because it is not subject to a causality by concept: the artist does not know what he does, the amateur does not know what it is he tastes. Neither consults "rule or precept" (*Regel oder Vorschrift*: ibid.) when estimating form. Their judgment is guided by a "subjective standard" (*subjektive Richtmaße*) that works as "mere nature in the subject" (ibid.).

Furthermore, what sets this standard, what may "serve" (ibid.) as a purely reflective measure for aesthetic finality, is the principle of the supersensible substrate. Why is this? Simply because the supersensible guarantees, prior to all schemas, prior to all rules and norms, that the synthesis of the manifold, of even the most heterogeneous manifold, is always possible. Even the synthesis of the manifold faculties themselves—imagination, understanding, theoretical reason, desire, and feeling—is possible. The action, the *Wirkung* of its action, is reassuring, liberating, and generous, and is experienced immediately in the aesthetic paradox of a singular feeling claiming universal validity. Once it is known that the "aesthetic and unconditioned finality" to be found in art "has to [*soll*] make a warranted claim to being bound to please everyone [*jedermann gefallen zu müssen*] (ibid.), the claim can only be fully legitimated by the principle according to which the nature of thought is to feel pleasure on the occasion of forms, or by the principle according to which it is in the nature of forms to provide immediate pleasure for thought.

Thus when taste demands its possible communication, it signifies that reflective thought, in its most subjective relation to itself and its most immediate relation to the object (form), is naturally in accord with itself and with its givens in general. This, I think, is what allows one to understand the "digression" of paragraph 40 (150–54; *145–47*) where the critical analysis appears suddenly to stray from the description of the aesthetic *sensus communis* in order to list the "maxims of common human understanding" appurtenant to the ways of thinking in general. The line of argument seems to have been interrupted. However, in saying that thinking must always think for itself, in accord with all other thought, and in accord with itself, the said maxims simply attest, in the language of popular wisdom, to the certainty of always being able to think: this is what thinking concludes from the principle of harmonious accord. I have said (see Chapter 1, pp. 36–43) that these maxims all involved reflection. I will add that if reflection can risk itself in trying to understand something it does not understand (heuristic), using to guide itself only the subjective feeling (tautegorical), it owes this ability to the assurance of the accord given it by the supersensible. One must not forget that it is reflective thought itself that discovers the principle of this guarantee in the supersensible substrate. Hence "the subjective condition of all judgments is the judging faculty itself, or judgment [*das Vermögen zu urteilen selbst, oder die Urteilskraft*]" (143, t.m.; *137*).

The Procedure of Communication

Thus it is easy to show how the presupposition of a *sensus communis* owes nothing to experience. Consequently a "psychological" but also a sociological interpretation (84; *81*) of the aesthetic community is to be rejected. An interpretation of this order interferes with the critical procedure, which cannot be inductive and must begin with the given in order to establish the conditions of its possibility; the critical procedure returns to the given in order to legitimate or delegitimate that for which it "gives" itself. The demand for possible communication as it is given in the feeling of the beautiful induces a *sensus communis* as its condition of possibility, which, in turn, is founded upon the supersensible principle of harmonious accord. It goes without saying that the mere empirical fact of unanimity, or even a simple majority opinion, favorable to a singular judgment that declares a form to be beautiful, can do nothing to legitimate the intrinsic claim of this judgment to be communicable to all. The "universal voice" is not the result of a vote. Communicability is a transcendental characteristic of taste, and it in turn requires a transcendental supplement, i.e., the Idea of the supersensible.

However, a number of passages in the "Analytic of the Beautiful" seem to call for both a sociologizing and "egologizing" reading, so to speak, or at least an anthropological one. To begin with the definition of *sensus communis* given in paragraph 40 (151; *144*), I will quote the passage directly in a translation I feel is respectful to the letter of the text but no more caught up in the anthropological bias than is necessary, in order that the reader bear witness to what I say and in order to shorten the discussion: "By the name *sensus communis* is to be understood the Idea of a communal sense [*gemeinschaftlichen Sinnes*], that is, a critical faculty, which in its reflective act takes into consideration, in thought (*a priori*) [*in Gedanken (a priori)*], the mode of representation of any other [*jedes anderen*], in order, *as it were*, to weigh its judgment with the collective reason of mankind, and thereby avoid the illusion arising from subjective and personal conditions which could readily be taken for objective, and might exert a prejudicial influence upon its judgment" (151, t.m.; *144*). The end of the passage is translated a bit freely in order to make the sentence a little easier going than it is.

The crucial point is the *jedes anderen*. It is generally understood to mean "everyone else." It seems to me that the expression echoes another, rather strange formulation: *eines Beurteilungsvermögen*, " *a* power of estimation," takes into account (*Rücksicht nimmt*) another (*anderen*) power of estimation whatever it may be, *jedes*. In the same way, *gleichsam*, "as it were," is italicized in the text, which indicates that the comparison (we are in the middle of reflection) of a judgment with other judgments is made "almost as if" thinking sought, by the comparison, to "attach" the judgment to human reason in general. It does this consequently in the mode of the *als ob*. In the same way, the "communal" (*gemeinschaftlich*) nature of the *sensus communis* (and there is no reason to translate it by "common to *all*") seeks to compare "in thought" (*in Gedanken*) (and not "in thinking") and to compare *a priori* (and not in experience) a singular aesthetic estimation with another estimation, whatever it may be. The aesthetic "community" is not primarily constituted by the convergence of opinions given by individuals. It is "deployed," so to speak, by a work of variation that "thought," and thought alone (*in Gedanken*) effects in order to remove itself from its "private" condition, deprived as it is of the Other by the singularity of its act of estimation. One could say that reflection reduces the estimations of the form that it judges beautiful in order to ensure that its estimation, immediate and singular, is reasonably universalizable. In this case it hardly matters whether the empirical individual in charge of this mental variation is the same as the one whose estimation it was in the first place. Were he to find himself "on an uninhabited island" (43; *41*), the demand and the procedure of this communication would be no less necessary to ensure that his estimation, like the disinterest of this estimation, was a pure aesthetic judgment.

Thus the only remaining anthropological resonance in the text is the evocation of the "collective reason of mankind." Although what follows sounds very similar: "This is what happens by weighing one's judgment [*sein Urteil*], not so much with actual, as rather with the merely possible, with the judgments of others [*an anderer . . . Urteile hält*] and by putting ourselves in the position of everyone else [*in die Stelle jedes anderen*], as the result of a mere abstraction from the limitations which contingently affect our own estimate [*unserer eigenen Beurteilung*]" (151, t.m.; *144–45*). Here it seems difficult to support the purely transcendental thesis of the meaning of "communal." "One" has one's own estimate, one puts oneself (*versetzt*) in the place of another to escape the contingency of one's own singular judgment: does this not refer to human individuals who practice these gymnastics? It is true that these gymnastics belong more to the order of the possible than to the real. Yet are they not the inevitable condition of human "sympathy," given that the ego can be in the place of the "you" only in an imaginary transference?

I do not deny that the conception of *sensus communis* still bears traces of what the critique itself calls its "empirical realism." The *dieses geschieht nun dadurch,* the "this is what happens," of the last passage cited shows obvious signs of this realism. The latter is an essential factor of the critical procedure along with transcendental idealism. Yet in order that this feeling be properly aesthetic, it is important not to confuse the two movements, for it is not the fact of the call for a *sensus communis* present in aesthetic feeling that needs to be established, but, rather, the legitimacy of this fact that is its necessity *a priori*. And on this subject, the text does not allow for any hesitation. It ceases to be anthropological and becomes truly critical when it comes time to elaborate the procedure by which aesthetic thought seeks to emancipate itself from the contingent particularities that might weigh on its estimation. One reaches this "abstraction" "by so far as possible letting go the element of the matter, i.e., sensation [*Empfindung*], . . . and confining attention to the formal peculiarities of our representation or general state of representative activity" (151; *145*).

However one interprets it, the "communal" operation thus always demands a kind of purification of the representation of the object judged beautiful or of the "subjective state" that responds in thought to this representation. There is a kind of skimming off of everything that might be "matter" in the representation or the subjective state it produces. One can promise oneself the "agreement of everyone" only for "the delight remaining" once consciousness has separated out "everything belonging to the agreeable and the good" (57; *54*).

The "matter" of sensation must be eliminated from aesthetic pleasure because it exercises a "charm" over thought. When thinking is subjected to this charm, its judgment is a "judgment of sense" (65; *62*), also called a "material aesthetic judgment": such a judgment only expresses the "agreeableness or disagreeableness" (ibid.) of the object. Thus the matter of representation creates an interest. A delight owing to matter is an emotion. There is nothing aesthetic in all of this, at least from the point of view of taste (the sublime is an emotion, but not owing to matter; it is due to the absence of form, which is not the same thing: see Chapter 2, pp. 56–67).

The matter of representation is called *Empfindung*, "sensation," in the sense of the first *Critique*. In agreeableness, "sensation alone" (*lediglich Empfindung*: 66, t.m.; *63*) suffices to provide pleasure. The state of thought is euphoric, but it cannot lay claim to a universal and necessary communication. This agreeable state can itself be called "the matter of delight" (65; *62*) because it is a delight owing to matter. It does not result from the good proportion of the faculties of knowledge in play in pure aesthetic judgment.

The faculties of knowledge can only be in accord, even for just a moment—the moment taste arises—if each lends itself to the play of the other, to the "rules of the game" of the other. Thus they can only be in accord insofar as understanding moderates its appetite for concepts and gives up "investigating" (*geschäftig . . . durchzuspähen*: KRV A, 147; *185*) appearances in order to ascribe some rule to them. But they can also only be in accord insofar as the imagination concentrates on pure forms, free of concepts and also free of matter: fanciful constructions of relations in which understanding will believe itself able to give free rein to its rules. Thus the imagination gives understanding "the wealth of material" (*Stoff*) which overwhelms it, and which is not the matter of sensation, but the proliferation of forms (see Chapter 2, pp. 60–67). Only then does agreeableness give way to "favor," which is the subjective state of thought, the delight corresponding to the estimate of forms.

This purge is the way aesthetic thought succeeds in putting itself in the place of the other and in laying claim to the communication of its judgment. From this we conclude that judgment can only lay claim to its communication when it has been purged of material charms. The argument here proceeds from a critical (transcendental) purification to a possible empirical communication. However, there is an argument that works in the opposite direction. For example, one finds the following lines at the end of paragraph 40, after the passage we have just examined: "We might even define taste as the faculty of estimating what makes our feeling in a given representation *universally communicable* without mediation of a concept" (153; *147*). From which one would conclude instead that communicability is what ensures the purity of the judgment of taste.

There is no need to "choose" between these two versions of the procedure of communication. Transcendentally, the critique proceeds from the purity of taste (its quantity of disinterest) to its communicability (its universal quantity and necessary modality), passing through its finality (that is, its relation; see Chapters 2 and 3). The disinterest of delight is always put forward to introduce the paradox of a universality without concept. But empirically, the purity of the judgment of taste is estimated according to the possibility of its communication. One could say that communicability is in fact the *ratio cognoscendi* of the purity of taste, the way in which taste is recognizable when it occurs, but that this same purity is the *ratio essendi* of the possible communication, which would be impossible without it.

All of this, Kant concludes, may seem *künstlich*, "artificial." And yet "nothing is more natural" than purging aesthetic pleasure of charm and emotion if it is to have an exemplary and universal value (152; *145*). This is because the nature of taste is artistic, and art is nature. Even the supersensible principle is like a "nature" in thought that oversees its harmonious accord (212–13; *202–3*). This does not prevent the Idea of this principle from being the fruit of an art of thinking that is *künstlich* (85; *82*).

§9 The Communication
of Sublime Feeling

A Mediatized Communication

One must ask oneself whether sublime feeling also demands to be universally communicated, like taste, and whether it is justified in doing so according to the same principle of *sensus communis* with its supreme finality in the supersensible. This question is raised in paragraph 39, which examines the communicability of a sensation *(der Mitteilbarkeit einer Empfindung*: 148–50; *142–44*). The examination of the communicability of the sublime takes up very little space.

The text distinguishes four kinds of sensation, according to whether the sensation is due to the senses, to morality, to the sublime, or to the beautiful. This repeats the division made at the beginning of the "Analytic of the Beautiful" in the name of the quality of taste (42–50; *40–48*). The pleasure in the beautiful, "favor" (*Gunst*), is the only delight "free" of all interest. The pleasure in the senses is "conditioned" by the interest the senses take in the existence of the object, in its "material" presence. As for the delight taken in doing or judging what is good, what is "esteemed, approved" (49; *47*), it is determined by the interest that results from the obligation of the empirical will to realize moral law. Moral obligation, the *Gebot*, the commandment, does not result from an interest, and in this it is altogether different from the necessity experienced by the senses; however moral obligation creates an interest in the realization of the good (54–57, 112, 159–60; *46–48, 118, 152*).

In the "First Moment" of the "Analytic of the Beautiful," the critique distinguishes three kinds of delight (see Chapter 7, pp. 159–63). In paragraph 39, a fourth delight is added, the delight provided by "the sublime in nature" (*die Lust am Erhabenen der Natur*: 149; *142*). Furthermore, the category or the reflective space overseeing the examination is no longer the quality of the delight, but its possible communication, its *Mitteilbarkeit*, which has a modal character. Thus the entire elaboration of communicability in taste is to be reconsidered here in relation to the sublime. By this I mean that the quality of sublime feeling, disinterested like the feeling of the beautiful (they please "on their own account": 90; *87*), but in which pleasure and displeasure combine "dynamically" (see Chapter 5), is not enough to determine its communicability. As with the beautiful, one must proceed with the examination of sublime judgment according to its quantity and modality. The question is to know whether a singular sublime judgment immediately requires one to obtain, as taste does, a universal and necessary agreement, and whether a sublime judgment requires this immediately, that is, whether its very occurrence carries with it this demand, prior to all concepts, as the simple sign of the subjective universality necessary in all thought.

To this question, the text clearly says "no." We must remember, however, that the feelings of the beautiful and the sublime were easily assimilated to one another with regard to their universalization: "The judgments: 'That man is beautiful' and 'He is tall' do not purport to speak only for the judging subject, but, like theoretical judgments, they demand the assent of everyone" (95;[14] *92*). Our text, on the contrary, asserts that sublime feeling "lays claim also to universal participation" (*macht zwar auch auf allgemeine Teilnehmung Anspruch*: 149; *143*), but this *call* cannot be immediate in the same way as it is in taste. The demand for universality that is proper to the sublime passes "through [*vermittelst*] the moral law [*des moralischen Gesetzes*]" (ibid.). The pleasure in the sublime is said to be a pleasure "of rationalizing contemplation" (*als Lust der vernünftelnden Kontemplation*), the pleasure that we have in contemplating while reasoning (149; *142–43*).

We have seen (see Chapter 4, pp. 115–22) that, as pleasure, the contradictory feeling of the sublime holds exclusively to the "soul-stirring delight" provided by the Idea of the absolute (as whole and as cause) and that only rationalizing thought, reason, can represent this unpresentable object, which is, properly speaking, an Idea. This pleasure is the "attractive" component of the sublime emotion (or "shock"). This component corresponds to the observation of an object that is a being of reason. The "repulsion" that takes hold of thought and prevents it from pursuing the contemplation of the object comes from its powerlessness to present it through a synthesis of the imagination.

Thus the communicability of sublime feeling as delight would only belong to reason as a universal capacity, and its universality would in fact be that of moral law. The text suggests this so strongly that it almost breaks the precarious unity of the paradoxical feeling and almost destroys the dynamical synthesis that constitutes it. However, the very notion of a pleasure tied to the exercise of rational thought, even if only contemplative (and not directly ethical), is not a simple one. For if the demand for universal communication is mediatized in sublime feeling by the representation of "moral law," we also know that the concept of this law translates or is experienced subjectively as a feeling, respect, whose specific quality is that it is neither pleasure nor pain (KPV, 78–92; *89–104*). Yet the text we are discussing seems to escape this objection. It suggests that pleasure as a component of sublime feeling only claims to be communicated because "it already [*schon*] indeed [*doch*] presupposes another feeling [*ein anderes Gefühl*], that, namely, of its supersensible sphere" (149, t.m.; *143*). (I emphasize the *doch*; the *seiner* of "*its* . . . sphere" relates the sphere to thought.) Yet this "other feeling," however "obscure" (*dunkel*) it may indeed also (*auch*) be, still has "a moral foundation" (*ein moralische Grundlage*: ibid.).

The Other Feeling

This "other feeling" is not named in the passage. Yet what is mentioned about it suffices to identify it. It is a very obscure feeling; it has a moral foundation; it signals the supersensible sphere of thought. We recognize respect, the *Achtung* or regard that the second *Critique* carefully isolates as the only moral feeling. "And the capacity [*Fähigkeit*] of taking such an interest in the law (or of having respect for the moral law itself) is really moral feeling" (KPV, 83; *94*). The "interest" in question is free of all motive. Respect does not satisfy the need thinking has to obey the law. On the contrary, as we have seen, listening to the law may simply produce in thought an interest in doing good (ibid.). This reversal is the central motif of the second *Critique* and a recurrent one in the third *Critique*. The regard thought feels for the law is not interested (in the sense of motivation). However the categorical imperative, without content (without "matter"), that is, the commandment issued from the mere form of the moral law, determines the interest thought has in certain objects—good actions that have been done and remain to do (49, 122–24, 159; *47, 118–19, 152*).

The law must not prescribe what is good, for then the will would be affected "pathologically" (KPV, 83; *94*) and could not claim to be freely determined. Because it is not "pathological," because respectful thought is not subject to any heteronomy, respect is "singular" (*sonderbar*) and unlike any other feeling. Its manner is not like any other but is, rather, of a "peculiar kind" (*eigentümlicher Art*: ibid., 79; *89*). It is obscure because it is "blank" in relation to pleasure and pain. It is not a pleasure. One only "reluctantly gives way to it as regards a man." One even makes an effort to defend oneself against the respect due the law. Nor, however, is respect a displeasure (ibid., 80–81; *90–91*). One cannot "ever satisfy oneself [*nicht sattsehen*] in contemplating the majesty of the law" (ibid., 81, t.m.; *91*).

These strange properties converge in the following property: respect is "the only case wherein we can determine from *a priori* concepts the relation of a cognition (here a cognition of pure practical reason) to the feeling of a pleasure or a displeasure" (ibid., 75; *85*). Respect is produced "by an intellectual cause," which is the law, and as such it is the only feeling "that we can know completely *a priori*" (ibid., 76; *86*). To say that it is produced by the law is going too far. It "is not the incentive to morality"; it is the "presence" of the law regarded subjectively, its "sign," "morality itself regarded subjectively as an incentive" (ibid., 78; *89*). Because of its *a priori* status it does not wait for the occasion with which an object might provide it in order to appear; respect is "there" as the signal in thought of its disposition to desire the Good. It is the subjective *a priori* of moral thought. In this sense respect does not belong to the faculty of pleasure and displeasure. Respect is indeed the disposition and the sign of the disposition of thought, but only insofar as it wants or "desires," and not insofar as it suffers.

Thus it is "another feeling" altogether from the sublime feeling. The sublime feeling is an emotion, a violent emotion, close to unreason, which forces thought to the extremes of pleasure and displeasure, from joyous exaltation to terror; the sublime feeling is as tightly strung between ultraviolet and infrared as respect is white. This does not prevent sublime pathos from "presupposing" an "apathetic" respect. For if thought did not have the power of concepts in the form of an Idea, if it did not have the absolute (free) causality that founds the law for which and from which it feels respect, it would have no chance of feeling the magnitude and force of "raw" nature so intensely as signs negatively indicative of the "presence" of this Idea. Sublime feeling is not moral feeling, but it requires the "capacity" of taking a pure interest in the law. On the basis of this presupposition it is argued that sublime feeling cannot be recognized as having a "communicability" analogous to that of taste. There is no sublime *sensus communis* because the sublime needs the mediation of moral feeling, and the latter is a concept of reason (freedom as absolute causality) that is felt subjectively *a priori*. Because it is felt subjectively by thought, this concept does indeed translate as a feeling (although an altogether different one). But as a concept that is felt, this feeling proceeds *a priori* from a faculty of knowing, i.e., reason in its practical usage.

This is the movement invoked by the text of the Deduction to explain why sublime feeling has no need for a deduction in the critical sense. The affinity (or finality) of the form of an object with the faculty of feeling pleasure or displeasure, or taste, even as it is expounded in detail according to the four "headings" of reflective judgment, still requires a "deduction." The critique must reveal what is presupposed as an *a priori* condition for such an affinity (which is real, for taste exists) to be possible. This condition is the *sensus communis*, and beyond it the supersensible substrate. Such is not the case with the sublime. Its critical "exposition" is "at the same time" (*zugleich*) its deduction (134; *129*). Through the simple analysis of sublime feeling, this exposition discovers in it directly "a final relation of the cognitive faculties," a paradoxical relation: final for pure practical reason, "contra-final" for the imagination. But this paradoxical relation attests by this very fact that it is *a priori* "at the basis of the faculty of ends (the will)" (*dem Vermögen der Zwecke [dem Willen]* a priori *zum Grunde gelegt werden muß*: ibid.). This is because the sublime contains the concept of absolute causality, or free will, or practical reason which is the concept of a causality of the end. This end is the universalization of practical freedom. This is why sublime feeling is legitimate in demanding its universalization, without needing its own deduction (ibid.). It owes this privilege to its close cousinship with moral feeling: free will is a universal Idea, and respect, which is this Idea felt subjectively, is also universal.

This must be explained further still. The concept of freedom as absolute causality is not determinant. Its object, freedom, remains indeterminate (in the sense demanded by understanding), "incomprehensible" (*unbegreiflich* for the understanding), "inscrutable" (*unerforschlich*: KPV, 7, 48, 49; *8, 56, 57*). But as such this object of the pure Idea of reason is indispensable (KPV, 7; *8*) to the realm of morality; it is its foundation, its condition of possibility. For this indetermination makes the determination of what freedom is impossible and keeps the law from having a content. It prescribes that one must judge the good and the bad, when thought so desires. But the decision about what is good and bad belongs to the thought that desires. Thus the thought that desires can desire freely, that is, morally. The law only provides it a guiding thread with which to help it in this decision.

Furthermore, this thread or regulative Idea is precisely that of the possible universal communication of the "maxim" supporting thought in its decision. "So act that" (*Handle so, daß*: κpv, 30; *36*), "Act as if" (*Handle als, ob*: *Foundation of the Metaphysics of Morals, Akad., 4, 421*): these clauses modalize the rule of universalization (that is, the quantity of the imperative) in order to allow this rule its merely regulative character. But the content of the rule, thus modalized, is clearly the demand for a universal communication: "that the maxim of your will will always hold at the same time as a principle establishing universal law" (κpv, 30; *36*). Thus we see how the communication required by morality is mediatized. It is mediatized by the law. More precisely still, it is required by the very form of the law. In fact it is the whole of the form. This form is borrowed from the form of a conceptual, cognitive rule and transposed analogically into the practical realm. The law is not a rule, but is formulated according to the "type" of a rule of knowledge, retaining from this rule only the principle of its universal validity. This is what the typic of the second *Critique* explains (κpv, 70–74; *79–84*).

Universality, which is thus transposed from knowledge to the practical, loses through the analogy its determined character and assumes its function as "guiding thread"—as indicated by the *als ob* and the *so, daß*. Meanwhile the concept of understanding is transformed into an Idea of reason, and the phenomenon, on the side of the object, is henceforth grasped as a sign. All voluntary action given in experience gives way to knowledge according to the series of conditions of which it is the conditioned. But the same action, subjected cognitively to the syntheses of intuition, of the imagination and understanding, can also be judged morally, as the effect (the sign) of a free causality. Thus the criterion for evaluating the action resides in the clause of a possible universalization. However, in spite of the profound transformation of the nature of universality as it passes from knowledge to morality, universality retains its conceptual foundation. The concept belongs henceforth to reason and no longer to understanding, yet as Idea it remains what legitimates the demand for universalization made of the moral maxim. Moreover, because this demand is the only demand heard in sublime feeling (and suffices to authorize or "deduce" it in its claim for possible communication), one must say that the latter is in fact "mediatized" by the concept of reason.

In conclusion we see that the demand to be communicated is of an altogether different nature in the sublime than it was in the beautiful. Twice different. First, the demand in sublime feeling does not properly belong to sublime feeling. The demand comes to sublime feeling from the demand to be communicated inscribed in the form of the moral law, and this latter demand is authorized by the simple fact that the law rests on the the Idea of freedom. The demand is authorized by the faculty of concepts and the faculty of desire. Far from being "immediate" like the demand of taste, far from being a universality "apart from a concept" (60; 58), the universality in question in sublime feeling passes through the concept of practical reason. If one does not have the Idea of freedom and of its law, one cannot experience sublime feeling. Furthermore, the sublime differs from taste in the quality of the feeling. Violent, divided against itself, it is simultaneously fascination, horror, and elevation. This splitting can also be expressed in terms of a possible communication. For what authorizes sublime feeling to demand its communication is that part of itself, that component, which is the aesthetic analogue of respect. This alone, consequently, lays claim to the concept. The communication of the beautiful does not refer to any concept; this is why the critique must deduce it. Taste is immediately a thought that feels itself, the thought that does not think the object but feels itself on the occasion of the form of an object. The sublime is a thought that is felt on the occasion of an absence of the object's form. But this absence is only due to the thought of another object by means of a concept, the Idea of absolute causality and magnitude. Sublime thought is a "rationalizing" contemplation. It is in this name that sublime thought demands to be communicated. Thus it only makes its demand under the direction of a concept. This is what gives the sublime its violence. It is an aesthetic feeling, and not merely any delight, because it demands to be universally communicated. But what demands this communication in this aesthetic feeling is not the aesthetic, but, rather, reason itself.

The Other Object

I will briefly point out a remarkable effect of the status given to the communicability of the sublime by the critique. The analytic of this feeling insists at various points that the sublime is only in thought (91–92, 92–93, 114, 134; *88–89, 89–90, 110, 129*), and that there is no sublime object strictly speaking. The critique also insists on calling the sublime a *Geistesgefühl* (see Chapter 7, pp. 181–87) in order to show the extent to which nature, which in the beautiful addresses itself to thought through the "cipher" of its forms, is discredited in sublime feeling. As if thought were turning away from any given object only to be exalted by its power to think an "object" that it gives itself.

Things are not quite so simple. For if it were only a question of thinking the absolute, one would be faced with a case of speculative reason, which would not belong to the aesthetic at all. Whereas here we do indeed have an aesthetic delight, and this implies the presentation of an object or at least the presentation of the form of an object by the imagination, even if the presentation is negative and the object formless. Thus there is an object that gives rise to the sublime, if not a sublime object. Paragraph 39 refers to "the pleasure in the sublime in nature" (149; *142*). Moreover, the argument that refuses sublime feeling its universal communication also invokes the formless character of the object that may give rise to sublime feeling. "There is simply [*schlechthin*] no authority for my presupposing that other men will pay attention to this object and take delight in contemplating the uncouth dimensions of nature [*in Betrachtung der rauhen Größe*]" (149, t.m.; *143*).

This argument against the hypothesis of a sublime *sensus communis*, which proceeds by way of the strangeness of the "sublime object," no doubt supports the argument we have just analyzed that appeals to the "other feeling" hidden in sublime feeling. But instead of exploring the subjective state of thought seized by the sublime, the argument contents itself with remarking the uncertain status of the object that occasions this state. The object is indeed a phenomenon (pyramid of ice, ocean, volcano, etc.) and as such falls under the general rule of knowledge, the schematism. The

"Savoyard peasant" perceives and conceives the phenomenon, whereas Herr von Saussure, who finds in the same object occasion for a sublime emotion, seems unquestionably foolish (115; *111*). The first has good sense, understanding; he is *verständig*. The second feels in the object the "presence" of something that transcends the object. The mountain peak is a phenomenon that indicates that it is also something more than a phenomenon. It indicates this precisely in that it "almost" exceeds the capacity of the imagination's comprehension and forces the latter to beat a retreat. Space and time, which it must give up synthesizing (which are thus no longer space and time as forms of intuition), signal the unpresentable "presence" of an object of thought that is not an object of experience, but which cannot be sentimentally deciphered anywhere except upon the object of experience. The analogy with morality imposes itself once again by way of this phenomenist or para-phenomenist means of access. For the virtuous act, if it exists, is a phenomenon, but if it is virtuous it points to the Other of phenomenality, absolute causality and its law.

One could say that the object's Other is not an object and that the sign is what de-objectifies the object. This is only true if one identifies the object with the phenomenon. However, in the vocabulary of the critique, this should not be done. An object is what offers itself to thought. The Ideas of reason have objects, those limits of understanding constituted by the absolute whole, the absolute cause, and the like. Although one cannot find a corresponding intuition for them, one can still think them, and thus take them as objects. These are the objects that Kant calls "intelligible" (KRV, 467, 483–84; *527, 547*). When thought grasps a phenomenon as a sign, it thinks it in two different ways at once: as a given and conditioned object of experience, and as the effect of a transcendent causality. These two manners of thinking are transcendentally "localized" in two different facultary realms. They are heterogeneous and characterize the same object in a heterogeneous way. The object that is presented to reason in the phenomenon is never "big" enough with respect to the object of its Idea, and for the imagination the latter is always too "big" to be presentable.

The differend cannot be resolved. But it can be felt as such, as differend. This is the sublime feeling. This feeling makes the raw
magnitude of nature a sign of reason while remaining a phenomenon of experience. The sublime feeling does this with the help of
the dynamical synthesis. Still one must have the "sense," the
Fähigkeit of the heterogeneous and of the necessity that forces the
heterogeneous ways of thinking to meet, without, however, reducing their differend in the least.

The Aesthetic Feeling Inspired by Moral Judgment

The following point remains to be examined: the "soul-stirring
delight" felt by "rationalizing" (*vernünftelnd*: 149; *143*) thought in
the sublime is not respect for the moral law itself. Rather, this delight is an echo of respect in the order of the aesthetic, that is, in
the order of contemplation and not of practice. Should one therefore see this exaltation as the sensation that must subjectively accompany moral judgment or the "maxim" of moral will in general?

Kant examines this sensation at the end of the "Methodology of
Pure Practical Reason" (KPV, 163–65; *182-85*). The question of
method in morality concerns the learning of moral correctness.
There are two dispositions to acquire. One must first learn "to
make judging according to moral laws" into something of a
"habit," that is, to acquire and/or have acquired a competence that
allows one to distinguish between "essential duties" and "non-
essential duties" (ibid., 163; *182*). The next step is to learn and/or
teach how to judge whether an act is done not only in accordance
with the moral law but "for the sake of the moral law" (ibid., 163;
183). For in the first case, the action or, rather, its maxim offers
only a rightness of deed; it has a moral value only in the second
case.

What is of interest to our discussion here is that this exercise of
moral discernment in which reflection is formed in the practical
realm—the reflection whose responsibility it is to "decide" what is
good—must "gradually produce a certain interest even in its [rea-
son's] own law [*selbst am Gesetze derselben*]" (ibid., 164; *183*). This

interest is signaled by a feeling that should be the sensation we are trying to isolate: the state in which thought, discovering the purity of a maxim, finds itself and recognizes the "sign" of the moral law's "presence" in the maxim. This "sign" signifies not only that the will obeys an interested motivation, including the one that may push it to accord itself with moral law, but that pure practical reason, the free (absolutely first) causality, is implicated in the determination of the will. This sensation is a kind of liking: "We ultimately take a liking [*wir gewinnen endlich . . . lieb*] to that the observation of which makes us feel that our powers of knowledge are extended" (ibid.). Our powers of knowledge are "extended" (*erweiterte*), because pure practical reason enters into the picture in the maxim of an empirical desire. It is this feeling of "liking" that thought feels when it discerns (recognizes) true morality, beyond mere factual rectitude.

Thus there is a kind of subjective happiness in the observation of a pure practical judgment or of a strictly moral maxim—a happiness projected as a liking for the latter. This happiness can be critically analyzed as the harmonious accord of the "faculties of knowledge," i.e., the powers of thought insofar as they are directed at the object. This happy sensation stems from the way "reason, with its faculty of determining according to *a priori* principles what ought to occur [*was geschehen soll*], can find satisfaction [*allein gut finden kann*]" (ibid., t.m.). Rational thought can thus "find satisfaction" because its power of determining *a priori* "the ends of freedom" is in "accord" (*Übereinstimmung*) with freedom "in the moral sphere" (*im Sittlichen*: 215; *205*). This is the definition given in the third *Critique* of the third supersensible Idea, the one which precisely authorizes the accord, the *Übereinstimmung*, of the *a priori* law of freedom and the maxim of moral desire. The "extension" of the faculties of knowledge is thus considerable; it is even maximal, for it requires that the supersensible principle guarantee pure *a priori* desire its actualization in a concrete maxim (but always and only as a sign).

Moreover, with this accord, this harmony, and this happiness one cannot help thinking, by analogy, of the state that characterizes the thought judging the beautiful. Accord, harmony, and happiness are guaranteed to thought by the second Idea of the supersensible, according to which, I will remind the reader, there is a "subjective finality of nature for our cognitive faculties" (ibid.). The analogy is inevitable because the text concerns practical methodology and the (subjective) feeling with which a moral judgment provides thought, and not the practical actualization of the law by the maxim. Kant does in fact make the analogy. This exercise of moral judgment "only enables one to entertain himself with such judging and gives virtue or a turn of mind based on moral laws a form of beauty [*eine Form der Schönheit*] which is admired [*bewundert*] but not yet sought" (KPV, 164; *183*). *Bewundert, noch nicht gesucht*: one admires virtue. It is an aesthetic feeling, but one does not yet seek it; it is not an ethical obligation. Thinking entertains itself, is entertained by its accord on the occasion of virtue taken as an object. It does not, however, engage itself to practice virtue. The good ratio in which the faculties of knowing find themselves with each other, the power to prescribe absolutely and the power to realize the prescription, is so pleasant that thinking "dwells" in its subjective state, "lingers," marks a pause, a *Verweilung* (64; *61*), and thus defers the putting into action of virtue.

The subjective state occasioned by the observation of moral rectitude should be compared to the feeling of the beautiful. "The existence of the object remains indifferent to us, as it is seen only as the occasion [*die Veranlassung*] for our becoming aware of the store of talents [*Talente*] within us [*in uns inne zu werden*] that elevate us [*erhabenen*] above the mere animal level" (KPV, 164, t.m.; *183*). "Talent" belongs to the terminology of the beautiful, their elevation, *erhabenen*, to that of the sublime. It is less important for the moral maxim (the "object") to "manifest" a transcendence of free will in relation to all other motivation ("animal," "pathological"); it is more important for the object to be grasped as the occasion of a pleasure, which is the case with taste. We have the proof in what follows: "It is the same with everything whose contemplation produces subjectively a consciousness of the harmony of our powers of representation by which we feel our entire cognitive faculty (understanding and imagination) strengthened [*gestärkt*]" (ibid.). The formulation leads directly to the Analytic of the Beautiful, in particular to what goes by the name of animation (see Chapter 2, pp. 60–67).

One must not forget the determination of the "satisfaction" thus described in the relative clause attached to it and with which the German sentence ends: "produces a satisfaction that can be communicated to others [*das sich auch anderen mitteilen läßt*]" (KPV, 164; *183*). This specification returns us to the question of communication. The aesthetic feeling provided by moral judgment demands, "it too," to be communicated. We recognize the obligation to be communicated, the *Sollen*, inherent in taste. But let there be no mistake: that my taste should be communicable does not entail that duty should be. Taste is subjective, and duty is objective. In the Methodology of Practical Reason the first "you must" is "still" in a relation of analogy with the second, and the aesthetic feeling produced by virtue is only a means of instilling the habit of recognizing and practicing virtue. As the means to something other than itself, this feeling cannot be identified with pure taste. Furthermore, as something aesthetic, taste cannot be confused with moral feeling—strictly speaking, respect—nor can it be confused with the obligation of putting the law into action. There is even some danger in this kind of learning: the pleasure in admiring virtue may deter thought from the desire to practice it.

Thus the term to compare, in the order of the aesthetic, with the feeling provided by the ethical maxim is not sublime feeling but the feeling of the beautiful. Sublime feeling is in no way a happy disposition of thought. The powers of thought in sublime feeling in no way relate to one another according to a good proportion; they "disproportion" themselves violently. The object that occasions the sublime is assuredly a "sign," the sign of a supersensible sphere, but it disarms the presentation and goes so far as to discredit the phenomenality of the phenomenon. The analogy (that one might suppose possible) between the "raw" magnitude or force of nature and virtue, insofar as they both inspire a sublime feeling, finds its limit here. To judge a maxim to be morally estimable leads thought to feel it as beautiful. To judge the ocean "too big" for presentation leads one to experience it as sublime. Duty can and must be called sublime: "Duty! Thou sublime and mighty name that dost embrace nothing charming [*nichts Beliebtes*]" (KPV, 89; *101*). However, duty differs from the sublime in the strict sense in that it does not move thought "by threatening aught that would arouse natural aversion and terror" (ibid.), and that the law it prescribes "itself finds entrance into the mind" (*ein Gesetzt... welches von selbst im Gemüte Eingang findet*: ibid.). Thus in the description of the sublimity of duty one finds characteristics that make the *feeling* of duty, respect, *not* in fact a sublime feeling. If virtue were itself sublime, the sign of the law of freedom in it would not be graspable by subjective thought except by "submerging" the phenomenality of the virtuous act, which would be too big or too strong to be presentable. This act would not be an act: the pure and free desire of which it would be a sign would prevent empirical will from actualizing it, just as the absolute of reason prevents the presentation of the phenomenon by the imagination.

All that can be conceded to sublime feeling in the consideration of morality is resistance (see Chapter 6, pp. 147–50), the resistance of virtue to passions, to "fear," "superstition," "the frailty of human nature," and its "shortcomings" (112–14; *108–10*). The courage of a soldier, or of a people at war, the submission of one who believes to God can be experienced by thought as something sublime, on condition that the maxim orientating the will of the soldier, of the people, of the one who believes, be virtuous. But even then it is not morality itself that is felt to be sublime, it is its resistance to temptations, its triumph over them, reducing them to naught. The sublime and aesthetic effect results from the disproportion of pure will to empirical desire. However, virtue consists in the simple "presence" of the former in the latter according to their "natural" accord, without resistance, and this is why virtue evokes beauty.

Morality thus intrinsically demands to be universally communicated, and it is analogous in this respect to the feeling of the beautiful. But it is analogous only, for this demand is legitimated by an Idea immediately or unconditionally present, always present, and present *a priori* to the thought that desires: the concept of freedom. Whereas the demand to be immediately communicated in taste must be deduced from a principle of *sensus communis,* that, in turn, is legitimated by a "supersensible" Idea that is hidden and according to which the forms in nature are in affinity with the states of thought. As for the sublime, it escapes both demands for universal communication. In the face of the raw magnitudes and forces of nature (or the resistance of virtue) "there is simply no authority for my presupposing that other men will pay attention to it [*darauf Rücksicht nehmen*]" (149, t.m.; *143*). The Idea of the absolute is not present to thought here in the necessary form of respect. The Idea of the finality without concept of a form of pure pleasure cannot be suggested by the violent contra-finality of the object. The sublime feeling is neither moral universality nor aesthetic universalization, but is, rather, the destruction of one by the other in the violence of their differend. This differend cannot demand, even subjectively, to be communicated to all thought.

Index

Index

In this index an "f" after a number indicates a separate reference on the next page, and an "ff" indicates separate references on the next two pages. A continuous discussion over two or more pages is indicated by a span of page numbers, e.g., "57–59." *Passim* is used for a cluster of references in close but not consecutive sequence. Entries are alphabetized letter by letter, ignoring word breaks, hyphens, and accents.

MERIDIAN

Crossing Aesthetics

Library of Congress
Cataloging-in-Publication Data

Lyotard, Jean-François
[Leçons sur l'Analytique du sublime. English]
Lessons on the Analytic of the Sublime : Kant's Critique of
Judgment, [sections] 23–29 / Jean-François Lyotard;
translated by Elizabeth Rottenberg.
p.   cm. — (Meridian)
Includes index.
ISBN 0–8047–2241–2 (cloth) : —
ISBN 0–8047–2242–0 (paper)
1. Kant, Immanuel, 1724–1804. Kritik der Urteilskraft. 2.
Sublime, The—History—18th century. 3. Judgment (Logic)
4. Aesthetics. 5. Teleology. I. Title. II. Series :
Meridian (Stanford, Calif.)
B2784.L9613   1994
121—dc20
93–10683
CIP

⊗ This book is printed on acid-free paper.
It was typeset on a Macintosh IIci
at Stanford University Press.